The International LGBT Rights Movement

The International LGBT Rights Movement

A History

LAURA A. BELMONTE

BLOOMSBURY ACADEMIC
LONDON • NEW YORK • OXFORD • NEW DELHI • SYDNEY

BLOOMSBURY ACADEMIC
Bloomsbury Publishing Plc
50 Bedford Square, London, WC1B 3DP, UK
1385 Broadway, New York, NY 10018, USA

BLOOMSBURY, BLOOMSBURY ACADEMIC and the Diana logo
are trademarks of Bloomsbury Publishing Plc

First published in Great Britain 2021

Cover design: Terry Woodley
Cover image © Agensia Brasil / Antonio Cruz

A catalogue record for this book is available from the British Library.

Library of Congress Cataloging-in-Publication Data
Names: Belmonte, Laura A., author.
Title: The international LGBT rights movement : a history / Laura A. Belmonte.
Description: New York, NY : Bloomsbury Academic, 2021. | Series: New approaches to
international history | Includes bibliographical
references and index.
Identifiers: LCCN 2020035917 (print) | LCCN 2020035918 (ebook) | ISBN 9781472513236
(hardback) | ISBN 9781472511478 (paperback) | ISBN 9781472511225 (ePDF) |
ISBN 9781472506955 (eBook)
Subjects: LCSH: Gay rights–History. | Sexual minorities–Civil rights–History. |
Human rights–History.
Classification: LCC HQ76.5 .B45 2021 (print) | LCC HQ76.5 (ebook) | DDC 306.76/609–dc23
LC record available at https://lccn.loc.gov/2020035917
LC ebook record available at https://lccn.loc.gov/2020035918

ISBN: HB: 978-1-4725-1323-6
         PB: 978-1-4725-1147-8
         ePDF: 978-1-4725-1122-5
         eBook: 978-1-4725-0695-5

Typeset by Integra Software Services Pvt. Ltd.,
Printed and bound in Great Britain

To find out more about our authors and books visit www.bloomsbury.com
and sign up for our newsletters.

For Susie

CONTENTS

ILLUSTRATIONS

ACKNOWLEDGMENTS

It is cliché to describe this book as a labor of love, but love is what propelled me to propose and write it. And love in many forms has inspired me and supported me throughout the complicated, often exhausting, process of maintaining an active scholarly agenda while taking on successive administrative roles of increasing scope.

I must start with the love shared by men and women who dared and continued to dare to defy social convention, the law, and religious tradition to love same-sex partners, to celebrate same-sex desire, and to be their authentic selves. I am in awe of the pathbreaking activists who have challenged and are challenging, sometimes at enormous personal risk, the cultural, political, and legal forces that have constrained, demonized, and criminalized lesbian, gay, bisexual, and transgender (LGBT) individuals in different eras and nations.

Then there are those who build careers on love for the life of the mind. I thank the brilliant archivists at IHLIA LGBT Heritage at the Amsterdam Public Library, the Hall-Carpenter collection at the London School of Economics, the ONE National Lesbian & Gay Archives at the University of Southern California, the Amnesty International collection at the Columbia University Libraries Rare Book & Manuscript Library, and the GLBT Historical Society in San Francisco, California. The outstanding team at Oklahoma State University's (OSU) Interlibrary Loan office fielded a mountain of requests with record speed. The late David Oberhelman, a gifted OSU librarian who left us far too soon, generously helped me expand the library's holdings in LGBT history.

Beloved colleagues from around the world have been essential to this project, graciously sharing ideas and sources. As he finishes an extraordinary career, Mel Leffler remains the finest of mentors and the best of humans. Elizabeth Williams, a dear friend and brilliant historian of Modern Europe and medicine, provided a remarkable close read of the manuscript that greatly enriched and improved the final product. I am exceedingly grateful to scholars who shared observations and citations that made this book richer and more inclusive. A long list includes Julio Capó, Jr., Víctor M. Macías-González, Eric Huneke, Mona Russell, Jun Pierre Pow, David Paternotte, Matt Schauer, Emily Graham, Jason Lavery, Dave D'Andrea, Ian Lekus, Christopher Ewing, and Sébastien Tremblay. I am incredibly fortunate to belong to the Society of Historians for American Foreign Relations (SHAFR), a community I prize for its warmth and comradery as much as its intellectual and professional sustenance. In an extensive list of SHAFR types who've made the protracted road to this book one I've never traveled alone (and who have provided some wonderful diversions along the way), I thank Anne Foster, Justin Hart, Mark Bradley, Petra Goedde, Kelly Shannon, Andy Rotter, Ara Keys, Frank Costigliola, Richard Immerman, Tom Zeiler, Katie Sibley, Julia Irwin, and many others. While writing this book, I became Dean of the College of Liberal Arts and Human Sciences at Virginia Tech, leaving OSU after twenty-three years. I greatly miss the OSU faculty writing group who provided great commentary on Chapter One. I am indebted to Susan Oliver, Exa von Alt, Lori Scanlon, and Tasia Persson, all of whom are outstanding administrative assistants. Their talent and dedication were essential to my being able to balance academic leadership and academic scholarship.

I am a passionate travel lover and one of the advantages of doing an international history of something is that people invite you to talk about it all over the world. I thank those who have provided priceless opportunities to present this work to varied foreign and domestic audiences, many of whom have forced me to rethink key assumptions and broaden my evidentiary base. I am particularly grateful to the History Department at Grand Valley State University, Shanon Fitzpatrick at McGill University in Quebec, Jessica Gienow-Hecht at the JFK Institute at Freie University in Berlin, the Brewster Lecture Committee at East Carolina University, Nick Cull at the Center for Public Diplomacy at the University of Southern California, Christopher Nichols at the Center for Humanities at Oregon State University, and Ann Wilson and Andrew Juster Shield of the Queer History Workshop at the University of Leiden. Special thanks to Maria Montoya, with whom I bonded for life over the travails of writing a major textbook with six co-authors, for inviting me to lecture at NYU-Shanghai.

I am gifted beyond measure with the love of dear friends. Much love to Kyle and Maria Longley, Rebecca Sheehan, Michelle and Jimmy Jarrard, Felicia Lopez and Bob Threeton, Farida Jalalzai and Chad Hankinson, Anna Zeide, Eric Ramirez-Ferrero, Stacy Takacs and Betsy Myers, Pat Hobbs and John Orsulak, Barry Friedman, Isabel Álvarez-Sancho and Erik Ekman, Helen Laville, and Judith and Skip Wolfe.

Finally, I'd need a much bigger word count than this short volume allows to articulate my love for my family. Mom and Dad and my sister Susan have been my biggest champions and unfailing support. I cannot fathom having spent hours of isolated work without the humor and affection of my furry research assistants William Howard-Taft, James Madison, and the late Truman. And, at long last, Susie gets a richly deserved, long overdue acknowledgment. Susie is not an academic and had she known what being married to one sometimes entails, I am pretty sure she would have skipped flying out to Los Angeles to meet me for dinner on a first date that coincided with my research trip to the Reagan Library. I am certain she never imagined that she would be scanning PDFs of materials at LGBT archives just a few years later—mostly so I could finish working and we could go have fun. Each day with Susie is filled with laughter, friendship, and a love that deepens every passing day. Thank you, sweetheart, for being my fellow traveler on adventures big and small, a lifetime of joy, and a true partnership in every conceivable way.

GUIDE TO ACRONYMS

ACLU—American Civil Liberties Union

ACT-UP—AIDS Coalition to Unleash Power

AIDS—Acquired Immune Deficiency Syndrome

AI—Amnesty International

AKOK—Apeleftherotiko Kinima Omofilofilon Kiprou (Cyprus)

ASK—Association for Social Knowledge (Vancouver, Canada)

BIA—Board of Immigration Appeals

BSSSP—British Society for the Study of Sex Psychology

CAMP—Campaign Against Moral Persecution (Australia)

CAPR—Committee of Revolutionary Pederastic Action (France)

CDU—Christian Democratic Union (Germany)

CHA—Communidad Homosexual Argentina

CIA—Central Intelligence Agency

CLESPALA—Club Littéraire et Scientifique des Pays Latins (France)

CoE—Council of Europe

CRH—Council on Religion and the Homosexual (San Francisco, California)

DOB—Daughters of Bilitis

ECHO—East Coast Homophile Organizations

ECHR—European Commission on Human Rights

ECtHR—European Court of Human Rights

ECOSOC—United Nations Economic and Social Council

EP—European Parliament

EU—European Union

F-48—Forbundet af 1948 (Denmark)

FBI—Federal Bureau of Investigation

FHAR—Front Homosexuel d'Action Révolutionnaire (France)

FLH—Frente de Liberación Homosexual (Argentina, Mexico)

FRG—Federal Republic of Germany

FUORI—Fronte Unitario Omosessuale Rivoluzionario Italiano (Italy)

GAA—Gay Activists Alliance

GALZ—Gays and Lesbians of Zimbabwe

GDR—German Democratic Republic

GLF—Gay Liberation Front

HLRS—Homosexual Law Reform Society (United Kingdom)

ICCPR—International Covenant on Civil and Political Rights

ICD—*International Classification of Diseases*

ICM—International Council Meeting (Amnesty International)

ICSE—International Committee for Sexual Equality

IEC—International Executive Committee (Amnesty International)

IGA—International Gay Association

ILGA—International Lesbian and Gay Association

INS—Immigration and Naturalization Service

IPC—Indian Penal Code

ISIS—Islamic State of the Levant and Iraq

ISS—Institute for Sexual Science

LCE—League for Civil Education

LGBT—lesbian, gay, bisexual, and transgender

LHV—League for Human Rights

NACHO—North American Conference of Homophile Organizations

NAMBLA—North American Man/Boy Love Association

NGTF—National Gay Task Force

NIGRA—Northern Ireland Gay Rights Association

NWHK—Nederlandsch Wetenschappelijk Humanitai Komittee, Dutch offshoot of the Scientific Humanitarian Committee

NWHLRC—North West Homosexual Law Reform Committee (England)

PiS—Law and Justice party (Poland)

PoC—Prisoner of Conscience

RCMP—Royal Canadian Mounted Police

RFSL—Riksförbundet för sexuellt likaberättigande, National Organization for Sexual Equality (Sweden)

SHC—Scientific Humanitarian Committee

SHR—Society for Human Rights

SIR—Society for Individual Rights

SMG—Scottish Minorities Group

SMUG—Sexual Minorities Uganda

SPD—Social Democratic Party (Germany)

STAR—Street Transvestite Action Revolutionaries

SVR—Stichting Vrije Relatierechten (Foundation for Free Relationship Rights) (Netherlands)

UMAP—Military Units for the Aid of Production (Cuba)

UN—United Nations

UNCHR—United Nations Commission on Human Rights

UNHRC—United Nations Human Rights Committee/Council

VSG—Vereinluer Sexuelle Gleichberechtigung (Germany

WHO—World Health Organization

WLSR—World League for Sexual Reform

WWII—World War II

KEY WORDS

Age of Consent

Bisexual

Decriminalization

Gay

Gay Liberation

Gay Pride

Gay Rights

Gender Identity

Gross Indecency

Homophile

Homosexuality

Human Rights

Lesbian

LGBT Activism

LGBT Advocacy

Same-Sex Desire

Same-Sex Relations

Same-Sex Marriage

Sexual Minorities

Transgender

Transnational Activism

Unnatural Acts

Introduction

The global landscape of international lesbian, gay, bisexual, and transgender (LGBT) rights is fraught with geopolitical complexities and stark contrasts. In 2019, 123 of the 193 member states of the United Nations (UN) had legalized consensual same-sex sexual acts, but 68 countries criminalized such behavior, including 6 nations that imposed the death penalty. Another twenty-six states punished same-sex sexual acts with sentences ranging between ten years and life imprisonment. While twenty-six countries had legalized same-sex marriage and seventy-three had nondiscrimination protections for gays and lesbians, thirty-two nations had "morality" laws that restricted freedom of expression relating to sexual orientation and gender identity usually under the guise of protecting youth or "propaganda" laws modeled on Russia's June 2013 law banning the promotion of homosexuality and advocacy for LGBT equality.[1]

These triumphs and challenges reflect a long arc of transnational LGBT advocacy efforts dating from the mid-nineteenth century to the present day. It is a trajectory that has involved individuals, informal networks, nongovernmental organizations (NGOs), and states that have not always worked in concert and that often meet resistance from a similar constellation of actors determined to stop the global movement for LGBT equality. While progress toward LGBT equality has been marked in many nations, there are several others where LGBT people are brutally repressed. The global community is working toward making LGBT rights an integral element of universal notions of human rights, but its ability to enforce these norms and close dramatic disparities in the experiences of LGBT people around

---

[1] International Lesbian, Gay, Bisexual, Trans and Intersex Association: Lucas Ramón Mendos, *State Sponsored Homophobia 2019*, 13th ed. (Geneva: ILGA, 2019), https://ilga.org/downloads/ILGA_State_Sponsored_Homophobia_2019.pdf.

the world is so far limited. Using selected historical figures, organizations, and events to illuminate critical junctures in the global LGBT movement, this book asks readers to contemplate whether "victory" for global LGBT equality is possible, what such success might look like, and what actions the global community could take to facilitate that aim.

While there is an enormous body of work documenting gay rights movements in individual countries or regions,[2] the transnational connections among LGBT activists have only recently drawn sustained scholarly attention.[3] International relations experts are assessing how LGBT rights have become a norm in global human rights discourse, examining the interconnections between LGBT rights and other worldwide political struggles, and exploring why the trajectories toward legal recognition of marginalized peoples differ among states.[4] Historians of sexuality are addressing how transnational flows and connections are shaped by sexual interactions and inform legal structures, definitions of citizenship, power dynamics between individuals and the state, and global debates on liberalism, globalization, and Westernization.[5] Concurrently, scholars are documenting the history of the human rights revolution. They are providing cogent insights into the legal and philosophical underpinnings

---

[2]See, for example, John D'Emilio, *Sexual Politics, Sexual Communities: The Making of a Homosexual Minority in the United States, 1940–1970* (Chicago: University of Chicago Press, 1983); Julian Jackson, *Living in Arcadia: Homosexuality, Politics, and Morality in France from the Liberation to AIDS* (Chicago: University of Chicago Press, 2009); Laurie Marhoefer, *Sex and the Weimar Republic: German Homosexual Emancipation and the Rise of the Nazis* (Toronto: University of Toronto Press, 2015); Jeffrey Weeks, *Coming Out: Homosexual Politics in Britain from the Nineteenth Century to the Present* (London: Quartet Books, 1977); Omar G. Encarnación, *Out in the Periphery: Latin America's Gay Rights Revolution* (New York: Oxford University Press, 2016); Jyoti Puri, *Sexual States: Governance and the Struggle over the Antisodomy Law in India* (Durham, NC: Duke University Press, 2016); and Ashley Currier, *Out in Africa: LGBT Organizing in Namibia and South Africa* (Minneapolis: University of Minnesota Press, 2012).

[3]David S. Churchill, "Transnationalism and Homophile Political Culture in the Postwar Decades," *GLQ: A Journal of Lesbian and Gay Studies* 15:1 (2009): 31–65; Leila Rupp, "The Persistence of Transnational Organizing: The Case of the Homophile Movement," *American Historical Review* (October 2011): 1014–39; David Minto, "Special Relationships: Transnational Homophile Activism and Anglo-American Sexual Politics" (PhD diss., Yale University, 2014); Michael J. Bosia, Sandra M. McEvoy, and Momin Rahman, eds. *The Global Handbook of Global LGBT and Sexual Diversity Politics* (Oxford University Press online, 2019), https://www.oxfordhandbooks.com/view/10.1093/oxfordhb/9780190673741.001.0001/oxfordhb-9780190673741.

[4]Phillip M. Ayoub, *When States Come Out: Europe's Sexual Minorities and the Politics of Visibility* (Cambridge, UK: Cambridge University Press, 2016); Dennis Altman and Jonathan Symons, "International Norm Polarization: Sexuality as a Subject of Human Rights Protection," *International Theory* 7:1 (2015): 61–95; Manon Tremblay, David Paternotte, and Carol Johnson, *The Lesbian and Gay Movement and the State* (Burlington, VT: Ashgate, 2011).

[5]For a brilliant overview of these trends, see Joanne Meyerowitz, "AHR Forum: Transnational Sex and U.S. History," *American Historical Review* (December 2009): 1273–86.

of human rights law, the roles of NGOs advocating for human rights, and the evolution of the international human rights agenda. But most of this scholarship pays insufficient attention to the myriad ways that LGBT rights intersect, enrich, and complicate this larger human rights history.[6]

In this book, I draw on these approaches and provide a synthesis of transnational LGBT activism since the mid-nineteenth century. Although there were intellectual exchanges among early Japanese, Indian, European, and American sexologists,[7] I initially focus on a core of individuals and organizations largely composed of Americans and Europeans because the first individuals to articulate demands for full political and legal inclusion of LGBT citizens and to challenge notions of homosexuality as criminal or pathological were situated in these regions, as were the first transnational LGBT networks and organizations. Although the LGBT rights movement did not have fully global dimensions until the late twentieth century, it has had international dimensions since its inception and supranational organizations like the UN and the European Union have long been forums where LGBT equality has been advanced and contested. I adopt an expansive concept of movement, using it to describe collective action taken against states, authorities, or cultural mores in the form of coordinated public protest or private resistance.[8] I define advocacy as both informal and formal networks of individuals and organizations who exchange information; highlight the plight of marginalized people at risk of violence or who are being denied full civic equality; pressure states to use their economic, political, and legal

---

[6]Examples include: Samuel Moyn, *The Last Utopia: Human Rights in History* (Cambridge, MA: Belknap Press, 2010); Sarah B. Snyder, *From Selma to Moscow: How Human Rights Activists Transformed U.S. Foreign Policy* (New York: Columbia University Press, 2018); Barbara Keys, *Reclaiming American Virtue: The Human Rights Revolution of the 1970s* (Cambridge, UK: Harvard University Press, 2014); Elizabeth Borgwardt, *A New Deal for the World: America's Vision for Human Rights* (Cambridge, UK: Belknap Press, 2007); and Akira Iriye, Petra Goedde, and William I. Hitchcock, eds. *The Human Rights Revolution: An International History* (New York: Oxford University Press, 2012). Ryan Thoreson's work on the International Lesbian and Gay Human Rights Commission (which was renamed OutRight Action International in September 2015) and the edited collection *Envisioning Global LGBT Human Rights* are exceptions to the larger human rights literature's inattention to LGBT rights. Ryan Thoreson, *Transnational LGBT Activism: Working for Sexual Rights Worldwide* (Minneapolis: University of Minnesota Press, 2014); Nancy Nicol, Adrian Jjuuko, Richard Lusimbo et al., eds. *Envisioning Global LGBT Human Rights: (Neo)colonialism, Neoliberalism, Resistance, and Hope* (London: ICwS, School of Advanced Study, 2018); Michael K. Lavers, "Exclusive: IGLHRC to Change Its Name," *Washington Blade*, September 28, 2015, http://www.washingtonblade.com/2015/09/28/exclusive-iglhrc-to-change-its-name/.

[7]On the transnational origins and evolution of sexology, see Veronika Fuechtner, Douglas E. Haynes, and Ryan M. Jones, eds. *A Global History of Sexual Science, 1880–1960* (Berkeley: University of California Press, 2017).

[8]For a helpful synthesis of scholarship on social movement and political activism, see Sidney G. Tarrow, *Power in Movement: Social Movements and Contentious Politics*, 3rd and rev. ed. (New York: Cambridge University Press, 2011).

power to champion a specific cause or issue; and then hold them accountable for enforcing any protections that are enacted.[9]

In this book, I provide a synthetic overview of transnational LGBT activism since the mid-nineteenth century. I not only integrate a wide array of secondary sources, but also utilize primary sources from archives typically ignored by scholars of foreign relations such as the IHLIA LGBT Heritage at the Amsterdam Public Library, the Hall-Carpenter Archives at the London School of Economics, the ONE Archive at the University of Southern California, and a variety of LGBT publications including *The Advocate*, *The Washington Blade*, and *ONE Magazine*.[10] These collections are replete with material on the individuals, issues, and organizations that drove the rise of international LGBT rights advocacy—trends largely omitted from currently accessible traditional diplomatic history resources like the Foreign Relations of the United States series, US Department of State records, and presidential documents. This book interweaves historiography on the histories of human rights and sexuality and provides a much-needed introductory volume targeted at a mass audience.

There are limits to this approach. A synthesis by definition will not offer exhaustive treatment of every region, every issue, and every era. Indeed, even if one were inclined to produce such an encyclopedic work, critical gaps in both the primary and secondary source materials would complicate such an endeavor. Archivists, professional and amateur alike, make decisions about what is deemed worthy for preservation. These decisions are shaped by class, racial, and gender biases and notions of morality. In practice, this has often meant that materials on lesbians and people of color, as well as those that were sexually explicit, were less likely to be retained, thus creating omissions in historic documentation that one must be careful not to assume are indicative of the nonexistence of these communities or the absence of sexualized reflections of LGBT life.[11] In addition, while there were unquestionably women who engaged in same-sex emotional and physical relationships in all historical eras, men who engaged in similar intimacies drew far more attention from legal and political authorities and there are consequently more extant sources about certain aspects of their experiences in some time periods. After World War II, when both men and women began mobilizing for gay rights, they rarely did so within the

---

[9]For more on the definitions and components of advocacy, see Margaret E. Keck and Kathryn Sikkink, *Activists beyond Borders: Advocacy Networks in International Politics* (Ithaca, NY: Cornell University Press, 1999).

[10]For excellent overviews on archives with material on same-sex sexuality in Africa, Asia, Australia and New Zealand, Europe, Latin America, and North America, see the respective essays by Xavier Livermon, Howard Chiang, Graham Willett, Christopher Ewing, Pablo Ben, and Rachel Corbman in *Global Encyclopedia of Lesbian, Gay, Bisexual, Transgender, and Queer (LGBTQ) History*, Howard Chiang, ed. (Chicago: Gale, 2019), 1: 91–118.

[11]Marc Stein, "Canonizing Homophile Sexual Respectability: Archives, History, and Memory," *Radical History Review* 120 (Fall 2014): 53–73.

same organizational contexts; and when they did, tensions along gendered lines often appeared. The international LGBT movement still wrestles with challenges of sexism, racism, economic inequality, differences between the developed and developing world, and intersectionality. Furthermore, there are significant national disparities—especially in countries where homosexuality remains illegal—in efforts to preserve LGBT-related archival materials and the production of scholarly monographs documenting LGBT individuals and communities.

Terminology presents another set of challenges. Historians of sexuality have long distinguished the sexual *acts* in which people engage from their *identity* as individuals. Religious, legal, and medical authorities defined people based on their same-sex sexual practices long before such people identified themselves as members of a distinct subgroup. *Sodomite, pederast, Uranian, homosexual, homophile, gay, lesbian, queer*: these are only a few of terms used at different times by different people as markers of condemnation or signifiers of proud defiance. Throughout the text, I try not to apply anachronistic terms, but there are times where a desire for clarity and a lack of alternative language make anachronisms unavoidable.

Different interpretations of sexuality and resistance to externally imposed models of advocacy further complicate matters. In many Middle Eastern nations, the Western conflation of sexual behavior with sexual identity and the definition of sexual orientation as a protected category in human rights law are highly problematic. In several Arab cultures, Western discourse on LGBT identity does not neatly correlate to local terminologies describing those who engage in same-sex sexual relations. The view that there should be universal civil rights based upon sexual conduct is also disputed. Furthermore, Western countries' invocation of Muslim and Arab societies' hostility to LGBT rights as a means of characterizing these nations as backward or violent not only evokes charges of imperialism, but also reduces non-heteronormative Arabs to passive victims. Not surprisingly, many activists in the Middle East emphatically reject this characterization. While they reject the Western notion of "coming out" as the sine qua non for challenging homophobia, they engage in subtler forms of advocacy like social media organizing or blogging. Rather than publicly promoting "gay rights," they call for expanded privacy protections or radical forms of liberty that would allow people to act on their same-sex desires in safety, beyond the reach of authorities and the law. Rather than "come out" to the wider community and one's family, these individuals choose to "come in" by sharing their private lives with only a selected few. They recognize that in these societies, visibility is often dangerous, not liberating.[12]

---

[12]Carl F. Stychin, "Same-Sex Sexualities and the Globalization of Human Rights Discourse," *McGill Law Journal* 49:4 (2004): 951–68; Jason Ritchie, "How Do You Say 'Come Out of the Closet' in Arabic? Queer Activism and the Politics of Visibility in Israel-Palestine," *GLQ: A Journal of Lesbian and Gay Studies* 16:4 (2010): 557–75.

These distinctions are also evident in Latin America and Africa. In Latin America, sexual practices associated with "macho" culture and sexual cultures of indigenous societies are not easily subsumed into the categorical assumptions undergirding the Western model of LGBT advocacy.[13] In sub-Saharan Africa, few gay, lesbian, bisexual, and transgender people currently embrace the term or the identity "queer," which is perceived as a predominately Western concept. In 2017, ILGA-Africa estimated that there were more than 250 LGBT organizations spread across forty nations on the continent, but many of these groups operate clandestinely. LGBT advocacy organizations are more plentiful and better funded in nations like Uganda, Kenya, and Nigeria whose governments are actively suppressing LGBT rights and espousing anti-LGBT rhetoric, but local activists put themselves at great risk of physical violence or arrest when they publicly confront such policies. They are also sometimes accused of abetting Western imperialism by accepting foreign funding and adopting priorities of outside organizations that may not always align with the demands and needs of local LGBT communities.[14] Furthermore, the professionalization and bureaucratization required by many NGOs as a prerequisite for funding can divert activists' resources and energies from grassroots organizing and service provision—a phenomenon described as "NGO-ization."[15]

This book is organized into six chapters. Chapter One provides a quick overview of the historic context in which sodomy laws first arose. It then examines the origins and evolution of LGBT advocacy from the mid-nineteenth century until the outbreak of World War I. Chapter Two surveys how global conflict brought the first wave of international organizing to a standstill, but also set the stage for the first mass movements for homosexual emancipation and renewed international activism in the interwar years. Although the rise of fascism led to a chilling escalation in the persecution of non-heteronormative and non-binary individuals, World War II (WWII) also provided gay men and women new opportunities for self-awareness and community-building that proved instrumental to the emergence of the post-WWII transnational homophile movement. Beginning with the ongoing persecution of gay men in Germany in the immediate aftermath of World War II, Chapter Three then addresses how the rise of the Cold War led to a global Lavender Scare—a fusion of antigay hysteria and national security concerns that negatively affected gays and lesbians in many Western countries. Both undeterred and animated by the repressive

[13]For a variety of perspectives, see Javier Corrales and Mario Pecheny, eds. *The Politics of Sexuality in Latin America: A Reader on Lesbian, Gay, Bisexual, and Transgender Rights* (Pittsburg: University of Pittsburgh Press, 2010).

[14]Marc Epprecht, *Sexuality and Social Justice in Africa: Rethinking Homophobia and Forging Resistance* (London: Zed Books, 2013).

[15]Aziz Choudry and Dip Kapoor, eds. *NGOization: Complicity, Contradictions and Prospects* (New York: Zed Books, 2013).

political climate, a new wave of homophile groups arose and forged transnational ties. Although unsuccessful at the time, they demanded inclusion in new definitions of international human rights. By 1965, a time of cultural and political ferment, more militant homophiles were rejecting assimilationism and were poised for more confrontational forms of advocacy. Chapter Four traces the international impact of the Stonewall uprising and a wave of legislation that decriminalized same-sex relations in several nations. A more assertive and visible international LGBT rights movement took shape and activists began coordinating transnational demonstrations aimed at specific countries. Advocates also won a major victory in the European Court of Human Rights that had sweeping long-term ramifications. At the same time, LGBT people living under authoritarian political regimes forged tentative ties to the international LGBT movement, a strategy imbued with both benefits and risks. Chapter Five examines how state inaction in the face of the HIV/AIDS pandemic inspired new transnational forms of protest. It also describes the impact of the end of the Cold War and subsequent expansion of supranational institutions in Europe in greatly expanding LGBT rights across the continent. Chapter Six follows the contentious and protracted process by which LGBT equality and LGBT organizations entered the discourse and institutions of the UN. The chapter concludes by illuminating the tensions not only between those advocating LGBT rights and their opponents, but also among LGBT advocates themselves.

The historical trajectory I trace is punctuated with thrilling victories and crushing defeats. Fiercely courageous pathbreakers coexist with those driven by faith or fear or political opportunism (or all three) to destroy them. The path toward LGBT liberation moves forward and backward in different places in different historical circumstances and is experienced quite differently depending on sex, culture, class, race, region, and context. While the international LGBT rights movement has unquestionably made significant advances, it is unlikely that universal acceptance of LGBT equality will ever be achieved.

CHAPTER ONE

Origins

While formal organizations aimed at securing LGBT political and legal equality were rare prior to World War II, there were transnational dimensions of LGBT advocacy long before then. In the nineteenth century, as distinct homosexual subcultures were emerging in London, Paris, Amsterdam, and New York,[1] a handful of Europeans challenged entrenched ideas about homosexuality and began calling for the decriminalization of same-sex sexual activity. News of their work spread internationally and sparked transatlantic connections among like-minded intellectuals.

At the same time, the rise of imperialism and the emergence of a new medical model of homosexuality contributed to escalating repression of gay activity and identity. Great Britain imposed laws mandating harsh penalties on same-sex sexual activities in its colonies throughout the world. Medical authorities argued that homosexual behavior stemmed from physical and mental abnormalities, creating new anxieties about same-sex attracted men and women already widely viewed as sinful and criminal. A series of highly publicized scandals exacerbated fears of a growing homosexual subculture threatening social order. But state persecutions of gay men like the 1895 trials of Irish writer Oscar Wilde also increased gay visibility and inspired the first international gay rights organizing efforts. Then, as now, movement toward more accepting views of homosexuality and decriminalization of homosexual behavior coexisted with fierce condemnation of same-sex attraction and severe legal, political, and social punishment of those confirmed or perceived to be gay.

---

[1]On the emergence of urban homosexual subcultures in the late nineteenth century, see Matt Cook, *London and the Culture of Homosexuality, 1885–1914* (New York: Cambridge University Press, 2008); David Higgs, ed. *Queer Sites: Gay Urban Histories since 1600* (London: Routledge, 1999); George Chauncey, *Gay New York: Gender, Urban Culture, and the Making of the Gay Male World, 1890–1940* (New York: Basic Books, 1994).

IMAGE 1.1 A depiction of same-sex love among the ancient Greeks on a fresco in the Tomb of the Diver, in what is now southern Italy and created in approximately 475 BC.

Attitudes about homosexuality changed dramatically from ancient times to the latter 1700s. Ancient Indians, Chinese, Egyptians, Greeks, and Romans tolerated homosexual practices. With the rise of Judaism, Christianity, and Islam, acceptance morphed into denunciation in many places. The Torah's Book of Leviticus contained two passages widely interpreted as negative references to homosexual acts. Leviticus 18:22 declares: "Thou shalt not lie with mankind, as with womankind; it is detestable." Leviticus 20:13 reads: "And if a man lie with mankind, as with womankind, both of them have committed abomination; they shall surely be put to death; their blood shall be upon them." These Jewish edicts informed early Christian interpretations of the story of Sodom and Gomorrah found in the Bible's Book of Genesis. Where Jewish writings depicted the divine destruction of the cities as retribution for the people's immorality and inhospitality toward Lot and his heavenly guests, Christian writers viewed homoeroticism as the sin that sparked God's wrath. The biblical story of Sodom and Gomorrah is also told in the Qur'an and male homosexuality is denounced in Sura 4:16: "If two men among you are guilty of lewdness, punish them both. If they repent and amend, leave them alone; for God is Oft-returning, Most Merciful." Unlike the Old Testament, the Qur'an did not call for homosexual behavior to be punished by execution. However, certain hadiths—sayings attributed to the Prophet Muhammad written almost two centuries after his death—described homosexuality as a profound "insult" to Islam meriting death by stoning.[2]

---

[2]The classic text is John Boswell, *Christianity, Social Tolerance, and Homosexuality: Gay People in Western Europe from the Beginning of the Christian Era to the Fourteenth Century* (Chicago: University of Chicago Press, 1980); Arno Schmitt and Jehoeda Sofer, eds. *Sexuality and Eroticism among Males in Moslem Societies* (New York: Harrington Park Press, 1992); Khaled El-Rouayheb, *Before Homosexuality in the Arab-Islamic World, 1500–1800* (Chicago: University of Chicago Press, 2005). See also Mustaka Akyol, "What Does Islam Say about Being Gay?" *New York Times*, July 28, 2015.

Despite these contested interpretations of the "sin of Sodom," codes making same-sex sexual activities crimes punishable by death or castration spread throughout Eurasia and into Africa. The legal definition of sodomy varied. Sometimes, it was limited to anal penetration of a man to the point of ejaculation. It did not always include oral sex, but some codes encompassed nonprocreative sex acts, regardless of the gender (and, sometimes, the species) of those involved. However, many indigenous societies in the Americas, sub-Saharan Africa, and the South Pacific accepted same-sex intimacy and in some cases, even celebrated those who defied gender norms.[3]

Following Henry VIII's break with the Catholic Church, English royal courts took the place of ecclesiastical courts in punishing sodomites. The Buggery Act of 1533, England's first sodomy law, did not define it, but punished with execution "the detestable and abominable vice of buggery committed with mankind or beast." The law targeted specific nonprocreative sexual *acts*, not specific groups of people. Preferring to handle legal matters through ecclesiastical courts, Mary I had the law repealed in 1553 when the jurisdiction of the Catholic Church was restored. Nine years later when Elizabeth I gained the throne, Parliament reenacted it, but it was not consistently enforced thereafter. In 1716, *Rex v. Richard Wiseman* defined heterosexual sodomy as a crime under the Buggery Act, but in 1817 *Rex v. Samuel* found that an adult man who performed fellatio on a boy did not violate the act. Eleven years later, as part of Prime Minister Robert Peel's plan to codify English criminal law, Parliament strengthened the 1553 anti-buggery law by dropping the requirement for proof of "the actual emission of seed" and making "proof of penetration only" sufficient grounds for conviction. It also added the law to the criminal codes of the East Indies and Ireland. Although the last executions for buggery in England occurred in 1835, it remained a capital offense in England, Wales, and Ireland until passage of the Offenses against the Person Act in 1861.[4]

Invoking biblical injunctions against "crimes against nature," civil and religious authorities led antisodomy campaigns in several Italian cities in the fifteenth century and across Spain in the sixteenth century. In 1553, Portugal's new Office of Holy Inquisitor broadened the legal definition of sodomy to include the anal penetration of either a man or a woman and the penetrator as well as the receiver. If found guilty, violators could be burned at the stake, have their property seized, or be deported and sentenced to

---

[3]There is a vast literature on these themes. For an overview, see Robert Aldrich, ed. *Gay Life and Culture: A World History* (New York: Universe Publishing, 2006); Marc Epprecht, *Heterosexual Africa? The History of an Idea from the Age of Exploration to the Age of AIDS* (Athens: Ohio University Press, 2008; see also Gay & Lesbian Vaishnava Association, *A Timeline of Gay World History*, http://www.galva108.org/single-post/2014/05/08/A-Timeline-of-Gay-World-History.

[4]Paul Johnson, "Buggery and Parliament, 1533–2017," *SSRN*, April 3, 2018, https://papers.ssrn.com/sol3/papers.cfm?abstract_id=3155522.

hard labor in Brazil, Africa, or India.[5] When the French, Spanish, Dutch, and English first settled in North America, virtually all of their colonies outlawed male same-sex sexual activity and attempted to impose European sexual norms upon indigenous peoples as a means of "civilizing" them.[6] Authorities also began to prosecute men and women who defied gender norms. In the 1690s, Massachusetts became the first American colony to outlaw crossdressing.[7] In the late seventeenth century, authorities in London, Paris, and Amsterdam periodically attempted to quash their emerging sodomitical subcultures through surveillance, arrests, and prosecutions. Throughout this era, Catholic and Protestant reformers alike condemned sodomy, sex outside of marriage, masturbation, and oral sex. Those found to have engaged in these behaviors faced harsh penalties including fines, imprisonment, whipping, stoning, disfigurement, branding, pillorying, dismemberment, execution, and execution followed by dismemberment.[8]

Authorities rarely prosecuted women who had sex with women. England's Buggery Act of 1533 did not mention lesbian sex. Indeed, few people of the era could conceive of sex that did not involve penile penetration. Trials of women charged with sexual offenses with other women were rare and usually involved women who had adopted male personas through crossdressing—seen as a dangerous threat to patriarchal ideals. But legal and religious records only tell part of the story. Women of this era expressed deep emotional ties to one another in letters, poetry, literature, and music. Some unmarried women shared households. Undoubtedly, some of these relationships were also sexual and the term "lesbian" was first used by the English in the 1730s, more than a century before the term "homosexual" was coined in Europe. But while lesbian sex was not illegal and same-sex intimacy between women was acknowledged, it was not condoned.[9] In 1740, when the Qing dynasty banned consensual homosexual sex between men and homosexual rape in China, the law's omission of women reflected

---

[5]James N. Green, *Beyond Carnival: Male Homosexuality in Twentieth-Century Brazil* (Chicago: University of Chicago Press, 1996), 20–2.

[6]Thomas A. Foster, ed. *Long before Stonewall: Histories of Same-Sex Sexuality in Early America* (New York: New York University, 2007), 5–6.

[7]Susan Stryker, *Transgender History: The Roots of Today's Revolution*, 2nd ed. (New York: Seal Press, 2017), 45–6.

[8]David F. Greenberg, *The Construction of Homosexuality* (Chicago: University of Chicago Press, 1988); Nicholas C. Edsall, *Toward Stonewall: Homosexuality in the Modern Western World* (Charlottesville: University of Virginia, 2003), 17–32; and Colin Spencer, *Homosexuality in History* (New York: Harcourt Brace & Company, 1995).

[9]Merry E. Wiesner-Hanks, *Women and Gender in Early Modern Europe*, 3rd ed. (New York: Cambridge University Press, 2008), 70–5, 293; Amy M. Froide, *Never Married: Singlewomen in Early Modern England* (New York: Oxford University Press, 2005), 71–4; Sara Mendelson and Patricia Crawford, *Women in Early Modern England, 1550–1720* (New York: Oxford University Press, 1998), 242–51.

male-centered Taoist notions of sex and a patriarchy that rendered women's sexuality invisible, not a tacit acceptance of lesbian relationships.[10]

In the late eighteenth century, the Enlightenment triggered a major shift in attitudes toward private sexual behavior. Frederick the Great of Prussia and Joseph II of Austria argued that "individuals should be free to believe, think, and even act as they wish, consistent with the rights of others, the maintenance of public order, and the ultimate authority of the state." Upon succeeding his father Frederick William I, Frederick the Great—possibly because of his own sexual inclinations—ended antisodomy crackdowns on taverns and male brothels in Berlin. He did not, however, repeal antisodomy laws. In France, Voltaire, Montesquieu, and other philosophes denounced sexual licentiousness and deviant practices like sodomy, adultery, and prostitution, but not on religious grounds. Bitterly critical of organized religion, the philosophes framed their objections to sexual deviance not in moral terms, but based on the view that sexual vice destabilized social order. In an age of frequent war and increasing economic competition, the philosophes deemed population growth essential to national prosperity and security. They therefore condemned nonprocreative sexual activities like sodomy. But they were even more critical of the state's brutal treatment of those convicted of sexual deviance.[11]

A leading French philosophe, the marquis de Condorcet, took this argument to its logical end and advocated the decriminalization of sodomy. He wrote: "Sodomy, so long as there is no violence, cannot be covered by criminal law. It does not violate the rights of any other man. It only exercises an indirect influence on the good order of society, like drunkenness and gambling." While he echoed his contemporaries in calling sodomy "a low vice, disgusting," he argued that the appropriate punishment was "contempt," not imprisonment or far harsher state-sanctioned penalties.[12]

In contrast to his French contemporaries' brief commentary on sexual deviance, British philosopher Jeremy Bentham wrote volubly about the subject. The founder of utilitarianism, Bentham wrote the longest essay on sodomy produced in the eighteenth century and the longest one written in English until the late nineteenth century. Although he chastised himself for worrying that publishing his work would destroy his professional reputation, Bentham chose not to release his essays on sodomy. They were not published until 1978, nearly two hundred years later.

In a 1785 essay, Bentham raised—and then demolished—all of the conceivable objections to pederasty, a synonym for sodomy without

---

[10]Bret Hinsch, *Passions of the Cut Sleeve: The Male Homosexual Tradition in China* (Berkeley: University of California Press, 1990), 142–4.

[11]Edsall, *Toward Stonewall*, 33–5; Bryant T. Ragan, "The Enlightenment Confronts Homosexuality," in *Homosexuality in Modern France*, Jeffrey Merrick and Bryant T. Ragan, eds. (New York: Oxford University Press, 1996), 8–29.

[12]Edsall, *Toward Stonewall*, 37.

the religious condemnation imbued in the latter term. In response to Montesquieu's claims about the debilitating impact of sexual deviance, Bentham pointed to the power of ancient Greeks and Romans who engaged in same-sex sexual activities. Because he believed that people with exclusively same-sex sexual lives comprised only a small portion of the population, Bentham scoffed at French philosophe Voltaire's fears that sexual deviance would inhibit population growth. In response to claims that pederasty threatened marriage, Bentham argued that adultery posed a far bigger danger. Bentham dismissed outright the notion that sodomy was a "crime against nature," asserting "If a pleasure is not a good, what is life for, and what is the purpose of preserving it?"[13]

Bentham stressed that punishing pederasty, not practicing it, was what harmed society and individuals. He warned that penalizing sodomy would radicalize those convicted and make them more, not less, likely to reengage in sexual deviance. Criminalizing behavior simply because a majority found it offensive could slide into tyranny. The mere existence of antisodomy statutes, Bentham claimed, created opportunities for extortion, blackmail, and fraudulent persecutions. He articulated many of the arguments still successfully used to justify the decriminalization of consensual homosexual relations between adults.[14]

While Bentham kept his views private, there were others who publicly called for the liberalization or abolition of statutes on moral offenses. In 1780, after an Englishman convicted of attempted sodomy choked to death during a pillorying witnessed by a vicious mob, Edmund Burke, a conservative member of the Whig Party, implored his colleagues in the House of Commons to abandon such barbaric punishments. Burke got some support in Parliament, but the press lambasted him for expressing sympathy toward a sodomite. Harsh physical penalties for sodomy remained British law for decades afterward.[15]

The Enlightenment's focus on individual rights and freedoms triggered more immediate change elsewhere. In the aftermath of the American Revolution, several US states reformed their legal codes. Thomas Jefferson failed to convince the Virginia legislature to make castration the penalty for sodomy instead of execution. In 1777, Georgia also rejected a call to make sodomy a noncapital crime. But ten years later, Pennsylvania opted to punish sodomy with imprisonment, not death. In 1796, New York and New Jersey made similar reforms and Massachusetts (1805), New Hampshire (1812), and Delaware (1826) soon followed.[16]

---

[13]Jeremy Bentham, "Offenses against One's Self," http://www.columbia.edu/cu/lweb/eresources/exhibitions/sw25/bentham/.
[14]Bentham, "Offences against One's Self."
[15]Edsall, *Toward Stonewall*, 39–40.
[16]Foster, ed. *Long before Stonewall*, 6.

In revolutionary France, calls for liberalization also yielded major changes in antisodomy laws. In 1791, fueled by expansive notions of individual rights and no longer bound by prerevolutionary codes that fused religion and law, France became the first nation in modern Europe to decriminalize consensual homosexual acts between adults in private. As part of a larger trend toward eliminating penalties for victimless crimes, the French omitted sodomy from both the 1791 penal code and the civil Code Napoléon promulgated in 1804. Jean-Jacques Cambacérès, whose homosexuality was well known among his colleagues in the National Assembly and by Napoleon himself, oversaw the drafting of the latter. The omission of "imaginary crimes" from French law signaled a major advance toward more humane state responses to same-sex sexual conduct. Although allegations of homosexuality remained a potent tool for smearing political enemies and state authorities still episodically repressed same-sex sexual behavior that they deemed a threat to public morality, the majority of Frenchmen who had sex with other men escaped police harassment and legal complications.[17]

French reforms triggered profound change elsewhere. Belgium, Spain, Portugal, and Scandinavia all adopted similar codes. Although some of these nations temporarily deviated from the French model, "virtually none of the countries of the European empires, other than the British, ever imposed criminal sanctions specifically on same-sex consensual activity in private."[18] When France invaded the Netherlands in 1811, it imposed the Code Napoléon, thus abolishing the Dutch law that made sodomy a capital offense. After the Dutch regained their independence two years later, no new sodomy law was enacted.[19] In 1830, eight years after Brazil gained its independence from Portugal, Dom Pedro I signed into law the Imperial Penal Code. Influenced by the French penal code of 1791 and the Code Napoléon, the new Brazilian code omitted all references to sodomy.[20] In 1839, the German state Württemberg abolished its sodomy statute and Hanover and Braunschweig followed suit the next year.[21] While France occupied Mexico from 1862 to 1867, it enforced the Code Napoléon and thus did not explicitly criminalize homosexual acts. When Mexico instituted

---

[17]Michael David Sibalis, "The Regulation of Male Homosexuality in Revolutionary and Napoleonic France, 1789–1815," in Homosexuality in Modern France, Merrick and Ragan, eds., 80–101.

[18]Michael Kirby, "The Sodomy Offence: England's Least Lovely Criminal Law Export?" in Human Rights, Sexual Orientation, and Gender Identity in the Commonwealth: Struggles for Decriminalization and Change, Corinne Lennox and Matthew Waites, eds. (London: Human Rights Consortium, Institute of Commonwealth Studies, University of London, 2013), 64.

[19]Timothy Murphy, Reader's Guide to Lesbian and Gay Studies (New York: Routledge, 2000), 413.

[20]Green, Beyond Carnival, 21–2.

[21]Gert Hekma, "Same-Sex Relations among Men in Europe, 1700–1900," in Sexual Cultures in Europe, Vol. 2, Themes in Sexuality, Franz X. Eder, Lesley Hall, and Gert Hekma, eds. (Manchester: University of Manchester Press, 1999), 90.

its own penal code in 1871, it too omitted references to sodomy, but outlawed attacks "on the morals and good customs" of the nation, language subject to wide and varied interpretation.[22] The divergence between states influenced by the French legal codes and states influenced by the British model or Islamic Sharia law shaped the global landscape for LGBT rights in ways that resonate to the present day.

Russia took an entirely different path. In the medieval era, homosexuality was tolerated and sodomy was only vaguely defined, encompassing any sexual act deviating from heterosexual missionary-style intercourse. The Orthodox Church considered homosexuality a sin, but rarely condemned its practice among lay people. Church punishments drew no distinctions between heterosexual and homosexual transgressions. There were no laws against sodomy and many foreign visitors to Russia in the fifteenth, sixteenth, and seventeenth centuries expressed astonishment at the open intimacy shared between men of all classes. In 1706, Peter the Great revised the Russian military code to criminalize "unnatural lechery" between soldiers, but ten years later, weakened the penalty from burning at the stake to lifelong exile. More than a century would pass before an 1832 criminal code outlawed consensual *muzhelozhstvo* (legally defined as anal intercourse) between civilian men, imposing a penalty of up to five years of Siberian exile, plus the loss of all civil and property rights. Nonetheless, the law was rarely applied and many elite Russian men with same-sex intimate inclinations, including composer Pyotr Tchaikovsky and explorer Nikolai Przhevalsky, lived relatively openly.[23]

Irrespective of nationality, many people's private lives were profoundly affected by sweeping economic, political, and legal changes during the nineteenth century. Industrialization dramatically changed preindustrial patterns of work and family life across much of Europe and North America. Infusions of job seekers leaving agricultural areas transformed dozens of cities from towns to sprawling metropolises. Middle- and upper-class families adopted a strict separation of work and home divided along gender lines. Houses were redesigned to create privacy. Sex, breastfeeding, and personal hygiene now occurred behind closed doors. But the divisions between urban and rural, the affluent and the working class, domestic servants and their employers also created new spaces for sexual attraction and deviation from expected norms. Despite the era's strong emphasis on marriage and domesticity, intimate friendships between men and between women flourished, though scholars disagree about how many such relationships were sexual. Urban life offered people interested in same-sex

---

[22]Len Evans, Chronology of Mexican Gay History, https://web.archive.org/web/2009072 9181055/; http://geocities.com/gueroperro/Chron-Mex.htm.
[23]Igor S. Kon, *The Sexual Revolution in Russia: From the Age of the Czars to Today* (New York: The Free Press, 1995), 15–16.

liaisons an escape from the close scrutiny of family and the ability to find people with similar inclinations.[24]

No one celebrated those newfound freedoms quite like Walt Whitman. Arriving in New York in 1841, he was electrified by the city. With a burgeoning population of 300,000, New York was as vibrant and diverse as any major European capital of the era. Whitman walked for hours, delighting in street life and cruising working-class men in public parks, the docks, ferries, streetcars, and the occasional bar. He kept detailed notes of his encounters with men. A few of these trysts blossomed into long-term love affairs.

IMAGE 1.2 Walt Whitman, sometime between 1855 and 1865.

[24]For a concise overview, see Annette F. Timm and Joshua A. Sanborn, *Gender, Sex, and the Shaping of Modern Europe*, 2nd ed. (New York: Bloomsbury Academic, 2016), 89–96.

Conflicted about his feelings for young men, Whitman turned to phrenology, then a trendy fad purporting to explain linkages between the shape of one's head and defining mental characteristics. In 1847, Whitman went to leading phrenologist Lorenzo Fowler to get his head read. Fowler concluded that Whitman had two very pronounced traits—amativeness (sexual love) and adhesiveness (comradeship). Whitman latched on to the concept of adhesiveness as a way to explain his intense attractions to men in a positive way. No longer conflicted about his feelings, he began to express them openly in his poetry. In 1860, Whitman added the Calamus poems to a new edition of *Leaves of Grass*, originally published five years earlier. Reflecting his embrace of adhesiveness, the poems boldly celebrated the "manly love of comrades." The poems further incensed critics who objected to the "obscene" nature of Whitman's work. But they also made Whitman an international hero to same-sex attracted men seeking to define their sexual identity including the British cultural critic John Addington Symonds, the Irish playwright Oscar Wilde, and the French author André Gide.[25]

In an age of resurgent conservatism following the European political revolutions of 1848, the increasing visibility of men like Whitman alarmed legal authorities and medical scientists investigating the causes of social deviance. Many US cities passed ordinances making it illegal for individuals to wear clothing "not belonging to his or her sex."[26] In 1857, French physician Bénédict A. Morel wrote *Treatise on Degenerations*, linking same-sex sexual attraction to degeneracy. That same year, Ambroise-Auguste Tardieu, France's leading expert on forensic medicine, published *Medico-Legal Study of Indecent Assaults*. Based on his physical examinations of hundreds of men convicted of crimes, Tardieu claimed that he could identify "true pederasts" because frequent homosexual sex gave their anuses and penises distinctive shapes. He warned that such men could pass through society undetected, making their presence known only to their own kind. Accordingly, Tardieu called for the rigorous enforcement of laws against public indecency and the physical inspection of suspected pederasts in order to minimize the destabilizing impact they had on society. Identifying and classifying sexual deviants became powerful legal and medical weapons against those who defied sexual and gender norms.[27]

These attitudes were evident among white authorities ruling British colonies throughout the world. While some European men flocked to overseas colonies in order to escape the constraints of sexuality imposed in their mother countries, imperial authorities imposed legal codes designed to

---

[25]Edsall, *Toward Stonewall*, 69–80.
[26]Stryker, *Transgender History*, 46–7.
[27]Edsall, *Toward Stonewall*, 129–30.

police native peoples seen as especially prone to "vice."[28] Although there were variations among them, the codes shared a common condemnation of same-sex activity under British imperial law. In no case did subjugated peoples have input on the construction or imposition of these laws, regardless of their local cultures or traditions. Sodomy laws were unilaterally imposed by white rulers persuaded of their moral superiority and intent on controlling sexual activities deemed corrupt.

The most widely imposed model was the Indian Penal Code of 1860, principally authored by Thomas Babington Macaulay. Its Paragraph 377 read: "Whoever voluntarily has carnal intercourse against the order of nature with any man, woman, or animal shall be punished with imprisonment for life, or with imprisonment ... for a term which may extend to 10 years and shall also be liable to a fine." Participants in these acts were equally condemned, regardless of assumption of the passive or active role, age, consent, or occurrence in public or private space. Adopted in over three dozen British territories across Asia, Africa, and the Pacific, Paragraph 377 was a blunt instrument that lumped together consensual private same-sex intimacy with violent sexual crimes like rape and pedophilia.[29] Having tacitly abandoned the use of the death penalty for sodomy offenses in 1836, Great Britain officially codified the change a year after implementation of Paragraph 377 in India. The Offenses against the Person Act of 1861 modified sodomy law in England, Wales, and Ireland, lessening the penalty from execution to imprisonment for ten years to life.[30]

Just a year later, Karl Heinrich Ulrichs penned a trenchant critique of sodomy laws and began articulating a theory about same-sex attracted men that had transnational ramifications. Born in 1825 in Aurich, Germany, Ulrichs studied law in Göttingen and Berlin and then became a junior attorney for the Kingdom of Hanover. In 1861, in Frankfurt am Main, Ulrichs became secretary to Justin T.B. von Linde, the representative of

---

[28]On British efforts to impose their moral and sexual standards on colonized peoples, see Ann Laura Stoler, *Carnal Knowledge and Imperial Power: Race and the Intimate in Colonial Rule* (Berkeley: University of California Press, 2002). On the allure of colonies in Africa, South and Southeast Asia, the South Pacific, and the Caribbean for men seeking sexual openness, see Robert Aldrich, *Colonialism and Homosexuality* (New York: Routledge, 2003).

[29]Kirby, "The Sodomy Offence," 64–7. Asian and Pacific colonies that instituted variants or replicates of Paragraph 377 included: Australia, Bangladesh, Bhutan, Brunei, Fiji, Hong Kong, India, Kiribati, Malaysia, Maldives, Marshall Islands, Myanmar (Burma), Nauru, New Zealand, Pakistan, Papua New Guinea, Singapore, Solomon Islands, Sri Lanka, Tonga, Tuvalu, and Western Samoa. In Africa, Paragraph 377 was imposed in Botswana, Gambia, Ghana, Kenya, Lesotho, Malawi, Mauritius, Nigeria, Seychelles, Sierra Leone, Somalia, Swaziland, Sudan, Tanzania, Uganda, and Zimbabwe. See Human Rights Watch, "This Alien Legacy: The Origins of 'Sodomy' Laws in British Colonialism," December 17, 2008, 6, https://www.hrw.org/sites/default/files/reports/lgbt1208_webwcover.pdf.

[30]The full text of the act is posted at http://www.legislation.gov.uk/ukpga/Vict/24-25/100/contents. In 1885, the British strengthened their sodomy law in ways that made it even harsher than Paragraph 377, an episode explained later in this chapter.

Lichtenstein, Reuss, and Homburg to the diet of the German Confederation. In 1862, after his friend, Johann Baptist von Schweitzer, an activist in the social democracy workers' movement, got arrested for public indecency with a young boy in Mannheim, Ulrichs wrote a defense and sent it to Schweitzer, but part of it was intercepted and turned in to authorities.

Although he had no medical training, the incident inspired Ulrichs to examine the origins of same-sex attraction. After informing his stunned family of his intentions, he began writing "The Race of Uranian Hermaphrodites, i.e., the Man-Loving Half-Men." He completed the first volume in 1863 and published it under the pseudonym "Numa Numantius" the next year. He did not publicly reveal himself as author of the text until 1868. Between 1864 and 1879, Ulrichs published twelve volumes called *Forschungen über das Rätsel der männerlichen Liebe* [*Researches on the Riddle of Love between Men*]. His initial analysis was based mostly on his own experience, which he assumed all same-sex attracted men shared.

Immersing himself in the new field of embryology, Ulrichs noted that human embryos in the earliest stages of development do not have differentiated sexual organs. (Chromosomal markers for sex were not discovered until 1905). Ulrichs seized on this fact to link sex organs and sexual desire (a connection now rejected) and to argue that both could develop naturally in either direction. A man could experience the disjuncture of having a masculine body and a feminine psyche, thereby manifesting a "third sex." Drawing not on science but on the speech on love by Pausanias in Plato's *Symposium*, Ulrichs coined the term "Urning," a reference to Aphrodite Uranus, to describe the hermaphroditic half-man, and "Dioning" to describe heterosexual men. "Urningin" and "Dioningin" were his comparable terms for women. After he met others with same-sex sexual inclinations, Ulrichs expanded his lexicon with other terms describing a variety of combinations of physical attributes and sexual inclinations. Because one's sexual inclination was set at birth, Ulrichs argued, same-sex intimate relations were "natural" and therefore deserving of legal protection as long as they were consensual. While some critics dismissed his "third sex" theory outright since Ulrichs himself was admittedly attracted to men, it presented a strong case for the abolition of legal restrictions on "unnatural" acts between consenting adults.

This was not merely an intellectual exercise for Ulrichs, but a matter of political urgency. Because his homeland Hanover did not criminalize consensual homosexual acts, he was justifiably worried that Prussia would impose its strict antisodomy law when it invaded Hanover in 1866. That is precisely what happened and when Ulrichs challenged the new government, he was twice imprisoned.[31] During the course of his

---

[31]A similar situation arose in Italy. In 1859, Victor Emmanuel II promulgated a penal code for the Kingdom of Sardinia that criminalized homosexual acts between men. When Italy united a year later, the sodomy laws of Sardinia were applied nationally, with the exception of Sicily.

second arrest in 1867, police raided his home and confiscated his "third sex" research materials. Having been ridiculed by the press, Ulrichs left Hanover upon his release from prison and moved to Bavaria, where same-sex sexual relations between men were still legal. There, on August 19, 1867, at the Congress of German Jurists in Munich, Ulrichs gave a public speech defending the rights of same-sex attracted men and women, a bold act that marked the beginning of the gay rights movement in Germany. He was shouted down, but wrote privately of his pride in taking a step on "a trail to freedom."

But Ulrichs's courage did not prevent the nationwide adoption of Prussia's antisodomy laws when the German Empire united in 1871. Paragraph 175 of the new German penal code made "unnatural" sex acts between men a crime punishable by imprisonment. While Ulrichs penned an essay lamenting the tragic impact of outlawing "love between men" in 1879, he fled to Italy the following year. He spent the remainder of his life in L'Aquila, cobbling together enough money to survive through language instruction and publishing a Latin journal. He died there on July 14, 1895, his work being challenged by the new medical model of homosexuality.[32]

Ulrichs's ideas greatly inspired Karl-Maria Benkert, a German-Hungarian translator, journalist, and human rights advocate who coined the terms "homosexual" and "heterosexual." Born in Vienna in 1824, Benkert moved with his family to Budapest as a child. As a young man, he worked as a bookseller's apprentice. Benkert was profoundly affected by the suicide of a close friend who had sex with men and was being blackmailed by another man. After serving in the Hungarian army, Benkert worked as a journalist and travel writer, publishing over twenty-five books on a broad array of topics. In 1847, granted permission by Viennese police to use the name of his aristocratic Hungarian relatives, he changed his name to Károly Mária Kertbeny. Although he never married and professed to be "normally sexed" in his writings, Kertbeny's diaries describe a number of encounters with men. He struck up a correspondence with Karl Heinrich Ulrichs and was terrified when Ulrichs was arrested.[33]

That fear did not dissuade him from writing extensively about homosexuality. In 1869, while the new penal code for the North German Federation was being drafted, he wrote two anonymous pamphlets calling for the abolition of Paragraph 143 of the Prussian Penal Code, the section that criminalized consensual private sexual acts between men (and which became Paragraph 175 of the unified German legal code in 1871). He framed his argument in classically liberal arguments about individual rights. Recalling his late friend, Kertbeny argued that blackmailers exploited the

[32]Hubert C. Kennedy, "The 'Third Sex' Theory of Karl Heinrich Ulrichs," *Journal of Homosexuality* 6:1/2 (Fall/Winter 1980/81): 103–11.
[33]Judit Takács, "The Double Life of Kertbeny," conference paper presented at "Past and Present of Radical Sexual Politics," University of Amsterdam, October 3–4, 2003, http://www.policy.hu/takacs/pdf-lib/TheDoubleLifeOfKertbeny.pdf.

law to target same-sex attracted men and that the state had no right to interfere in the private sexual lives of its citizens.

In these pamphlets, Kertbeny publicly used his terms homosexual and heterosexual for the first time.[34] A union of the Greek term "homos" ("same") and the medieval Latin word "sexualis," Kertbeny offered a way for same-sex attracted men and women to describe themselves in a neutral, legalistic, and scientific way. He provided an alternative to pejorative terms like "sodomite" and "pederast." Both homosexuality and heterosexuality, he argued, were congenital and immutable. But while Kertbeny did not believe same-sex sexual behavior was criminal or sinful, he associated it with sickness and deviance. He died in 1882 and did not live to see the wide application of his terminology.[35]

While Ulrichs and Kertbeny hoped to spark liberalization of laws against homosexuality, there were others who were greatly alarmed by questioning of sexual norms and who began pushing aggressive measures to guard traditional morality. In the 1860s, British authorities passed a series of Contagious Disease Acts that allowed authorities to order any woman suspected of prostitution to be tested for sexually transmitted diseases. But the laws prompted a furious outcry from moralists who believed the acts condoned prostitution, reformers who viewed prostitutes as victims of patriarchy and moral double standards, and civil libertarians opposed to increasing police power. Although they did not succeed in getting the acts repealed until 1886, the coalition grew and a powerful Social Purity Alliance arose. Throughout the 1870s, hysteria about girls and women forced into prostitution (often called "white slavery") soared. Tabloids stoked interest in lurid scandals and heightened popular fears of social disorder.[36]

Throughout this era, historical toleration of male homosexuality in Japan was rapidly eroding. Nanshoku ("love of males"), a tradition of same-sex intimacy that arose among aristocrats, Buddhist monks, and samurai warriors hundreds of years earlier, became commodified when bourgeois men began patronizing male prostitutes in the tea houses of early modern Tokugawa Japan. Ruling from 1603 to 1867, the shoguns prohibited trade with Westerners and suppressed Christianity. This self-imposed isolation and absence of religious opposition to homosexuality created a culture where male same-sex subcultures flourished and there were no moral taboos against the practice of sodomy. But the opening of Japanese ports to foreign trade in 1859 shifted popular attitudes. After the shogunate collapsed and the Meiji Restoration returned imperial control in 1868, Japan began to modernize

---

[34]Kertbeny first used the term "homosexual" in a May 1868 letter to Ulrichs.
[35]Takács, "The Double Life of Kertbeny."
[36]Judith Walkowitz, Prostitution and Victorian Society: Women, Class, and the State (Cambridge, UK: Cambridge University Press, 1980).

and Christian morality infiltrated society. In 1873, the government outlawed sex between men. Ten years later, when Japan adopted a legal code inspired by the French model, the antisodomy law was repealed and never reenacted. Nonetheless, the culture of *nanshoku* was forced underground as Japan developed close commercial and political ties to the West.[37]

Rapid societal changes also reshaped homosexual cultures elsewhere.[38] In 1884, a time of intense agitation for Irish home rule, a scandal in Dublin revealed the dangers that the shifting public mood posed to those in an increasingly visible homosexual subculture. That year, Irish nationalists not above using salacious allegations to advance their cause claimed that staff at Dublin Castle, a building used as a metaphor for the English government then ruling Ireland, were participating in gay orgies. William O'Brien, a member of Parliament representing Cork and the publisher of the *United Ireland* newspaper, accused Gustavus Cornwall, head of the General Post Office in Ireland, of being homosexual. Incensed, Cornwall sued O'Brien for libel. Witnesses in the subsequent five-day trial related their sexual trysts with Cornwall and revealed the existence of a thriving gay subculture in Dublin. The Irish and British press covered the proceedings extensively. When the trial ended with the dismissal of Cornwall's libel suit, Irish nationalists across the country rejoiced. But the consequences for gay men in Ireland and Great Britain were severe.

In the wake of the trial, newspapers unleashed fiercely homophobic commentary and police targeted gays. Cornwall, who had fled to his brother-in-law's house in Scotland, was arrested and placed on trial in Dublin for buggery and corrupting young men. Other suspected homosexuals were arrested and interrogated including James Ellis French, a detective director in the Royal Irish Constabulary. Many fled Ireland to escape persecution. Eight men, including three who ran male brothels, were tried. French received two years' imprisonment at hard labor. Although Cornwall was found not guilty of buggery, the judge said it was clear that he was guilty of "vices and practices equally loathsome" even though legal. Cornwall, he declared, belonged to "a vile gang [that] existed in the city, leagued together for the pursuit of unnatural depravity and vice." At another defendant's trial, the prosecutor described the accused as "musical," a euphemism for homosexual that endured for years.[39]

---

[37]Adrian Carton, "Desire and Same-Sex Intimacies in Asia," in *Gay Life and Culture: A World History*, Robert Aldrich, ed. (New York: Universe Publishing, 2006), 313–21.

[38]For context on changing attitudes toward homosexuality in Europe from the 1860s to 1914, see Dagmar Herzog, *Sexuality in Europe: A Twentieth-Century History* (New York: Cambridge University Press, 2011), 31–44.

[39]James H. Murphy, "'Disgusted by the Details': Dr. Jekyll and Mr. Hyde and the Dublin Castle Scandals of 1884," in *Back to the Future of Irish Studies*, Maureen O'Connor, ed. (New York: Peter Lang, 2010), 177–90; Brian Lacey, *Terrible Queer Creatures: Homosexuality in Irish History* (Dublin: Wordwell Ltd., 2008), 135–45.

In England, the Dublin Castle scandal contributed to the passage of a portion of the Criminal Law Amendment Act of 1885, which had devastating, long-lasting ramifications for British and Irish gay men. The legislation raised the age of consent from thirteen to sixteen and levied harsher penalties for sexual offenses like seduction through fraud or drugs and abduction of girls under the age of eighteen for the purposes of seduction. Late in the debate, supposedly out of his concern about the rise in male prostitution and degeneracy in urban areas, Henry Labouchère, Liberal MP for Northampton and founding editor of the muckraking *Truth* magazine, introduced an amendment that made "gross indecency" a crime in the UK. Although the amendment excluded lesbian sexual activity, it covered a much broader array of sexual activities between men than the 1861 antisodomy statute. Where the older law only criminalized anal intercourse that could be physically proved, Labouchère's amendment encompassed fellatio, mutual masturbation, and other nonpenetrative sexual activities and it required no physical proof. Any man found guilty of "gross indecency" with another man, "in public or in private," could be imprisoned for two years with or without hard labor. An additional codicil permitted the prosecution of anyone who aided "the commission of" gross indecency. Very late on August 7, 1885, with virtually no debate in an almost empty chamber, the House of Commons passed the amendment as Section 11 of the Criminal Law Amendment Act. Whatever the intentions of those who drafted and supported it, the Labouchère amendment's inclusion of private as well as public acts and definition of sexual contact between men in extremely vague terms irrespective of age or consent gave police, prosecutors, and blackmailers a potent tool for targeting gay men or allegedly gay men. No other nation would pass as proscriptive a law until the Nazis broadened Germany's Paragraph 175 in 1935.[40]

The emergence of medical theories positing that homosexuality was a mental illness compounded the difficulties same-sex attracted men and women faced. In 1886, the Austro-German psychiatrist Richard von Krafft-Ebing published *Psychopathia Sexualis*, a compendium on sexual deviance intended as a scientific reference tool for legal and medical professionals. As a means of deterring general readers, he used a Latin title and wrote some of the text in Latin. Nonetheless, the book sold well, went through twelve editions, and was translated into several foreign languages.

Categorizing as aberrant any sexual act not intended for procreation, Krafft-Ebing drew on case studies of homosexuals that he conducted while working at a mental asylum and with private patients. Articulating an elaborate theory on homosexuality, Krafft-Ebing argued that homosexuality developed in utero and resulted in a "sexual inversion" of the brain. The evolutionary development of homosexuals stalled, leaving them with

---

[40]Edsall, *Toward Stonewall*, 112–14.

primitive psychosexual centers of the brain. Although he popularized the term originally coined by Kertbeny and shared his and Ulrichs's view that homosexuality was innate and natural, Krafft-Ebing emphasized a medical model defining homosexuality as deviant and pathological. Because he considered homosexuality a sickness and deficiency resulting from an inherited neurological or psychological condition, he believed it should be treated or cured, but not outlawed. He therefore challenged the laws criminalizing male homosexuality in Germany and the Austro-Hungarian Empire.[41]

Although Krafft-Ebing eventually revised his view that homosexuality was pathological, scientific claims about linkages between homosexuality and degeneration persisted and animated those intent on guarding traditional morality. In 1889, Finland, having had no law against same-sex relationships under criminal laws adopted in the 1730s, criminalized both male-male and female-female sexual contact (with a maximum penalty of two years' imprisonment) in a major revision of its penal code. Rejecting prevailing ideas that women were sexually passive and thus only engaged in sexual activities initiated by a man (a consensus soon challenged by the sexologists' depiction of lesbians as "inverts" with masculine sexual desire), Finland became one of the only nations in the world to include lesbianism in its definition of sodomy at the time.[42] Other states chose not to recriminalize sodomy, but used broadly interpreted statutes on "public indecency" and "vagrancy" to restrict homosexual behavior and identity. In 1889, a new Brazilian penal code retained the nation's long-standing decriminalization of sodomy, but gave police the ability to arrest anyone crossdressing or wearing make-up in public, engaging in sexual trysts in public places, or engaging in male prostitution.[43] The same year, Italy adopted a new criminal code that omitted references to same-sex sexual adults, but including similar provisions outlawing public indecency.[44] Same-sex attracted men in a wide array of cities including New York, Chicago, San Francisco, Washington, DC, London, Berlin, Amsterdam, Paris, Havana, Mexico City, Buenos Aries, and Rio de Janeiro learned to both fear and evade such statutes.

Sex scandals only strengthened the convictions of those who viewed such visible homosexual subcultures as evidence of increasing social decay. In

---

[41]Edsall, *Toward Stonewall*, 131–2.
[42]Special thanks to my colleague Jason Lavery for background on this significant change. See also Jan Löfström, "A Premodern Legacy: The 'Easy' Criminalization of Homosexual Acts between Women in the Finnish Penal Code of 1889," *Journal of Homosexuality* 35:3–4 (1998): 53–79; Ministry of Justice, The Criminal Code of Finland, http://www.finlex.fi/en/laki/kaannokset/1889/en18890039.pdf.
[43]Green, *Beyond Carnival*, 22–3.
[44]Yuri Guaiana and Mark Seymour, "From Giarre to Civil Unions: The 'Long March' for Same-Sex Relationships in Italy," in *From Sodomy Laws to Same-Sex Marriage: International Perspectives since 1789*, Sean Brady and Mark Seymour, eds. (London: Bloomsbury Academic, 2019), 167.

IMAGE 1.3 Drawing from an anti-LGBT broadside denouncing a drag ball in Mexico City that was raided by the police in 1901. The caption reads: "The 41 fags found at a dance on Calle de la Paz on November 20, 1901." The son-in-law of Mexican President Porfirio Díaz was rumored to be the forty-second guest at the infamous "Dance of the 41," but authorities never confirmed his attendance. Although the other forty-one men had broken no laws, the government punished them by forcing them to clean streets while dressed in women's clothes and to dig trenches for soldiers fighting Mayans in the Yucatán. Mexican LGBT activists later reclaimed the number "41" as a symbol of resistance and courage.

1889, London police arrested a fifteen-year-old Post Office messenger boy suspected of theft. When interrogated, the boy divulged that he had earned the large sum of money he was carrying by working as a prostitute at a male brothel on 19 Cleveland Street. He claimed that three of his fellow messengers also worked as male prostitutes there. Testimony from the boys as well as police surveillance soon revealed that a number of high-profile British men were clients, including Lord Arthur Somerset, an equerry to the Prince of Wales. Unsubstantiated rumors that Prince Albert Victor, the eldest son of the Prince of Wales and second-in-line to the British throne, had visited 19 Cleveland Street added extra intrigue.

Yet police only arrested two men: an associate of the proprietor and a messenger boy implicated in the seduction and recruitment of other messenger boys. Both pled guilty to indecency and received short terms at hard labor. Lord Somerset and Charles Hammond, proprietor of the brothel, both quickly and easily fled the country. Unsure how to proceed on such an explosive matter, police delayed for months before issuing a warrant for Somerset's arrest. By that point, Somerset was already safely abroad and since no extradition order was ever issued, he spent the rest of life in exile in the south of France. By January 1890, sixty suspects had been named, but twenty-two of them fled England to escape charges. The mainstream British press barely covered the story.

But Ernest Parke, editor of the radical weekly *The North London Press*, soon ensured the story received international attention. Suspicious when one of his reporters told him about the light sentences imposed on the convicted male prostitute (the usual penalty for "gross indecency" was two years), Parke discovered that the boys had implicated prominent aristocrats. He ran stories about the investigation, first without naming specific individuals, then alleging that Henry Fitzroy, earl of Euston, was involved in "an indescribably loathsome scandal in Cleveland Street." Euston sued Parke for libel and won, but the trial was chockful of widely reported details of the homosexual underworld in London. On February 28, 1890, persuaded there was merit to Parke's allegations of a cover-up, Henry Labouchère introduced a motion in Parliament to launch an official investigation. Although he denied that "a gentleman of very high position" (presumably Prince Albert Victor) was involved in the affair, Labouchère alleged that Prime Minister Lord Salisbury, the Lord Chancellor of England, and the Attorney General Richard Webster colluded to quash the investigation. Webster hotly denied the allegations and after seven hours of debate, the House of Commons roundly defeated the motion in a 206–66 vote. While the scandal soon faded from public memory, it fueled the view that male homosexuality was an aristocratic vice that corrupted working-class youth.[45] Similar claims resurfaced when forty-one men were arrested in a 1901 raid on a drag ball in Mexico City and two years later, when French police charged Baron d'Adelswärd-Fersen and Albert Hamelin de Warren with public indecency and "inciting minors to debauchery" after they invited school boys to their apartment for poetry readings and tableaux vivants.[46]

Passage of the Labouchère amendment and the Cleveland Street affair both angered and terrified those calling for social acceptance of homosexuality. John Addington Symonds, an independently wealthy literary scholar and essayist best known for his seven-volume cultural history of the Renaissance, was a good example. As a young man, Symonds had been tormented by his feelings for other men and squeamish about physically expressing them. Falsely accused of corrupting a choir boy while at Oxford, he left the university and took refuge in travel abroad and marriage. In frail

[45]Morris B. Kaplan, *Sodom on the Thames: Sex, Love, and Scandal in Wilde Times* (Ithaca, NY: Cornell University Press, 2005), 166–213.
[46]Robert McKee Irwin, Edward J. McCaughan, and Michelle Rocio Nasser, eds. *The Famous 41: Sexuality and Social Control in Mexico* (New York: Palgrave Macmillan, 2003); Florence Tamagne, "The Homosexual Age, 1870–1940," in *Gay Life and Culture: A World History*, Aldrich, ed., 172.

health much of his life, the stress took its toll and he suffered a nervous breakdown. As he recovered, Symonds decided to accept his sexual identity. After falling in love with a seventeen-year-old boy, he confessed his feelings for men to his wife. He proposed that they have a celibate marriage and he promised to be discreet in his sexual relationships with men in exchange for remaining an ideal husband and father. Surprisingly, she agreed.

Deeply affected by the Calamus poems, Symonds began writing homoerotic poetry and translating classical poetry with homosexual themes. In 1871, he started a long correspondence with Walt Whitman and over the next twenty years, he repeatedly asked the poet to identify the specific types of interactions between men his concept of adhesiveness included. Whitman dodged the question for years. In 1873, Symonds wrote *A Problem in Greek Ethics*, a passionate defense of emotional and physical love among men in ancient Greece. In Symonds's view, male homosexuality was in no way effeminate, pathological, or deviant. Yet it would be another decade before he shared ten privately printed copies of his work with friends.

As part of his ongoing efforts to reconcile his public and private selves, he began writing *A Problem in Modern Ethics*, a survey of contemporary medical, psychological, and literary attitudes toward homosexuality. In 1890, hoping Whitman would echo his positive views on inversion, Symonds wrote the poet a letter in which he bluntly asked Whitman's views on sexual intimacy between men. Always cautious in his private writings and leaving his poetry open to myriad interpretations, Whitman emphatically denied that sex was an element of his notions of comraderie between men—a claim Symonds justifiably found dubious. Having privately printed fifty copies of *A Problem in Modern Ethics* in 1891, Symonds decided to seek a wider audience for frank discussion of sexuality. Although he feared public exposure of his homosexuality and worried his lack of scholarly credentials undermined his authority, Symonds forged an alliance with Havelock Ellis, England's first sexologist.

Extremely shy and very limited in his own sexual experience, Ellis was nonetheless intellectually voracious and a leading writer among British left-wing intellectuals. After spending much of his youth in rural Australia, Ellis returned to England to study medicine and became active in socialist and avant-garde circles in London. In 1890, he published *The New Spirit*, a treatise on individual freedom. In 1891, at age thirty-two, he entered a celibate, unconventional marriage with Edith Lees, an openly lesbian feminist. His marriage and friendships with gay men including Edward Carpenter, an openly gay socialist poet and writer, stoked Ellis's intellectual interest in homosexuality. After exchanging several letters with Symonds, the two agreed to collaborate on medical study of homosexuality. Where Symonds, a literary critic and gay man, was hell-bent on disproving medical claims that homosexuality was a pathology, Ellis, a doctor and a heterosexual, was more trusting of medical authorities and animated more

IMAGE 1.4 Married in 1891, Edith Lees and Havelock Ellis had a very unconventional union. Openly lesbian, Lees had several affairs with women, with Ellis's knowledge. A novelist and women's rights activist, she was an active intellectual and strong supporter of her husband's work in sexology.

by intellectual curiosity than personal crusade. Despite their differing approaches and having never met in person (Symonds lived abroad most of the time), they began collecting case studies and enlisted Edward Carpenter on their project. But after Symonds died at age fifty-three in 1893, Ellis opted to complete the work alone and Carpenter embarked on his own project.

Profoundly moved by *Leaves of Grass* while in his twenties, Carpenter was a prolific author and advocate of varied issues, including feminism, sexual liberation, socialism, Eastern mysticism, and vegetarianism. In 1883, he published *Towards Democracy*, a book predicting a socialist revolution that would trigger a new age of democracy that celebrated sexual freedom and "comradeship." At age forty-five, he met twenty-year-old George Merrill, a working-class man who became his life partner. In 1894–5, he wrote a pamphlet on "homogenic love" (preferring the entirely Greek term to the odd Greek-medieval Latin fusion of "homosexual"). Drawing on Ulrichs's conception of the "third sex," Carpenter argued that everyone has a blend of male and female characteristics, with more masculine and feminine extremes evident in some people. He rejected the view that homosexuality was a pathology and argued that sexual inversion almost always "quite instinctive, mentally and physically, and therefore twinned in the very roots of individual life and practically ineradicable." Homogenic love, Carpenter claimed, benefitted society by fostering a more democratic community beyond the immediate family and across class lines.[47]

But just as Ellis and Carpenter finished their works and began seeking publishers, the most notorious gay sex scandal of the age erupted and the trials of Oscar Wilde overshadowed any effort to promote more positive images of homosexuality. A poet, novelist, editor, journalist, and playwright, Wilde was then one of the most famous people in the world. Born in Dublin in 1854, Wilde studied at Trinity College and Oxford University, developing a reputation for his brilliance as a classics scholar, sharp wit, and flamboyant style. An adherent of aestheticism, Wilde rejected middle-class respectability and valued beauty and taste above all other ideals. In 1884, he married Constance Lloyd. Just two years later, while Constance was pregnant with their second son, Wilde was seduced by seventeen-year-old Robert "Robbie" Ross. He and Constance remained together, raised their children, and often entertained at their lavishly decorated home. Nonetheless, rumors about Wilde's sexuality began to swirl, particularly after the first edition of *The Picture of Dorian Gray* (1890) included homoerotic passages that critics savaged as "unclean" and "poisonous." Wilde expunged most of the objectionable content in a second edition of the novel, but the original version came back to haunt him later.[48]

After his affair with Robbie, Wilde spent increasing amounts of time cavorting in the West End, mingling with aspiring writers and pursuing young men from the urban underclass. In June 1891, he was introduced to Lord Alfred "Bosie" Douglas, a student at Wilde's alma mater, Magdalen College, Oxford, and youngest son of the Marquess of Queensberry. Wilde was immediately smitten and the pair were soon inseparable. The two were brazen about their affair and openly intermingled with male prostitutes and crossdressers at restaurants and hotels in the West End, his home, and his

---

[47]Edsall, *Toward Stonewall*, 70, 78–80, 100–9; Weeks, *Coming Out*, 34–5.
[48]For an extensive and engaging account of Wilde's life and trials, see Kaplan, *Sodom on the Thames*, 224–51.

rooms at St. James Place, often joined by Wilde's friend Alfred Taylor. By 1895, Wilde was riding high. His play *An Ideal Husband* was a smashing success and a second play, *The Importance of Being Earnest*, was about to premiere.

On February 18, 1895, after months of trying to end Wilde and Bosie's relationship, the Marquess of Queensberry paid a visit to the Albemarle Club and left a card inscribed: "For Oscar Wilde, posing somdomite [*sic*]." Queensberry, a Scotsman best known for lending his name to the approved rules for amateur boxing, was a controversial figure. After divorcing his wife for a much younger woman, he had his second marriage annulled. He

IMAGE 1.5 Oscar Wilde and Lord Alfred "Bosie" Douglas, 1894. Introduced in 1891, Wilde and Douglas had a tumultuous relationship that ended for good a few months after Wilde's release from prison in May 1897. In 1902, Douglas married Olive Custance, a bisexual heiress and poet, and later converted to Roman Catholicism. He remained a controversial figure who denounced homosexuality, espoused anti-Jewish views, and became entangled in several libel cases.

was estranged from his five children and had a string of mistresses. After his British peers in the House of Lords failed to reelect him because of his atheism, he was enraged when the government appointed his eldest son to his seat.

The episode made the Marquess even more intent on keeping Wilde away from Bosie. He stopped by Wilde's house and insinuated that Bosie and Wilde were engaging in sodomy. Although Wilde thwarted the Marquess's plans to disrupt the opening of *The Importance of Being Earnest*, he decided— against the warnings of friends—to file criminal libel charges against Queensberry. Whether Wilde was inspired by Lord Euston's success in his libel case against Ernest Parke in the Cleveland Street scandal is unknown. He seems not to have anticipated that Queensberry would engage a private detective to gather evidence to prove his allegations, the surest way to rebut Wilde's libel case.

Despite his own questionable reputation, Queensberry presented himself as a concerned father trying to save his son from being corrupted by an older man. The trial was a media sensation, rife with drama and reflecting the age's anxieties about culture, gender, class, and moral decay. In Queensberry's formal plea, his legal team presented a devastating portrait of Wilde's solicitation and commission of "indecent" acts with at least ten men and boys in several locations, allegations impossible to refute given Wilde's indiscretion about these public assignations. The plea also pointed to the excised homoerotic passages of the first edition of *The Picture of Dorian Gray* as evidence of Wilde's familiarity with "the relations, intimacies, and passions of certain persons of sodomitical and unnatural habits, tastes, and practices." Sir Edward Carson, Queensberry's attorney, skillfully portrayed both Wilde's writings and his sexual actions as corrupting influences on the young.

At the trial, Carson and Wilde had many riveting exchanges. Wilde presented himself as a friend of the Douglas family and a frequent guest at their home. He relayed Bosie's depiction of Queensberry as divisive and unforgiving—an assertion seemingly validated when Queensberry and his eldest son were arrested after a public fistfight. Sir Edward George Clarke, Wilde's attorney, tried to defuse potential controversy by introducing two suggestive letters that Wilde had written to Bosie, one of which had been obtained by blackmailers who unsuccessfully attempted to extort money from Wilde. Wilde characterized one of the letters as a work of art with no salacious intent. When Carson aggressively cross-examined Wilde about his literary work, the writer responded with wit and charm, rejecting the suggestion that art could be moral or immoral.

In the end, Wilde's own recklessness proved his undoing. Carson peppered him with questions about his escapades with young working-class men, repeatedly hammering the class and age differences between Wilde and his consorts. At first, Wilde claimed there was nothing licentious in these interactions and defended his passion for youth, but he grew flustered when Carson insinuated that the men were often prostitutes whom he met through Taylor and that Wilde had kissed a servant boy. Cornered, Wilde stammered, "Pardon me, you sting me, insult me, and try to unnerve me in every way. At times one says things flippantly when one should speak more seriously, I admit that, I admit it—I cannot help it. That is what you are doing to me." Having woven together Wilde's private letters, literary work, and public conduct and associates, Carson virtually guaranteed that Wilde's libel suit would fail.

Wilde's lawyers unsuccessfully tried to withdraw their case. They admitted that Wilde had "posed" as a sodomite in writings, but denied that he had engaged in sexual improprieties. The judge declared Queensberry not guilty, a verdict that reflected the truth of Queensberry's claims and the belief that the public interest was served by his revelations. Under the Libel Act of 1843, Wilde was now liable for Queensberry's considerable legal expenses.

Carson, however, was not finished. He sent all of his trial notes and witness statements to the public prosecutor and urged them not to let Wilde escape justice. To make sure the government did not shirk its duties, Carson sent a copy of his cover letter to London newspapers. Unwilling to set themselves up for allegations of a cover-up like those that had plagued the Conservatives in the Cleveland Street episode in 1889–1990, the Liberal government directed law enforcement to prosecute Wilde. On April 5, 1895, after ignoring friends' suggestions that he flee to France, Wilde was arrested for multiple counts of gross indecency and imprisoned.

Three weeks later, his trial began. Wilde pled not guilty. Douglas, Robbie Ross, several others left England to escape being called as witnesses or being prosecuted themselves. Wilde responded eloquently when asked to define "the love that dare not speak its name." The trial ended with a hung jury. Wilde was granted bail and went into seclusion. Carson, Wilde's prosecutor in the first trial, privately asked the solicitor general "Can we not let up on the fellow now?"

With such sensationalism and attention surrounding the case, the answer was a resounding "no" and Wilde was tried again, this time with Alfred Taylor as a co-defendant. They were both charged with gross indecency and conspiracy to commit indecent acts. Taylor faced additional charges of procuring and attempted sodomy. The prosecution called a parade of working-class men who received immunity in exchange for their testimony about Wilde's and Taylor's sordid activities. Several other individuals provided corroborating evidence about Wilde's presence at specific events and places. Under the terms of the Criminal Law Amendment Act of 1885, which included the Labouchère amendment, defendants had the right to testify and Wilde's eloquence prompted applause from the courtroom audience.

Although Wilde and Taylor's cases were severed and the conspiracy charges were dropped, both men were convicted and sentenced to two years' imprisonment with hard labor.

In jail, Wilde was forced to walk on a treadmill for hours or to pick fibers out of old ropes. He was not allowed to speak to other prisoners and was barred from writing and reading anything other than the Bible for several months. His health deteriorated markedly, especially after a fall that ruptured his right eardrum. While in Reading Gaol, he wrote—but was not permitted to send—*De Profundis*, a 50,000-word letter to Bosie in which he dissects his life, takes responsibility for his downfall, and finds spiritual redemption. "To regret one's own experiences is to arrest one's own development." Wilde writes, "To deny one's own experiences is to put a lie into the lips of one's own life. It is no less than a denial of the soul." Robbie Ross arranged for its partial publication in 1905, five years after Wilde died in exile in France, impoverished and in poor health.[49]

The Oscar Wilde scandal drew media attention throughout much of the world and shaped popular attitudes toward homosexuality for decades afterward. Newspapers throughout Europe, North America, and the British Empire covered the Wilde trials. Most accounts strongly condemned Wilde's homosexuality, but some foreign commentators also portrayed Wilde as a victim of British sexual prudery.[50] Wilde's flamboyance, style, and brilliance inspired gay men to venerate him, while his persecution and tragic fate reinforced the dangers of homosexuality in a hostile culture. When the protagonist in E.M. Forster's novel *Maurice* goes to a medical specialist and confesses he is "an unspeakable of the Oscar Wilde sort," the passage perfectly evoked the fear of public ruin and the weight of private shame many gay men confronted and that Forster himself had experienced.[51]

But Wilde's imprisonment also inspired bold acts of resistance. In 1896, Havelock Ellis published a German language edition of *Sexual Inversion*. The following year, after removing much of the historical and literary analyses that John Addington Symonds had contributed to their joint project, Ellis published an English language version. Incensed at the unauthorized revisions, Symonds's literary executor bought and destroyed

---

[49]See Kaplan, *Sodom on the Thames*, 224–51.

[50]Greg Robinson, "International Significance of the Wilde Trials," in *Global Encyclopedia of Lesbian, Gay, Bisexual, Transgender, and Queer (LGBTQ) History*, Howard Chiang, ed. (Chicago: Gale, 2019), 3:1731–5.

[51]Inspired by the relationship between his friend Edward Carpenter and his partner George Merrill, Forster wrote *Maurice* in 1913–14. The novel was partially based on Forster's affair with Hugh Meredith while both were students at Cambridge University. Although he showed the manuscript to select friends and revised it as late as 1960, fear of scandal kept him from publishing it. The novel was released only after Forster's death in 1971. See Edsall, *Toward Stonewall*, 175–7.

all printed copies. Undeterred, Ellis turned to a disreputable publisher who issued a reprint a few months later. The text, the first medical account of homosexuality originally published in English, frankly described male same-sex relations as natural and undeserving of moral or legal condemnation—an emphatic rejection of rationale for the 1885 Criminal Amendment Act and Wilde's conviction. Even after authorities prosecuted a bookseller who sold the text for violating British obscenity law, Ellis continued writing and speaking publicly about sexuality until his death in 1939.[52]

Outrage at Wilde's imprisonment also inspired Magnus Hirschfeld, one of the most significant activists in the history of the international LGBT rights movement. A Jewish-German physician, Hirschfeld was haunted by two episodes that occurred early in his medical career. The first was a lecture on "sexual degeneracy" where a gay man who had been kept in an asylum for thirty years was paraded naked before his medical school class. The second was more personal. When Hirschfeld began treating people who expressed same-sex attractions, one of his patients was a German military officer who was engaged to a woman, but trying to reconcile his homosexuality with his social status and the masculine ethos of German culture. On the eve of his wedding, the soldier shot himself in the head, leaving behind a suicide note calling homosexuality "a curse against human nature and the law." Hirschfeld was shattered. Although he maintained the impartiality expected of a scientist in his time and thus never discussed his own homosexuality publicly, he redoubled his efforts to help homosexuals accept themselves.[53]

In 1896, Hirschfeld wrote *Sappho and Socrates*, a pamphlet building on the work of Karl Heinrich Ulrichs and calling for the repeal of Paragraph 175. In keeping with the Napoleonic Code, Hirschfeld argued that the state should not interfere with consensual sexual relations between adults. Challenging many of his contemporaries especially Albert Moll, Hirschfeld emphatically rejected the notion that homosexuality was a pathology. While some gay men flocked to his practice and were relieved when he told them they were perfectly healthy, others feared Hirschfeld's calls for legal reforms would draw unwanted attention to them.[54]

Hirschfeld enlisted key Social Democrats (SPD), including party chairman August Bebel, in his push for the repeal of Paragraph 175. In May 1897, Hirschfeld and a few SPD members co-founded the Scientific Humanitarian Committee (SHC) (Wissenschaftlich humanitäres Komitee, or WhK), the world's first advocacy organization for gay and transgender rights.

---

[52]Joy Dixon, "Havelock Ellis and John Addington Symonds," *Sexual Inversion* (1897), *Victorian Review* 35:1 (Spring 2009): 72–7.
[53]Ellen Mancini, *Magnus Hirschfeld and the Quest for Sexual Freedom* (New York: Palgrave Macmillan, 2010), 46–7.
[54]Mancini, *Magnus Hirschfeld and the Quest for Sexual Freedom*, 54–64.

Adopting the motto "Through science to justice," SHC called for research to debunk antigay bias and started a petition calling for the decriminalization of private, consensual homosexual conduct between men over the age of sixteen. Despite police surveillance, Hirschfeld campaigned vigorously and gathered over 900 signatures. In January 1898, Bebel presented the petition to the Reichstag, but it was decisively rejected. Although the effort to repeal Paragraph 175 failed, it catapulted gay rights into German political discourse and Hirschfeld continued his research on the nature and causes of homosexuality.[55]

Like their counterparts in Ireland and England, German politicians weaponized allegations of homosexuality in the hopes of tarnishing rivals and advancing their aims. In 1902, in a misguided attempt to win sympathy for the repeal of Paragraph 175 and advance the cause of socialism, the Social Democratic newspaper *Vorwärts* (Forward) revealed that authorities on the Isle of Capri had expelled German steel magnate Alfred Krupp because of his homosexual activities. Krupp's "bourgeois vice," the paper alleged, reflected the decadence of capitalist elites closely aligned with Kaiser Wilhelm II. After the distraught Krupp committed suicide in 1903, Wilhelm II eulogized his friend as a patriot and gifted businessman. News of the Krupp scandal swept Europe and new epithets associating homosexuality with Germany arose. Italians referred to "la Berlinese," the French "le vice allemand."[56]

But the Krupp affair also generated sympathy for homosexuals and helped to fuel the growth and internationalization of SHC. Chapters formed throughout Germany. Following a reorganization in 1906, SHC broadened the geographic composition of its board and integrated twenty-eight members from Germany, Austria, Switzerland, Holland, Denmark, England, Italy, and Belgium.[57] The organization continued advocating for the repeal of Paragraph 175. By 1907, it had gathered more than 6,000 signatures on a pro-repeal petition, including hundreds of doctors and luminaries like Hermann Hesse, Käthe Kollwitz, Albert Einstein, and Rainer Maria Rilke. It held regular forums on homosexuality. It published multiple editions of the pamphlet *Was Soll das Volk vom dritten Geschlecht Wissen? (What Should the People Know about the Third Sex?)* It organized public lectures (usually by Hirschfeld). It publicized its activities and Hirschfeld's research through the *Jahrbuch für sexuelle Zwischenstufen (Yearbook for Intermediate Sexual Types)* published consistently from 1899 to 1923 and a monthly report for members published through 1933. SHC sent these publications

---

[55]Mancini, *Magnus Hirschfeld and the Quest for Sexual Freedom*, 88–91.
[56]Mancini, *Magnus Hirschfeld and the Quest for Sexual Freedom*, 94–6.
[57]John Lauritsen and David Thorstad, *The Early Homosexual Rights Movement (1864–1935)*, rev. ed. (Ojai, CA: Times Change Press, 1995), 33.

and others to government officials considering penal code reforms and to libraries across Europe. As Hirschfeld's international reputation grew, individuals from Russia, the Netherlands, Scandinavia, Belgium, and Italy sought political and scholarly collaborations with him.[58]

IMAGE 1.6 A copy of Magnus Hirschfeld's *What People Should Know about the Third Sex* distributed by the Scientific Humanitarian Committee in Leipzig, Germany, in 1901.

---

[58]For a concise overview of Hirschfeld's life and work, see Ralf Dose, *Magnus Hirschfeld: The Origins of the Gay Liberation Movement* (New York: Monthly Review Press, 2014).

In the middle of these successes, Hirschfeld's role in a new scandal significantly undermined SHC. In 1907, Maximillian Harden, editor of a Social Democrat–aligned news magazine *Die Zukunft* (*The Future*), believed that Wilhelm II's foreign policy was weakening Germany internationally and that the emperor was too close to French diplomats working against Germany's national interests. He wrote an article accusing Count Kuno von Moltke and Prince Philip von Eulenburg—both friends and trusted advisors to Wilhelm II—of participating in homosexual parties at Eulenburg's castle, Liebenberg. Harden claimed Eulenburg was vulnerable to blackmail and that the prince's friendship with Raymond Lecomte, a French diplomat, was a security risk. Harden took special umbrage at Eulenburg's feminine manner, indecisiveness, and fondness for poetry and singing. Harden deemed these traits antithetical to the masculine ideals underpinning Realpolitik, the strategy used by his late friend Otto von Bismarck in unifying and empowering modern Germany before he was ousted as first chancellor by Wilhelm II in 1890. Incensed by Harden's claims, the kaiser barred Moltke and Eulenburg from his court and demanded that the pair respond to the journalist's slander.

Forced to defend himself, Moltke first unsuccessfully challenged Harden to a duel, then filed libel charges against him. Concurrently, Eulenburg was tried for perjury after lying under oath in a related slander trial. Throughout months of court proceedings extensively covered by the German and European press, Eulenburg and many other Prussian military officers and aristocrats linked to the kaiser were alleged to engage in homosexual activities. Rather than try to prove that Moltke had engaged in homosexual acts, Harden's defense argued that Moltke had a homosexual "orientation." They called his ex-wife Lilly von Elbe, who testified that Moltke and Eulenburg's friendship played a role in the failure of their three-year (and likely unconsummated) marriage. To substantiate their claims about sexual identity, the defense called Hirschfeld as an expert witness. Although he had never physically examined Moltke, Hirschfeld attested that Moltke was unconsciously homosexual and had not violated Paragraph 175 because he had not engaged in homosexual acts. Homosexuals, Hirschfeld asserted, could experience platonic love just like heterosexuals. Convinced that Moltke was homosexual (even without physically expressing it), the jury found Harden not guilty of libel.

Outraged by the verdict and its smears upon the kaiser, the Prussian attorney general appealed and the presiding judge ordered a second trial. Moltke's lawyers depicted Lilly von Elbe as vengeful and hysterical. Rescinding his original testimony, Hirschfeld said that Eulenburg and Moltke were only friends. Persuaded Moltke was heterosexual, the second jury found Harden guilty of libel and he received a four-month jail term. In the aftermath of the Eulenburg scandals, Hirschfeld's reputation was deeply damaged. He was vilified in the press and personally subjected to homophobic and anti-Semitic attacks. SHC's membership plummeted and Hirschfeld's detractors were emboldened.[59]

While SHC suffered setbacks in Germany, Russian homosexuals were enjoying newfound openness. In the late nineteenth century, visible homosexual subcultures developed in St. Petersburg and Moscow. Although criminal sanctions for consensual sodomy between men remained harsh, prosecutions became increasingly rare by 1900. Because of close ties between aristocrats and the tsarist autocracy, homosexual indiscretions were addressed privately and there was no Russian equivalent of the Cleveland Street scandal or Oscar Wilde trials. In 1903, Vladimir Nabokov, founder of the Constitutional Democrat Party and father of the author of *Lolita*, wrote an article on the legal status of homosexuals calling for the state to end its prosecutions for private, consensual same-sex activities.

After popular uprisings in 1905 persuaded Tsar Nicholas II to transform the Russian autocracy into a constitutional monarchy, liberals and socialists debated whether sexuality should be regulated. Print censorship ended. Openly gay people were prominent in the imperial court and Russian cultural circles. In 1906, gay writer and poet Mikhail Kuzmin published *Wings*, a well-received semiautobiographical coming-out novel. The following year, Lidiia Zinov-eva-Annibal published *Thirty-three Monsters*, a less successful novel with frank depictions of lesbianism. In 1908, the publication of the anthology *Liudi srednego pola* (*People of the Intermediate Sex*) gave Russians access to translated excerpts of critical contemporary work on homosexuality including research by Ulrichs, Krafft-Ebing, psychoanalyst Sigmund Freud, Edward Carpenter, and others; autographical accounts of "inverts" in several countries; and transcripts of the Oscar Wilde trials and a meeting of the SHC. Russian translations of complete texts on homosexuality were also released. In the years before the Bolshevik Revolution, commentators across the political spectrum hotly debated homosexual emancipation and the decriminalization of sodomy.[60]

Such changes encouraged Magnus Hirschfeld to persevere after the embarrassment of the Eulenburg scandal. He launched new research and publication projects, continued lecturing internationally, and collaborated with fellow activists and sexologists. Rejecting a fixed gender binary with artificially constructed male and female norms, Hirschfeld advanced the notion of gender fluidity. He studied intersexed people and coined the term "transvestite." While he never adopted the specific term "transgender," he was also the first researcher to distinguish crossdressing

---

[59]For a rich account of the Eulenburg scandals, consult Robert Beachy, *Gay Berlin: Birthplace of a Modern Identity* (New York: Vintage Books, 2014), 120–39. See also Dose, *Magnus Hirschfeld*, 43–5.

[60]Dan Healey, *Homosexual Desire in Revolutionary Russia: The Regulation of Sexual and Gender Dissent* (Chicago: University of Chicago Press, 2001), 92–110.

from transgenderism and from homosexuality. In 1909, when the German parliament considered expanding Paragraph 175 to outlaw sexual acts between women, Hirschfeld joined forces with leading German feminists in successfully lobbying against the proposed legal change.[61] In 1911, after the Dutch government criminalized homosexual sex between adults and young men or women under the age of twenty-one (the age of consent for heterosexual relations was sixteen), advocates led by liberal jurist Jacob Schorer and criminal anthropologist Arnold Aletrino launched the Nederlandsch Wetenschappelijk Humanitai Komittee—NWHK (Dutch Scientific-Humanitarian Committee), an offshoot of the SHC. NWHK ran a library, issued publications, and released reports aimed at students, legal authorities, and physicians. When Hirschfeld lectured before 2,000 physicians at the Fourteenth International Medical Congress in London in August 1913, his presentation of photographs and diagrams of male and female "intermediate types" electrified the audience, which included Havelock Ellis and Edward Carpenter. Recognizing the need to educate the British public about homosexuality, Carpenter and Ellis co-founded the British Society for the Study of Sex Psychology (BSSSP). The organizers of the First International Congress for Sex Research to be held in Berlin in November 1914 invited Carpenter to speak.[62]

But just as these transnational partnerships were beginning to gain momentum, political turmoil and war engulfed the European continent. Although international meetings of sexologists and homosexual rights advocates were suspended during the Great War, the alliances and intellectual exchanges among these individuals set the stage for future organizing efforts and generated new visibility for same-sex attracted people. Led by pioneers like Walt Whitman, Karl Heinrich Ulrichs, and Károly Mária Kertbeny, homosexuals had new frameworks and language for understanding their lived experience that did not exist fifty years earlier. But laws like Paragraph 175 and medical models that defined homosexuality as pathology also shaped gay identity and daily life. The possibility of exposure, scandal, arrest, or violence loomed over those engaging in—or perceived to be engaging in—same-sex sexual activities. But in the aftermath of two global wars, a more assertive and cohesive international LGBT rights movement arose.

---

[61]Mancini, *Magnus Hirschfeld and the Quest for Sexual Freedom*, ix–x, 25.
[62]Dose, *Magnus Hirschfeld*, 45–7; Lauritsen and Thorstad, *The Early Homosexual Rights Movement*, 30; Rob Tielman, "Dutch Gay Emancipation History," *Journal of Homosexuality* 13:2–3 (1986): 10–11; and Edsall, *Toward Stonewall*, 138–40; Weeks, *Coming Out*, 130–1.

CHAPTER TWO

Protest and Persecution, 1914–45

The outbreak of the Great War in August 1914 brought nascent transnational organizing efforts to a standstill. Although wartime tensions exacerbated suspicions about homosexuals, the conflict also created opportunities for gay men and women to demonstrate their patriotism and to interact intimately. Wartime sacrifices fueled demands for full citizenship. The 1920s became a time when the visibility of gay and lesbian subcultures greatly increased, the first homosexual emancipation mass movements arose, and transnational advocacy for homosexual emancipation was reinvigorated.

But new perils also surfaced. Authorities attempted to criminalize lesbian sex and censored cinematic and literary depictions of same-sex desire. Right-wing political groups demonized people who defied gender and heterosexual norms. With the rise of fascism, antigay laws and violence soared, bringing homosexual emancipation activities to a close across Europe. The outbreak of World War II again brought a mix of persecution and liberation for gay men and lesbians in the armed forces and on the home front. In the war's aftermath, new homophile organizations forged transnational ties and began articulating a vision for international LGBT equality, defying the postwar era's orthodoxies and Cold War tensions.

In the early twentieth century, popular understandings of sex and gender were shifting. In the United States, newspapers publicized cases of women who had been assigned female identities at birth, but had chosen to live as men.[1] Sexologists like Magnus Hirschfeld had begun to separate gender

---

[1]Emily Skidmore, *True Sex: The Lives of Trans Men at the Turn of the 20th Century* (New York: New York University Press, 2017). For a broader chronological and geographic perspective, see Jen Manion, *Female Husbands: A Trans History* (New York: Cambridge University Press, 2020).

identity and homosexuality, rejecting the idea that only those who did not outwardly conform to appropriate gender roles experienced same-sex desire. In the 1910s, Austrian physiologist Eugen Steinach began performing "transplantation" surgeries on rats and guinea pigs. He demonstrated that "castrated infantile male rodents, implanted with ovaries, developed certain characteristics, including sexual behavior, associated with females and that castrated infantile female rodents, implanted with testes, developed characteristics, including sexual behavior, of males." Steinach's work inspired his colleague Robert Lichtenstein to attempt transplantation on humans. Lichtenstein removed undescended testicles from healthy men and implanted them into the abdomens of men who had never developed testicles or had lost them due to injury or disease. Steinach and Lichtenstein also collaborated on a failed effort to "cure" a few homosexual men through Lichtenstein's surgical removal of one of their testicles followed by implantation of a testicle taken from a heterosexual man. By the early 1920s, a few European surgeons were performing experimental sex-change surgeries on humans.[2]

Beginning in 1905, Sigmund Freud added a psychological dimension to theories about sexuality, distinguishing between the *object* of one's sexual desire and its *aim* (in other words, what one wished to do to the object of one's lust). Freud argued that deviations from the norm could occur in both. He also claimed that humans are born with an instinctual libido that progresses through five psychosexual stages (oral, anal, phallic, latent, and genital). If an individual experienced sexual frustration in any of these stages, Freud argued, he or she would retain anxieties leading to neurosis in adulthood. While Freud himself did not draw a moral distinction between a heterosexual or homosexual outcome of this process, the idea of "arrested development" contributed to the belief that one's sexual identity could be shaped by a child's environment—and therefore "cured" if deemed abnormal.[3]

In August 1913, Havelock Ellis and Edward Carpenter co-founded the British Society for the Study of Sex Psychology (BSSSP), a forum to discuss recent theories on sexuality. Inspired by Magnus Hirschfeld's Scientific Humanitarian Committee (SHC), BSSSP initially focused on homosexual law reform, but broadened its agenda to include prostitution, sexually transmitted diseases, birth control, and many other sex-related issues. Welcoming women from the start, BSSSP organized public lectures, published pamphlets, and assembled a private library of works on sexuality.[4]

---

[2]Joanne Meyerowitz, *How Sex Changed: A History of Transsexuality in the United States* (Cambridge, UK: Harvard University Press, 2002), 16–18.
[3]Sara Flanders et al., "On the Subject of Homosexuality: What Freud Said," *International Journal of Psychoanalysis* 97:3 (June 2016): 933–50.
[4]Weeks, *Coming Out*, 132–5.

Although sex reformers tried to reshape popular attitudes despite escalating political conflicts among European states, a scandal involving Colonel Alfred Redl underscored the age's profound anxieties about homosexuality. The ninth of fourteen children born to an impoverished railway clerk and his wife in Galicia, Redl transcended his humble origins and attended an Austrian military academy and the Imperial War College. Fluent in Ukrainian, Russian, and Polish, he rose through the officer ranks of the Austro-Hungarian Army and became head of counterintelligence operations in 1907. He introduced innovations including a fingerprint database and the use of primitive surveillance equipment. But Redl was also operating as a double agent for Russia. Receiving generous payments in exchange for high-level military secrets, he adopted an opulent lifestyle that obviously exceeded his legitimate sources of income. He provided his male lover, an officer in the Austrian cavalry, with an elegant apartment. When his superiors suspected an intelligence leak in their ranks, Redl outwitted their efforts to discover its source.

Redl did not live to see the European continent plunged into war or the devastating consequences of his treachery. On May 25, 1913, after his successors at the Austro-Hungarian intelligence service confronted him with evidence of his espionage activities for Russia and intentionally left him alone with a revolver, Redl committed suicide. Authorities broke into his rooms and discovered perfumed letters, Austrian battle plans, and photographs of Redl engaged in sex acts with Austrian soldiers, many of whom were dressed in women's clothing and wearing makeup. Revelations of Redl's homosexuality combined with his duplicity stunned the Hapsburg Empire and fueled the idea that homosexuals posed a grave danger to national security. To divert attention from their own failures in intelligence oversight and military strategy, members of the Austro-Hungarian Army's General Staff blamed Redl for the enormous losses their forces sustained in Galicia and a failed invasion of Serbia at the beginning of World War I. For decades afterward, intelligence services worldwide cited the Redl affair as justification for barring homosexuals from sensitive government posts.[5]

But wartime patriotism inspired gay men and women to challenge such exclusion. In Austria, a new branch of the SHC founded in Vienna organized public lectures to combat antigay stereotypes exacerbated by the Redl scandal.[6] Although Great Britain found 22 officers and 270 soldiers guilty of homosexuality during the conflict, it did not prosecute thousands

---

[5]Some accounts claim that Redl was blackmailed into spying for the tsarist government after Russian agents discovered his homosexuality in 1901. Other scholars dispute this assertion, pointing to the rather open nature of homosexuality within the Austro-Hungarian officer corps and to simple greed as Redl's main motive for espionage. For a thoughtful assessment of the military and psychological effects of Redl's treachery, see John R. Schindler, "Redl—Spy of the Century?" *International Journal of Intelligence and CounterIntelligence* 18:3 (2005): 483–507.
[6]Lauritsen and Thorstad, *The Early Homosexual Rights Movement*, 41.

of gay men who served honorably. German military authorities adopted a similar attitude. Although they prosecuted male-on-male sexual assaults, they ignored most episodes of consensual sex between male soldiers, assuming such acts resulted from sexual deprivation in wartime and not wishing to highlight the presence of homosexuals in the ranks. Through military service or participation in groups like Britain's Boy Scouts or Germany's Wandervögel, gay men demonstrated masculine ideals that ran counter to stereotypes of effeminate homosexuals. Poets and writers like Wilfred Owen, Siegfried Sassoon, and Marcel Proust eloquently depicted the homosocial bonds among soldiers. The war also generated greater awareness of lesbianism. Recruitment campaigns for females to serve in ancillary roles in the armed forces stoked fears that such work was "unnatural." But the press later praised women performing well in traditionally "male" roles, thus helping to broaden accepted notions of femininity.[7]

Magnus Hirschfeld also embraced World War I as an excellent opportunity for homosexuals to prove their character and courage. Although the SHC had only 105 members in 1914, its visibility and prominent allies gave the organization political influence. Hirschfeld instructed thousands of German men and women on how to pass as "normal" soldiers. He successfully dissuaded German military authorities from imposing harsh penalties on soldiers who engaged in consensual homosexual activities or crossdressing. The SHC suspended its Paragraph 175 repeal petition campaign (which by then had nearly 5,000 doctors, professors, and others among its signatories) and focused on sending care packages to SHC members serving in the armed forces. Over the course of the war, however, Hirschfeld's experiences working at a Red Cross hospital outside of Berlin transformed him into a peace activist. Setting aside his hopes that combat service would help dispel antigay stereotypes, Hirschfeld turned his energies toward ending the war and joined the League for a New Fatherland, an alliance of pacifists from Germany, Switzerland, the Netherlands, and England. SHC published articles by its British members and emphasized the continued need for transnational solidarity among homosexuals.[8]

Such ties were difficult to sustain when wartime adversaries played on gender and sexual stereotypes to demonize each other. The sexologists' depictions of "inverts" and recent scandals fueled the notion that homosexuals were outsiders who were weak, cowardly, and easily preyed

---

[7]Tamagne, "The Homosexual Age, 1870–1940," 174–5, 370; Jason Crouthamel, *An Intimate History of the Front: Masculinity, Sexuality, and German Soldiers in the First World War* (New York: Palgrave Macmillan, 2014), 59, 124–5.

[8]Lauritsen and Thorstad, *The Early Homosexual Rights Movement*, 26; Mancini, *Magnus Hirschfeld and the Quest for Sexual Freedom*, 111–12; Marhoefer, *Sex and the Weimar Republic*, 24.

upon by blackmailers. In England, conservatives fused xenophobia and nationalism to attack the Liberal Party and Prime Minister Herbert Asquith. Playing upon perceptions fostered by the Eulenburg scandals of 1907, journalists like Lord Alfred "Bosie" Douglas alleged that Germany was trying to undermine the British war effort by exporting its homosexual degeneracy. Ironically, Douglas had been Oscar Wilde's infamous companion years earlier, but now considered himself a moral purity crusader. In a May 1916 article in the conservative *English Review*, Arnold White echoed Douglas's claims and denounced "the moral and spiritual invasion of Britain by German urnings [male homosexuals] and their agents for the purpose of undermining the patriotism, the stamina, the intellect, and the morals of British navy and army men, and of our prominent public leaders."[9]

As in peacetime, politicians found allegations of homosexuality a potent way to destroy an opponent or generate publicity. In the aftermath of the April 1916 Easter Rising, British authorities discredited Sir Roger Casement, an eloquent Irish nationalist, by exposing his homosexuality in the most lurid way possible. It was a remarkable turnabout from the honors the British government had previously bestowed upon Casement. Born in Dublin in 1864, Casement worked in the shipping industry in Liverpool and West Africa. He eventually joined the British Colonial Service and gained renown for detailing horrific labor abuses on rubber plantations in the Belgian Congo, findings that triggered major reforms in the colony. In 1910, Casement won additional acclaim for his report on terrible treatment of indigenous Amazonians on Peruvian rubber plantations. In 1911, in recognition of his groundbreaking human rights work, George V knighted Casement. After his retirement the following year, Casement joined the Irish nationalist movement, traveling to the United States to promote his cause. In October 1914, Casement went to Germany in a failed effort to persuade the German government to release Irish POWs so they could join a popular revolt against Great Britain. After he made the ill-advised decision to return to Ireland aboard a German U-Boat, the British captured and imprisoned him, sentencing him to death for treason. Citing Casement's famed humanitarianism, many Britons called for clemency.

Prosecutors were unmoved and set out to destroy Casement's reputation. They showed Casement's private "black diaries" from 1903, 1904, 1910, and 1911 to George V, members of Parliament, the Archbishop of Canterbury, and the US ambassador to Great Britain. The "black diaries" provided extremely graphic details of Casement's sexual encounters and male sexual partners (many of whom were paid) during his years in the Colonial Service. While not discounting the possibility that the diaries

---

[9] Tamagne, "The Homosexual Age, 1870–1940," 174.

could be forgeries, his Irish nationalist comrades were unwilling to defend a colleague whose behavior they found shameful and that violated British law. Casement was hanged on August 3, 1916.[10]

In early 1918, British MP and purity crusader Noel Pemberton Billing linked same-sex desire to a German-Jewish conspiracy he blamed for weakening the British war effort. To publicize these views, he directed Captain Harold Spencer, assistant editor of his newspapers the *Imperialist* and the *Vigilante*, to publish an article alleging that the German secret service kept a "black book" listing 47,000 British men and women, including "wives of Cabinet ministers, dancing girls, even Cabinet Ministers themselves," whose "sexual perversions" made them easy targets for blackmailers. On February 16, 1918, Spencer, who had been expelled from the British army for "delusional insanity," published an article called "The Cult of the Clitoris" in which he suggested that attendees at dancer Maud Allan's upcoming private performance of Oscar Wilde's *Salomé* were likely to be among the 47,000 listed in the notorious German "black book."

Just as Pemberton Billing hoped, Allan sued him for libel and gave him a much wider forum than the House of Commons to advance his claims of sedition and decadence in the Liberal Party and British elite society. In late May, when the seven-day libel trial began, it drew huge crowds and extensive newspaper coverage in Britain and Europe. Allan's notoriety added extra drama. Born in Canada, raised in San Francisco, and educated in Germany, she was a dancer celebrated for her erotic performances in *Salomé* at the Palace Theater in London. Allan had royal admirers and influential backers, but she had also been lambasted by purity crusaders. Her close relationship with Margot Asquith, wife of Prime Minister Herbert Asquith, sparked rumors of lesbianism. Beginning in 1910 and for twenty years afterward, Margot paid for Allan's apartment at Regent Park.

Homing in on the use of the word "clitoris" in Spencer's article, Allan's lawyers argued that the word itself suggested lesbianism and nymphomania— and thus smeared the reputation of "the lady whose name is coupled with it." In response, Pemberton Billing, who served as his own legal counsel, set out to prove his claims about Allan's sexual immorality. He presented her early piano training in Berlin as evidence of her German sympathies. Capitalizing on the well-known Oscar Wilde scandal, he insinuated that Allan's decision to perform the disgraced playwright's *Salomé*, along with her intimate friendship with Margot Asquith, reflected her own perversity. After Allan admitted under cross-examination that she was familiar with the term "clitoris," he argued that only a sexually deviant woman would

---

[10]Not published in full until 1995, the Casement "black diaries" remain controversial. Many scholars dispute their authenticity, finding it particularly suspect that they only exist for years when Casement's so-called white diaries exist and could therefore serve as context for Casement's supposed lurid activities. Aldrich, *Colonialism and Homosexuality*, 190–3.

IMAGE 2.1 Maud Allan as Salomé, shown with the head of John the Baptist.

possess such knowledge. His tactics worked. The judge cleared Pemberton Billing of libel as cheers erupted in the courtroom. Publicly humiliated, Allan stopped performing and began teaching dance. She later fled to Los Angeles, where she lived with Verna Aldrich, a female secretary who became her lover, until her death at age eighty-four in 1956.[11]

Like Pemberton Billing's acquittal, the suppression of Rose Allatini's 1918 novel *Despised and Rejected* reflected deep-seated anxieties in British society during the Great War. A pacifist, Allatini published the novel under the pseudonym A.T. Fitzroy and told the story of Antoinette, a female bisexual, and Dennis, a male homosexual and conscientious objector. Fearful the book's dual themes of sexual unorthodoxy and pacifism might dissuade men from joining the armed forces, the British government banned the book under the terms of the Defense of the Realm Act and destroyed all unsold copies.[12]

As the war neared its end, new hopes and new threats arose for gay men and lesbians around the world. In Russia, the overthrow of Tsar Nicholas II and outbreak of the Bolshevik Revolution sparked significant changes for homosexuals. Upon taking power in 1917, the Bolsheviks abolished the

---

[11]Rebecca Jennings, *A Lesbian History of Britain: Love and Sex between Women since 1500* (Westport, CT: Greenwood World Publishing, 2007), 94–7.
[12]Deborah Cohler, "Sapphism and Sedition: Producing Female Homosexuality in Great War Britain," *Journal of the History of Sexuality* 16:1 (January 2007): 68–94.

entire tsarist criminal code.[13] Rejecting the view that either the state or the Orthodox Church should regulate private sexual behavior, they advocated "free love" and legalized divorce, prostitution, abortion, and birth control. After years of slow deliberations, they adopted new Russian criminal codes in 1922 and 1926 that contained no provisions outlawing *muzhelozhstvo* (consensual anal sex between adult men). The Bolsheviks' abolition of legal penalties for male-male sodomy was hailed internationally as the biggest advance for homosexuals since France's decriminalization of male homosexual relations in 1791 and 1804.

But decriminalization of gay sex did not indicate the Bolsheviks' acceptance of homosexuality. In 1919, the Justice Commissariat prosecuted Bishop Palladi of Zvenigorod for "corruption of a boy" and for unnatural vice (pederasty) and sentenced him to five years' imprisonment. Although the trial stemmed from the Bolsheviks' larger attack on the Russian Orthodox Church, it also reflected the communists' association of homosexuality with bourgeois vice and the aristocratic decadence of prerevolutionary Russia. Furthermore, they embraced the medical view defining homosexuality as a pathology that could be cured. Even after the legal changes of 1922 and 1926, homosexuals could still be prosecuted (although none were) for "satisfaction of sexual lust in perverted forms"—vague language that was later interpreted to include sex between men, sex between women, or anal sex regardless of the partners' genders.[14]

News of the Bolshevik Revolution had electrified leftists and reformers across the globe. In Germany, the SHC firmly aligned itself with the forces calling for the end of monarchy and militarism. On November 10, 1918, the day before Germany officially surrendered, the League for a New Fatherland invited Hirschfeld to speak before a crowd of 4,000 gathered outside the Reichstag. With bullets flying overhead as the Red Guards and supporters of the kaiser clashed nearby, Hirschfeld gave a rousing address calling for a socialist revolution and the repeal of Paragraph 175. Upon the establishment of the Weimar Republic, SHC sent a delegation to the new government asking for the immediate release of all prisoners being held for violations of Paragraph 175. Although SHC's request was denied, the state's relaxation of restrictions on the media soon benefitted advocates of homosexual emancipation.[15]

In May 1919, Austrian director Richard Oswald released *Anders als die Andern* (*Different from the Others*), likely the world's first progay film.

---

[13]Homosexuality remained illegal in Georgia, Azerbaijan, Uzbekistan, and Turkmenistan. See Florence Tamagne, *A History of Homosexuality in Europe, Vol. I & II Berlin, London, Paris 1919–1939* (New York: Algora Publishing, 2006), 280.

[14]Scholars disagree about the Bolsheviks' motives for decriminalizing sodomy and there is little documentation describing their views on same-sex sexual activities. See Healey, *Homosexual Desire in Revolutionary Russia*, 110–25.

[15]Mancini, *Magnus Hirschfeld and the Quest for Sexual Freedom*, 110–26.

Co-written by Hirschfeld and Oswald, the movie opens with Paul Körner, a famous violinist, reading the vaguely worded obituaries of German men who committed suicide because of Paragraph 175. After Kurt Sivers asks Körner for violin lessons, the two men fall in love, much to the dismay of their families. Playing "the doctor," Magnus Hirschfeld makes several cameos in the film, delivering speeches explaining his intermediate sex theories and why homosexuality should not be illegal. As Körner and Sivers become more open about their relationship, they are spotted in a park by Franz Bollek, a man who had blackmailed Körner years earlier after meeting him at a costume party. Bollek later approaches Körner alone and demands money in exchange for not exposing Sivers's homosexuality. Through flashbacks, viewers learn how Körner originally became aware of his sexual identity, tried to change it through medical hypnosis, and then accepted it. Although Körner starts paying Bollek to protect Sivers, his blackmailer's demands escalate and Sivers flees when he discovers his lover is being extorted. Bollek then turns Körner in to the police and a judge sentences Körner to a week in jail. His reputation and career destroyed, Körner kills himself by ingesting cyanide. The film ends with a close-up of a hand crossing out Paragraph 175 in a law book.

Public screenings of the film were at first well attended. But Catholic, Protestant, and right-wing groups soon started protesting the film. The demonstrations triggered a nationwide debate about censorship. Defending the film, Hirschfeld showed it to members of the Weimar National Assembly and government officials. It did not help. In May 1920, Weimar lawmakers approved the creation of a national film review board. On the recommendation of a psychiatrist and two sexologists who were known opponents of Hirschfeld, the panel recommended that public screenings of *Different from the Others* be banned on the grounds that it was biased against Paragraph 175 and could confuse young people about homosexuality. The ban became law in October 1920. Nonetheless, censorship of sexual content occurred relatively infrequently during the Weimar era.[16]

---

[16]Hirschfeld continued to screen the film privately and in 1927, Hirschfeld inserted forty minutes of the original film into his own feature *Gesetze der Liebe* (*Laws of Love*), prints of which made their way into the Russian Film Archives. This became very significant later. For decades, scholars believed that the Nazis had destroyed all copies of *Different from the Others*. In the 1980s, film restorers began trying to piece together the original, but it was not until 2017 that they partially succeeded, using a high-grain master positive of *Laws of Love* purchased from Russia by the UCLA Film & Television Archive six years earlier. The footage has been restored and has been used to reconstruct as much of *Different from the Others* as possible, with guidance from Nazi censorship records and the insertion of still photos in place of missing scenes. See Robert Ito, "A Daring Film, Silenced No More," *New York Times*, November 15, 2011, https://www.nytimes.com/2013/11/17/movies/different-from-the-others-a-1919-film-on-homosexuality.html; and Daniel Wenger, "The Tragic Lessons of Cinema's First Gay Love Story," *The New Yorker*, February 14, 2017, https://www.newyorker.com/culture/cultural-comment/the-tragic-lessons-of-cinemas-first-gay-love-story.

IMAGE 2.2 Magnus Hirschfeld (with glasses and mustache in the bottom right-hand corner) holds the hand of his lover Karl Giese during a costume party held at the Institute for Sexual Science in Berlin, 1920.

As the controversy over the film raged, Hirschfeld used his own funds to purchase an ornate building in Berlin to serve as a repository for his vast collection of materials on sexuality and an international center for sex research and advocacy. Established in July 1919, the *Institut für Sexualwissenschaft* (Institute for Sexual Science or ISS) was the first institution of its kind established anywhere in the world. ISS offered free medical advice and its lectures and facilities were open to the public. Paintings and photographs of famous inverts and transvestites adorned the walls. Although it remained an independent organization, SHC opened offices in the building. ISS was an immediate success and 20,000 people a year visited for sex education, contraception, marital counseling, treatment of sexually transmitted diseases, and advice on gay and transgender issues. Famous visitors included Anglo-American author Christopher Isherwood, English poet W.H. Auden, French writer André Gide, and Russian director Sergei Eisenstein. Every German visitor was encouraged to sign the petition calling for repeal of Paragraph 175.[17]

---

[17]Lauritsen and Thorstad, *The Early Homosexual Rights Movement*, 26–9.

Like their counterparts in Europe, those with same-sex desires in the United States experienced a blend of opportunities and obstacles during the war years. Americans had been bitterly divided along ethnic and nationalist lines over entry into the conflict. The debates highlighted deep fissures over class, race, gender, and sexuality in US society. Military service was closely linked to ideals of masculinity and images of vulnerable women ravaged by German "Huns" punctuated government propaganda justifying American military intervention. On the home front, progressives fought to break barriers of exclusion that hindered women, African Americans, labor activists, political radicals, and pacifists.

Wartime mobilizations and social upheaval exposed many Americans to gay subcultures unknown to or ignored by the general public. Denizens of major cities like New York, San Francisco, and New Orleans had long been aware of the existence of men whose dress, language, and sexual desires openly defied gender norms. As urban populations grew, local tabloids published vivid accounts of police crackdowns on "perverts" in places as diverse as St. Louis, Boise, Long Beach, and Portland, Oregon.

But a scandal that erupted in Newport, Rhode Island immediately after the war generated national attention and engulfed top US government officials. Best known as an elegant seaside playground for the wealthy, Newport was also the site of a naval training station where approximately 24,000 sailors were based in 1918. Reports of sailors' cocaine use, excessive drinking, and solicitation of prostitutes dismayed Josephus Daniels, the head of the US Department of the Navy, and prompted the mayor of Newport to order the closure of brothels. He was not, however, able to stop the sexual interactions between sailors and men occurring off base.

In February 1919, Chief Machinist's Mate Ervin Arnold learned of these activities while being treated at the naval training station's hospital. A fellow patient named Thomas Brunelle shared details of his homosexual activities in Newport, describing a thriving gay scene among local homosexuals and naval personnel frequenting the Army & Navy YMCA and the Newport Art Club. After his medical treatment was complete, Arnold, a former detective, decided to verify Brunelle's claims and immersed himself in the world of fairies (effeminate and flamboyant gay men), trade (masculine men who assumed the active role in sex with other men, sometimes for money, and who may or may not have considered themselves homosexual), crossdressers, cocaine addicts, and hard drinkers. In the lobby of the Army & Navy YMCA, older men—including an Episcopal military chaplain named Reverend Samuel Neal Kent—openly solicited younger men for private assignations.

Although his motives for doing so remain unclear, Arnold reported his findings to his Navy superiors. Alarmed to discover sailors were engaging in flagrant same-sex sexual activity, the station commander appointed a court of inquiry. Assistant Secretary of the Navy Franklin D. Roosevelt, acting as head of the Navy in Secretary Josephus Daniels's absence, agreed that "a most searching and rigid investigation" was needed to root out and prosecute those spreading deviance. Roosevelt asked Attorney General A. Mitchell Palmer to lead the inquiry and was incensed when Palmer declined. Arnold and Lieutenant Erastus Hudson, the station's welfare officer, assured Roosevelt they knew what would be needed for a successful undercover operation.

Hudson and Arnold enlisted a team of young and attractive sailors to gather information about Newport's bars, "cocaine joints," prostitutes, and "cocksuckers and rectum receivers." They encouraged the agents to have sex with their fellow sailors, assuring them that they would not be prosecuted if they engaged in illegal behavior while achieving their mission. The investigators pursued these aims with gusto and submitted vivid reports of having oral and anal sex with men.

In early April 1919, arrests began and continued through the summer. Arnold's agents solicited sailors and frequented public spaces known to draw homosexuals. Several sailors were arrested and charged with sodomy, a felony under a recent revision of the Articles of War. After being imprisoned for weeks, individuals were tried by a military tribunal and encouraged to implicate others. Fifteen sailors were court-martialed. Some received sentences of imprisonment for as long as twenty years and were sent to a naval prison in Maine. Others received dishonorable discharges. Not content to limit prosecutions to sailors, Arnold and his team—with Roosevelt's approval and provision of additional secret funds—expanded their scope to target civilians. The decision proved unwise.

After they arrested Reverend Kent on eleven counts of "lewd and scandalous" behavior, a group of Rhode Island clergymen led by Bishop James DeWolf Perry publicly defended Kent, citing his long record of good works and bravery while ministering to victims of the 1918 flu pandemic. It seems not to have occurred to Perry and his colleagues that Kent's humanitarianism did not negate the possibility that he enjoyed having sex with men. The government and the prosecutors blithely detailed how the agents—some of them as young as seventeen—entrapped suspected homosexuals.

The revelations sparked a furor. Outraged that young men had been ordered to debauch themselves, the jury found Kent innocent. But the government did not let the matter end there. After Kent fled to a sanatorium in Michigan, federal agents tracked him down and charged him under a new law prohibiting immoral activities within ten miles of any US military installation.

When the second trial began in January 1920, it was a public relations disaster for the Navy. Kent's defense attorney shredded agents' testimony and emphasized how many of the young men reported enjoying their sexual escapades with men. Fourteen clergymen and civic leaders testified on Kent's behalf and he was again found innocent. Journalist John R. Rathom of the *Providence Journal* wrote scathing stories about the court proceedings and published a letter sent to President Woodrow Wilson by a group of Newport clergymen who condemned the Navy's "deleterious and vicious methods."

The *Providence Journal*'s decision to publish the letter drew national attention to the scandal and put the Navy on the defensive. Roosevelt lashed out, arguing that Rathom's reports would damage the reputation of the Navy and harm recruitment efforts. In a series of telegrams, Roosevelt and Rathom argued over whether or not Navy leaders had adequately supervised the investigation or authorized the agents' participation in illegal activities. Attempting to quash the controversy, Daniels ordered a high-level internal investigation. But two months later, after the commission released a report that whitewashed the Navy's coercion and corruption of the agents under its charge, the US Senate launched a more rigorous, independent investigation of the Navy's handling of the Newport cases. For the first time ever, Congress convened a subcommittee assessing the homosexual subculture and the government's treatment of homosexuals.

The three subcommittee members pored over court transcripts and interviewed the sailors serving prison sentences. The convicted men recounted how they were beaten, threatened, and forced to give self-incriminating testimony. The senators also interviewed Roosevelt (who had resigned his Navy post to accept the 1920 Democratic nomination for vice president), Arnold, Hudson, and several of the agents. When they released their final report in July 1921, they excoriated Daniels and Roosevelt for the investigators' methods. Senator Henry Keyes, a Republican representing Vermont, called for the release of all of the convicted sailors held at the Portsmouth naval prison. Two of the senators recommended that anyone in the US armed forces suspected of homosexuality be dishonorably discharged and provided medical care rather than be prosecuted and imprisoned. "Perversion is not a crime," Keyes argued, "but a disease that should be properly treated in a hospital." Edwin Denby, Daniels's successor as Secretary of the Navy, emphatically rejected the proposal. But the Newport scandal quickly faded from national consciousness and the Navy continued to criminalize sodomy. When Roosevelt ran for governor of New York in 1928 and for president four years later, his public refusals to accept responsibility for his role in the episode were forgotten.[18]

While the Newport investigations were being launched in the United States, the world's first mass movement for homosexual emancipation was developing in Germany. Kurt Hiller, a Jewish attorney, unsuccessfully tried to convince Hirschfeld and other fellow SHC members that "inverts" ought to publicly reveal themselves, form "their own political party," and run for seats in the Reichstag.[19] But at the first postwar SHC meeting in August

---

[18]Lawrence R. Murphy, *Perverts by Official Order: The Campaign against Homosexuals by the United States Navy* (New York: Harrington Park Press, 1988); Ben Brenkert, "Franklin D. Roosevelt's Forgotten Anti-Gay Sex Crusade," *The Daily Beast*, June 15, 2015, https://www.thedailybeast.com/franklin-d-roosevelts-forgotten-anti-gay-sex-crusade.

[19]Marhoefer, *Sex and the Weimar Republic*, 3–7.

1920, Hiller won support for restoring transnational alliances with other gay groups and led a coalition that blocked an effort to increase sentences for violations of Paragraph 175 to up to five years in jail. On March 18, 1922, SHC finally presented its signed petition for the repeal of Paragraph 175 to the Reichstag, twenty-five years after it was launched. Although the Reichstag voted to have the government reconsider Paragraph 175, the Weimar regime's attention was focused on the collapsing German economy and it took no action.

While twenty-five SHC chapters pushed for change in Germany, Hirschfeld renewed his international gay rights work. He resumed his foreign speaking trips, traveling to Holland, Czechoslovakia, and Italy. In 1921, he organized the First Congress for Sexual Reform, a meeting in Berlin which inspired the creation of the World League for Sexual Reform (WLSR). A multinational organization, WLSR soon drew representatives from dozens of countries and advocated for a diverse array of issues including decriminalization of private consensual homosexual acts between adults, liberalization of antiabortion laws, and the legalization of divorce. In 1928, WLSR convened in Copenhagen for its second congress and in London the following year. In 1931, its meeting in Vienna drew over 2,000 committee members. But the 1932 congress in Brno proved to be its last. With the rise of fascism and economic depression, few governments were responsive to demands for sexual reforms. Three years later, WLSR was disbanded.[20]

Hirschfeld, long a target of anti-Semites, paid a high personal price for resuming his public activities in a time of such economic and political volatility. In 1920, during a lecture on endocrinology in Munich, he was stoned and nearly beaten to death by right-wing thugs. In February 1923, members of a right-wing student group interrupted a lecture he was giving in Vienna, threw stink bombs, and opened fire on the audience. While Hirschfeld escaped injury, many audience members did not.[21]

Such hostility did not dissuade German gay men and lesbians from forming new homosexual liberation groups. Having sacrificed for their homeland during the war, some joined "friendship leagues" calling for the repeal of Paragraph 175 and state recognition of "the full citizenship rights of inverts." Within a year, they had formed an umbrella group called the German Friendship League.

In the fall of 1919, Karl Schultz capitalized on the relatively relaxed censorship laws under the Weimar Republic and began publishing 20,000 copies a week of *Die Freundshaft* (*Friendship*), a homosexual liberation magazine devoted to political news, readers' letters, short stories, and poetry. Almost immediately, purity crusaders led by Kurt Brunner accused the magazine of recruiting youth through sexualized content and seductive

[20]Tamagne, *A History of Homosexuality in Europe*, 81–5.
[21]Lauritsen and Thorstad, *The Early Homosexual Rights Movement*, 31–3.

personal ads. Forced to defend themselves in court, Schultz and the magazine's former publisher lost their case and were sentenced respectively to six weeks and two weeks in jail under the provisions of an imperial obscenity law retained by the Weimar government. *Die Freundshaft* appealed to the *Reichsgericht* and while Germany's highest court ruled that the contested issues of the magazine contained obscenity and upheld the two men's sentences, it rejected the notion that homosexual content in and of itself—whether sexually explicit or not—made a publication obscene. The case was an important victory for homosexual rights advocates.[22]

Gay rights leader Friedrich Radszuweit capitalized on the ruling. In 1923, the German Friendship League splintered when Radszuweit renamed the organization the League for Human Rights (LHR) and launched the *Journal for Human Rights*. Using his wealth from dealing textiles in the prewar years, Radszuweit bankrolled the publishing house that produced the flagship magazine *Die Freundin* (*The Girlfriend*) and *Die Transvestit* (*The Transvestite*). *Die Freundin* was especially notable since it reflected a new militancy among lesbians proclaiming their own identity and desire for inclusion in the homosexual emancipation movement. By the late 1920s, although they could not be displayed openly or sold to minors, there were more than twenty publications aimed at homosexuals, lesbians, and transvestites sold nationwide at newspaper kiosks and through subscriptions. The LHR became the largest of the new homosexual emancipation groups, peaking in 1929 with 48,000 members, about 1,500 of whom were women. League chapters operated in Braunschweig, Breslau, Mannheim, Weimar, Nuremberg, and Cologne. International LHV affiliates arose in Switzerland, Austria, Czechoslovakia, Brazil, Argentina, and New York.[23]

With much smaller ranks than their German counterparts, English gay rights activists also remobilized after World War I. BSSSP's gay subcommittee published pamphlets aimed at persuading heterosexuals that homosexuals should not be persecuted for their physically innate condition. But with only 234 members in July 1920, BSSSP was unwilling to emulate SHC's anti-Paragraph 175 petition campaign and advocate for the legalization of consensual private sex between adult men.[24]

Such timidity proved a weak stratagem in clashes with moral reformers who were alarmed by the ways the war reshaped gender boundaries. The militancy of the British suffragettes heightened concerns about "masculine" women. Such anxieties were evident in parliamentary debate over a proposal to criminalize sex between women. In August 1921, three MPs introduced an amendment to a bill aimed at protecting children under sixteen from

[22]Marhoefer, *Sex and the Weimar Republic*, 38–41.
[23]Marhoefer, *Sex and the Weimar Republic*, 17, 41–51; Tamagne, *A History of Homosexuality in Europe*, 76.
[24]Lauritsen and Thorstad, *The Early Homosexual Rights Movement*, 37.

sexual assault. Their proposed clause would outlaw "any act of gross indecency between female persons" in the same way that the Criminal Law Amendment Act of 1885 had for men. On August 4, 1921, the House of Commons approved the measure 148–53, but it failed in the House of Lords. Although there were no future attempts to criminalize sex between women, the bill's defeat did not signal a new acceptance of lesbianism. Its opponents did not champion the civil rights of women-loving women, but instead argued that the law's passage would not eradicate female perversion, would greatly increase popular awareness of lesbianism, and would create opportunities for extortionists to target women trapped in compromising situations.[25]

Widespread contempt for lesbians was evident in the furor generated by Radclyffe Hall's *The Well of Loneliness*. Hall was independently wealthy and a prize-winning author known for adopting chic men's clothing. In 1920, she gained notoriety when Sir George Fox-Pitt accused her of the immoral seduction of Una Troubridge, a sculptress married to Admiral Ernest Troubridge. Although Una divorced her husband after meeting Hall, Hall successfully sued Fox-Pitt for slander. Six years later, she decided to write a novel about sexual inversion featuring Stephen Gordon, an upper-class English "mannish woman." As a child, Stephen detests dresses and develops a crush on one of the family's female servants. Her father reads work by Karl Heinrich Ulrichs to understand his daughter. As a young woman, Stephen adopts a short hair style and wears masculine clothes. She discovers a book by Richard Krafft-Ebing in her father's library (assumed to be *Psychopathia Sexualis*). Concluding she has a mental defect, Stephen describes herself and other inverts as "hideously maimed and ugly," a view which did not square with sexologists like Havelock Ellis and later work by Krafft-Ebing which defined inversion as mere difference, not degeneracy.

While working as an ambulance driver in World War I, Stephen finds love with Mary Llewellyn, but their romance is met with social rejection. They move to Paris and throw themselves into the nightlife of the avant-garde. (By then, real-life Paris had a thriving gay and lesbian subculture with notable figures like Natalie Clifford Barney, Gertrude Stein, Alice B. Toklas, Jean Cocteau, André Gide, Sylvia Beach, and Romaine Brooks.) But Stephen concludes she cannot ensure Mary's happiness and feigns an affair with another woman in order to make Mary leave her for a man. The novel ends with Stephen's poignant plea to God for "the right to our existence!"

In July 1928, publisher Jonathan Cape issued a limited first edition of *The Well of Loneliness*. It met mixed reviews and initial sales were poor. There were no calls for its suppression until James Douglas, a moral reformer

---

[25]Jennings, *A Lesbian History of Britain*, 108–14.

who worked as editor of the *Sunday Express*, launched a campaign against it. Railing against the threat posed to children by the increasing visibility of "sexual inversion and perversion," Davis proclaimed: "I would rather give a healthy boy or a healthy girl a phial of prussic acid than this novel." As other newspapers echoed Davis's call for the censorship of *The Well of Loneliness*, its publisher asked Home Secretary Sir William Joynson-Hicks to decide if it was obscene. In August, although the novel had no explicit sexual references, Joynson-Hicks ordered the book withdrawn and its publisher complied. Secretly, Jonathan Cope leased the rights of the novel to an English language publisher in France and copies of the novel soon reappeared in Great Britain. Johnson-Hicks ordered the books seized, and bookstores, customs officials, and police officers battled over whether the novel was obscene and should be destroyed. Leonard and Virginia Woolf and E.M. Forster enlisted numerous literary luminaries in a public letter protesting the novel's suppression, but many balked when Hall insisted that they also attest to the novel's artistic merit.

While the French publisher continued distributing *The Well of Loneliness* internationally, the trial over its obscenity began on November 9, 1928. Jonathan Cape's solicitor had sent out letters to 160 potential witnesses, but many refused to appear in court or were reluctant to testify. Attempts to defend the book were futile and just a week later, the judge rendered a guilty verdict, declaring the novel filled with "the most horrible and disgusting obscenity." Despite protests from public intellectuals like George Bernard Shaw and T.S. Eliot, an appeals court upheld the ruling. *The Well of Loneliness* was banned in Britain, but sold over a million copies during Hall's lifetime. Efforts to ban it in the United States failed. Two additional British novels with lesbian themes were also published in 1928, but neither Virginia Woolf's *Orlando* nor Compton Mackenzie's *Extraordinary Women* was banned. For decades afterward, lesbians had diametrically opposing views of *The Well of Loneliness*. For some, it was transformative. Others found it unrelentingly bleak. Beginning in the 1970s, some feminists objected to its portrayal of bisexuality and its adherence to strict butch/femme roles. But the novel itself and the controversy surrounding its publication unquestionably increased awareness of lesbian lives, a reality that lesbians both praised and lamented.[26]

While the Newport investigations highlighted the existence of gay subcultures in the United States, Americans lagged far behind their German and English counterparts in advocating for homosexual emancipation. Long enmeshed in transnational radical political circles, Emma Goldman was one of the first public champions of gay rights. When the 1923 edition of SHC's *Yearbook* included an article by Goldman, Hirschfeld wrote an

---

[26]Jennings, *A Lesbian History of Britain*, 114–27; Tamagne, *A History of Homosexuality in Europe*, 320–4.

introduction describing her as "the first and only woman, indeed one could say the first and only human being, of importance in America to carry the issue of homosexual love to the broadest layers of the public." In the article that followed, Goldman wrote:

> I regard it as a tragedy that people of differing sexual orientation find themselves proscribed in a world that has so little understanding for homosexuals and that displays such gross indifference for sexual gradations and variations and the great significance they have for living. It is completely foreign to me to wish to regard such people as less valuable, less moral, or incapable of noble sentiments and behavior.

Goldman claimed to have embraced gay rights decades earlier, inspired by her acquaintance with lesbians who she met while serving time in prison for her political activities. "I firmly stood up in defense of Oscar Wilde," she declared, adding, "as an anarchist, my place has always been alongside the persecuted." While traveling in Europe after the Wilde trials, Goldman became acquainted with the works of sexologists like Havelock Ellis, Richard Krafft-Ebing, Edward Carpenter, and, most importantly, Hirschfeld himself, who heightened her awareness of "the crime perpetrated ... upon Oscar Wilde and people like him."[27]

Hirschfeld was also a major influence on Henry Gerber, an American gay rights pioneer. While working for the Allied Army of the Occupation in Germany in the aftermath of World War I, Gerber became enthralled with Hirschfeld's ideas and upon his return to Chicago in 1924, Gerber and six friends won state approval of their application to create a nonprofit corporation called the Society for Human Rights (SHR). Serving as SHR's secretary, Gerber published two issues of *Friendship and Freedom*, a newsletter that promoted SHR's aims of promoting tolerance, increasing its membership, and gaining support from medical authorities. But the first-known gay rights organization in the United States proved short-lived. In the summer of 1925, after the wife of SHR's vice-president reported the group's activities, police raided Gerber's home, seized his papers, and arrested him and the other SHR members for violating obscenity laws. Although the charges were dismissed after the men served three days in jail, the legal fees nearly bankrupted Gerber and he was fired from his job as a postal worker. After SHR disbanded, Gerber continued to write about homosexuality under a pseudonym. In 1929, while living in Los Angeles, Harry Hay learned of the SHR's existence from the partner of one of its former members. Twenty-one years later, Hay co-founded the Mattachine Society, one of the most significant gay advocacy groups in US history. In

---

[27]Emma Goldman article quoted in Lauritsen and Thorstad, *The Early Homosexual Rights Movement*, 40–1.

1963, after Gerber informed the group of his earlier advocacy efforts, *ONE Magazine* published a story about SHR.[28]

By the late 1920s, Hirschfeld's work continued and his international reputation spread, but his relations with other German gay rights activists were frayed. Adolf Brand, the anarchist publisher of the homosexual journal *Der Eigene* (*The Self-Owned*), and zoologist Bernard Friedländer had co-founded the Gemeinschaft der Eignen (Committee of Special People) in 1903. They had long rejected Hirschfeld's third sex theories and recoiled at the doctor's acceptance of transvestites and effeminate homosexuals. Their individualized vision of homosexuality celebrated the idealized masculine beauty of Ancient Greece. The Committee of Special People never attained the international visibility or membership numbers of SHC, but it offered an alternative to Hirschfeld's attempts to make homosexuality respectable through medicine and science. Brand and Friedländer repeatedly launched anti-Semitic attacks on Hirschfeld, arguing that his faith made him an unacceptable leader for the German homosexual rights movement.

Although SHC and the Committee of Special People briefly allied in the anti-Paragraph 175 coalition of the early 1920s, the tactical and worldview differences between the two groups never disappeared. After the coalition unraveled, Brand began calling for the public exposure of influential homosexuals, a position Hirschfeld emphatically opposed. Brand and Friedländer also attacked Hirschfeld for supporting the criminalization of sex with people under age sixteen. It would hardly be the last time that gay activists clashed over the politics of outing and age of consent laws.[29]

Such tactical and philosophical differences played a major role in splitting the homosexual emancipation movement just as it nearly won the long-sought repeal of Paragraph 175. In the summer of 1929, a Reichstag committee working on a reform of the German criminal code reviewed scores of reports on homosexuality, many submitted over the years by SHC, LHR, and the Committee of Special People. In October, the committee voted 15–13 to omit Paragraph 175 from a revised penal code; but the next day, it approved Paragraph 297. The new law legalized consensual acts between men in private, but imposed criminal penalties for men who had sex with men under the age of twenty-one, who coerced other men into sex, or who paid male sex workers. The decision outraged Hiller and fellow SHC activist Richard Linsert. Paragraph 175 had ignored male prostitution entirely. Under Paragraph 297, male prostitution could be punished with up to five years' imprisonment. They also recoiled at the proposed law's establishing a higher age of consent for homosexual sex than for heterosexual sex (the age of consent for women remained sixteen). By contrast, Radszuweit and

---

[28]Hayden L. Mora, "Henry Gerber's Bridge to the World," in *The Right Side of History: 100 Years of LGBTQ Activism*, Adrian Brooks, ed. (New York: Cleis Press, 2015), 10–15.
[29]Tamagne, *A History of Homosexuality in Europe*, 69–72.

the LHV called for an age of consent for men set at eighteen and were supportive of the criminalization of male prostitution. They, unlike SHC, believed that the homosexual movement needed to distance itself from "queens," pedophiles, and male prostitutes in order to win respectability and secure legal protections.[30]

These debates were rendered moot when the onset of the Great Depression and the dissolution of parliament entirely derailed the German criminal code revision effort. But the clash over Paragraph 175 led to a power struggle within SHC. Having led the organization since its inception in 1897, Hirschfeld was forced to resign in November 1929. Hiller and Linsert took SHC in a more radical direction and battled Hirschfeld over organizational funds and the future of ISS. While they supported Hirschfeld's view that homosexuality was an innate biological trait, they downplayed science and articulated a political discourse claiming homosexuals were entitled to full citizenship rights.

But the fractures in the movement, its small numbers, and its failure to integrate lesbians in any significant way left Germany's homosexual rights groups poorly positioned to respond to the rapidly shifting landscape of German politics. In early 1930, the Social Democratic government led by Hermann Müller collapsed before the effort to repeal Paragraph 175 was brought to the Reichstag. Under Müller's successors, first Heinrich Brüning and then Franz von Papen, Germany moved sharply right and the state became increasingly hostile to gay rights organizers.[31]

Despite his growing alarm at the political climate, Hirschfeld continued overseeing pioneering work in gender reassignment surgeries that he had begun in the early 1920s. His most famous patient was Dora "Dorchen" Richter. Born Rudolph in 1882, Dorchen hated her genitals as a child and began crossdressing. As an adult, she waited tables as a man at high-end hotels during summers, but presented herself as a woman for the rest of year. She was arrested multiple times for crossdressing and served some time in jail. After a sympathetic judge wrote to Hirschfeld, the doctor invited Dora to come to ISS and helped her secure a permit to crossdress in public legally. In 1922, she underwent castration and hormone treatment under Hirschfeld's supervision. She became a domestic servant at ISS, working with other transgender people. In 1931, ISS physicians performed the world's first complete male-to-female gender reassignment surgery on Dora, completing a penectomy and vaginoplasty. Hirschfeld also collaborated with the Danish physicians working with Lili Elvenes (born Einar Wegenar and better known as Lili Elbe), a Danish transgender woman who underwent castration at ISS.

---

[30]Tamagne, *A History of Homosexuality in Europe*, 77; Marhoefer, *Sex and the Weimar Republic*, 113–28.

[31]Tamagne, *A History of Homosexuality in Europe*, 78–81; Marhoefer, *Sex and the Weimar Republic*, 129–45.

In 1931–2, Elbe's subsequent gender reassignment surgeries in Dresden and death from post-operative infection drew widespread attention in Denmark and Germany. *Fra Mand til Kvinde* (*Man into Woman*), an account of Elbe's transformation originally published in Danish in 1931, was translated into German and English. Remarkably, Hirschfeld was able to convince the German government to pay for another man's sex change, a testament to his reputation as a scientific authority.[32]

Nonetheless, Hirschfeld started spending more time abroad. In November 1930, he began a lecture tour in the United States at the invitation of his colleague Harry Benjamin, a German-born endocrinologist who later gained international fame for performing sex change operations. Stopping first in New York and worried that he might need to emigrate, he made private inquiries about the possibility of moving to America. To minimize the controversy sparked by his lectures, he only spoke about homosexuality in German. When speaking in English, he presented himself as an expert on improving the sex lives of heterosexual married couples. Part of his reason for doing so was to boost sales of Titus Pearls, a patent medicine he developed at ISS and whose sales generated a considerable amount of his income. The remedy was manufactured and marketed by a Dutch company as a cure for "shattered nerves," exhaustion, depression, and dizziness—and as an aphrodisiac for both men and women. Hirschfeld hoped to capitalize on his fame as the "world-known authority on sexology" who invented the pills. The plan worked and soon many American newspapers referred to him as "the Einstein of sex."[33]

While in America, Hirschfeld concluded it was unsafe to return to Germany and opted to head onward to Asia and the Middle East. In 1931, he visited China and gave thirty-five lectures (in German with Chinese translations) on sexology, refuting views of homosexuality that had arisen after the collapse of the Qing dynasty in 1911. In 1907, the Qing government had rewritten the Chinese legal code and removed a 1734 law criminalizing anal sex between men. Upon taking power in 1912, the new Republican government did not recriminalize sodomy. The work of Hirschfeld and many other European sexologists, including Richard von Krafft-Ebing, Sigmund Freud, and Edward Carpenter, was translated (sometimes from Japanese sources) and disseminated. Translators crafted new terms for Krafft-Ebing's and Ellis's medical theories on homosexuality that defined same-sex attraction as "perversion" or "inversion." These theories transformed Chinese conceptions of same-sex relationships, moving away from the relative tolerance of homosexuality in the premodern era to hostility echoing

---

[32]Mancini, *Magnus Hirschfeld and the Quest for Sexual Freedom*, 69, 118. Meyerowitz, *How Sex Changed*, 15–21, 30.

[33]Heike Bauer, *The Hirschfeld Archives: Violence, Death, and Modern Queer Culture* (Philadelphia: Temple University Press, 2017), 103–8.

modern Western depictions of homosexuality as pathological. Hirschfeld emphatically rejected such condemnations of same-sex love.[34]

By the early 1930s, networks of sexologists spanned the world. In Tokyo, Hirschfeld reconnected with Japanese colleagues who he met originally in Berlin. In the Dutch East Indies, true to his socialist beliefs, he harshly criticized colonialism. In India, he supported the Indian independence movement and strongly refuted negative depictions of Indian sexuality in American author Katherine Mayo's *Mother India*, a white supremacist text met with popular outrage upon its publication in 1927. In Palestine, he visited former students from ISS who had established their own sexology practices in Tel Aviv. After stops in Athens and Vienna, Hirschfeld and Li Shiu Tong, a 24-year-old medical student who became Hirschfeld's companion after they met in Shanghai, settled in Zurich, Switzerland, in August 1932. He began writing an ethnography about his world tour.[35]

Already in failing health, Hirschfeld realized his life and his life's work were both in grave danger. In Germany, Franz von Papen, a conservative Catholic who was appointed Chancellor in July 1932, was orchestrating a harsh crackdown on "sexual immorality." Although ISS remained open, police harassed anyone associated with it. The domestic political situation grew even more perilous after President Paul von Hindenburg appointed Adolf Hitler chancellor on January 30, 1933. Hitler's Nationalist Socialists (Nazis) immediately launched a "Campaign for a Clean Reich" aimed at aligning German civil society with Nazi ideals. They shuttered most gay publications, outlawed gay rights organizations, and closed the vast majority of gay and lesbian bars and nightclubs throughout Germany. SHC, the Committee of Special People, and the LHR destroyed their membership lists and soon disbanded.

On May 6, the Nazis' antigay activities sharply escalated when members of the Nationalist Socialist Student League rampaged through ISS, shouting "Brenne Hirschfeld!" ("Burn Hirschfeld!") and assaulting staff. They seized Hirschfeld's client lists and the Gestapo later used them to track down and arrest gay men who were sent to concentration camps. Four days later, the Nazis burned thousands of books and documents from the ISS collection and works by "un-German" authors in a bonfire on Opernplatz. The same evening, the Berlin police pronounced ISS closed forever. With his German passport about to expire, Hirschfeld left Switzerland and raced to Paris, remaining in exile with his long-time partner Karl Giese and Li Shiu Tong. Although Hirschfeld recovered some ISS materials through purchases at auctions or from intermediaries who rescued them, his attempts to establish a new institute for sexual science

---

[34]Tze-Ian D. Sang, *The Emerging Lesbian: Female Same-Sex Desire in Modern China* (Chicago: University of Chicago Press, 2003).
[35]Bauer, *The Hirschfeld Archives*, 109–23.

IMAGE 2.3 Nazi soldiers burning thousands of materials from the Institute for Sexual Science and other works deemed "un-German" on the evening of May 10, 1933, in Berlin.

never came to fruition. He eventually moved to Nice and died there on May 14, 1935. He did not live to see his sister, Recha Tobias, and many of his associates perish in the Nazi death camps.[36]

The ascension of the Nazis unleashed a brutal suppression of the gay rights movement that spread throughout Europe. Just two months after the Nazis burned the Hirschfeld library, the Gestapo arrested SHC leader Kurt Hiller and sent him to the Oranienburg concentration camp. Released after nine months of imprisonment, Hiller fled to Prague and then to London. Thousands of other German gay men suffered even harsher fates. On June 30, 1934, Heinrich Himmler, commander of the Schutzstaffel (SS), led a murderous purge of 300 members of the Sturmabteilung (SA), the paramilitary wing of the Nazi Party whose violent methods help bring Hitler to power. The "Night of the Long Knives" consolidated Hitler's influence and secured the loyalty of the German Army.

Ernst Röhm, commander of the SA "brown shirts," was the most prominent casualty. Röhm was Hitler's closest friend in the Nazi leadership,

---

[36]Dose, *Magnus Hirschfeld*, 58–67.

the only one permitted to call him Adolf. The fact that Röhm was openly gay and had other openly gay men in the top ranks of the SA seems not to have bothered Hitler, though it did spark rumors that Hitler himself might be homosexual. In 1931, Hitler remained loyal even after leftists publicly outed Röhm and a Munich newspaper published Röhm's private letters to a friend detailing gay affairs. But three years later, Prussian Premier Hermann Göring, Propaganda Minister Joseph Goebbels, and Himmler conspired against Röhm. Using falsified evidence, they persuaded Hitler that Röhm was orchestrating a coup attempt, thereby ensuring Röhm would be destroyed. Subsequent Nazi propaganda emphasized Röhm's homosexuality as well as his disloyalty in contrast to the Third Reich's moral purity. But leftists around the world responded with homophobic rhetoric claiming homosexual depravity pervaded the Nazi Party and fascism itself.[37]

With their SA rivals eliminated and their hold on the German Army firm, the Nazis greatly intensified their campaigns against homosexuals. On June 28, 1935, acting on their view that homosexuality was a contagious form of degeneracy, the Nazis dramatically expanded Paragraph 175 to cover not only intercourse or intercourse-like acts between men, but also "unnatural vice" and "criminally indecent activities" between men. The statute was intentionally vague and applied retroactively, meaning that kissing, mutual masturbation, and even unconsummated same-sex desire were now criminalized. Under the auspices of the newly created Reich Office to Combat Homosexuality and Abortion, regional police offices were required to submit lists of homosexuals to the state. Arrests for Paragraph 175 violations doubled in 1935 and then doubled again the following year. By 1939, the Gestapo had amassed files on more than 90,000 gay men and police closely monitored private homes, bars, and cruising areas. Men who were detained were often tortured and coerced into naming other homosexuals. While some were released, approximately 60,000 men were convicted of sodomy. Of these between 5,000 and 15,000 were sent to concentration camps and forced to wear pink triangle patches identifying them as homosexual. Although homosexuals as a group were never targeted for mass extermination, they faced especially harsh treatment meted out by Nazi guards and fellow inmates alike. Some were subjected to medical experimentation aimed at eradicating homosexual desire, including castration and hormonal treatments.[38]

---

[37]Beachy, Gay Berlin, 243–5. For a cogent analysis of the Nazis' broader views on sexuality, see Dagmar Herzog, Sex after Fascism: Memory and Morality in Twentieth-Century Germany (Princeton: Princeton University Press, 2005), 10–63.

[38]Geoffrey J. Giles, "'The Most Unkindest Cut of All': Castration, Homosexuality, and Nazi Justice," Journal of Contemporary History 27 (1992): 41–61; W. Jake Newsome, "Homosexuals after the Holocaust: Sexual Citizenship and the Politics of Memory in Germany and the United States, 1945–2008" (PhD diss., State University of New York at Buffalo, 2016), 20–64.

IMAGE 2.4 Prisoners at the Sachsenhausen concentration camp forced to wear the pink triangle the Nazis used to identify homosexuals.

The Nazis' failure to criminalize sex between women under the broadened Paragraph 175 reflected their view that women were inferior and sexually passive. Lesbians not only posed no political or social threat, but also could serve the Nazi state as wives and mothers of Aryan children. While a few lesbians were arrested and sent to concentration camps as "asocials," the Nazis did not systematically persecute them. Still, the climate of fear compelled most lesbians to go underground, break ties with friends, or abandon unfeminine hairstyles and clothing. Some moved to new places to start new lives or married men—many of them gay—for protection.[39]

As totalitarianism spread in the interwar period, gay men and lesbians in other nations were forced to make similar choices. Upon taking power in 1922, the fascist government in Italy valorized "a new man" ideal deemed incompatible with homosexuality. It closed an Italian academic journal that published the work of scholars debating the theories of Edward Carpenter and Magnus Hirschfeld. Although homosexuality was not recriminalized in Italy, fascist authorities publicly condemned gay men, subjected them to confinement, and used informants to spy on gay enclaves and establishments. In 1938, police in the Sicilian city of Catania rounded up gay men and banished them to the island of San Domino. Housed in austere dwellings without running water or electricity, the men could roam outside until their daily 8 p.m. curfew. Ironically, this internal exile accorded some of these men their first exposure to a gay community away from the social and religious rejection of families and the Roman Catholic Church. After the outbreak of World War II in 1939, legal authorities returned the men to their hometowns and placed them under surveillance.[40]

Gay men living under other authoritarian regimes faced the recriminalization of homosexuality. After a May 1926 coup d'état in Portugal, the new right-wing government reinstated sodomy laws. In 1934, with the escalation of the Stalinist purges and the rising threat of Nazi Germany, the Soviet Union once again outlawed homosexuality under Article 121, describing it as "fascistic perversion." Writing in *Pravda* and *Izvestia*, Maxim Gorky declared, "Wipe out homosexuality and Fascism will disappear." Abandoning the Bolsheviks' policies on "free love," Stalinists linked homosexuality and fascism and homophobic rhetoric spread globally through the Communist International.

Soviet newspapers portrayed homosexuality as a crime against the state and behavior incompatible with socialism. Those convicted of violating the new Article 121 faced up to eight years in prison. Although some gay men in Moscow, Leningrad, Kharkov, and Odessa were arrested, the Stalinist regime never systematically persecuted homosexuals.[41]

In the United States, gays and lesbians found themselves constricted not by authoritarianism, but the onset of the Great Depression. In the 1920s, gay subcultures flourished in Harlem and Greenwich Village and a "pansy craze" punctuated by flamboyantly gay and lesbian performers swept Manhattan theaters and nightclubs in the early 1930s. Because of the variety of people who gathered to drink illegally in Jazz Age speakeasies and establishments, police did not have much success enforcing disorderly conduct laws, even those specifically aimed at gays. But as a major economic crisis gripped the country, many Americans blamed a decline in national morality and authorities began cracking down on public hedonism. When Prohibition ended in 1933, authorities recalibrated liquor laws to target "disreputable" individuals in bars. Police and liquor regulators joined forces in raiding bars condoning disorderly conduct. Viewed as both disreputable and a threat to public order, many gay bars and bathhouses closed. But while gay

---

[40]Lorenzo Benadusi, *The Enemy of the New Man: Homosexuality in Fascist Italy*, trans. Suzanne Dingee and Jennifer Pudney (Madison: University of Wisconsin Press, 2012); Alan Johnston, "A Gay Island Community Created by Italy's Fascists," *BBC News*, June 13, 2013, http://www.bbc.com/news/magazine-22856586.

[41]Healey, *Homosexual Desire in Revolutionary Russia*, 181–204; Tamagne, *A History of Homosexuality in Europe*, 280–2.

subcultures became less visible in many cities, they did not disappear and gay and lesbian private networks endured.[42] In 1934, under pressure from fundamentalist Protestants and the Catholic Church, Hollywood adopted the Motion Picture Production Code, banning cinematic portrayals of "sex perversion." For decades afterward, if films contained gay and lesbian characters, they were portrayed as menacing, suicidal, pathetic, or sissified—stereotypes that had international ramifications due to the popularity and reach of Hollywood.[43]

After World War II erupted, the Nazis extended their pro-Aryan policies and suppressed homosexuals in nations that fell under Nazi occupation. Having repealed its sodomy law seven years earlier, Poland found itself subjected to the expanded Paragraph 175 after the Nazis invaded in September 1939. After seizing control of the Netherlands in May 1940, the Nazis outlawed all sexual acts between men and dissolved the Dutch SHC, which had been active since 1911. But their efforts to persecute Dutch gays faltered when local police refused to cooperate.[44]

In German-occupied Vichy France, Nazi collaborators used the war as a pretext for criminalizing sexual behaviors that had been legal for over a century. In place of statutes that made no reference to sodomy and that drew no distinction between private homosexual or heterosexual relations between people over the age of consent (which was raised from eleven to thirteen in 1832), the Vichy regime under Marshal Philippe Pétain amended the penal code to criminalize "shameless or unnatural acts" between adult men and male minors under the age of twenty-one. A key element of the Vichy government's emphasis on "moral order," the August 1942 legal revision reintroduced a distinction between "natural" and "unnatural" sexual acts that had been expunged from French law since 1810. But the Vichy government did not criminalize homosexuality itself—a significant contrast to Paragraph 175 in Germany. Nor did the Vichy regime orchestrate mass persecution of French gay men. While approximately 200 gay men in Alsace and the Moselle were arrested under Paragraph 175 and sent to concentration camps after Germany annexed eastern France, the majority of French gay men escaped arrest and were not targeted by Vichy authorities on account of their sexual orientation. Nonetheless, the Vichy years left a long and negative impact on the legal status of gay men. After the liberation of France, the provisional government led by Charles de Gaulle did not revert to the Napoleonic Code and abandon the anti-homosexual provisions of the Vichy code, but instead set the age of consent for heterosexual relations at fifteen and left in place the prohibition on

---

[42]The classic text is: Chauncey, *Gay New York*.

[43]Vito Russo, *The Celluloid Closet: Homosexuality in the Movies*, rev. ed. (New York: Harper & Row, 1987).

[44]Tielman, "Dutch Gay Emancipation History," 11–12.

sex between men over twenty-one and male minors aged fifteen to twenty. The disparities in the ages of consent for heterosexual and homosexual sex were not equalized until 1982.[45]

World War II also triggered changes in nations not subject to Nazi occupation. For many, the war was a time of discovery and self-realization as gays and lesbians found each other in same-sex environments on the home front and in the armed forces. In 1940, after the United States instituted a peacetime draft in response to the outbreak of war in Europe, military psychiatrists—persuaded they could identify homosexuals— convinced the Department of War to revise its post–World War I policy of court-martialing and imprisoning soldiers found guilty of committing sodomy. Draft boards began screening suspected homosexual recruits with a number of procedures that were easily evaded by gay men and women motivated to serve their nation in time of war. Homosexuality alone was not initially deemed disqualifying for military service, but the government reversed the policy in 1941. Two years later, facing critical manpower needs to wage the war, US officials (and their German counterparts) began distinguishing between occasional and inveterate homosexuals. A soldier found to have engaged in homosexual acts on an isolated basis could be "redeemed" through counseling and retained in the military. To dissuade those who might claim homosexual identity as a means of evading service, military leaders—ignoring the opposition of psychiatrists—began informing local draft boards of any recruit claiming to be gay, a decision that had devastating consequences in some cases. While many gay and lesbian soldiers actively serving in the armed forces successfully concealed their identities, some were later discovered by military authorities and given administrative discharges (sometimes called "blue" discharges because of the color of the paper on which they were printed) and subsequently denied benefits granted to other US veterans. These discharges required no formal court-martial, only a hearing. The policy marked a significant change under which gay men and lesbians could now be prosecuted on the basis of their sexual identity alone, not just for homosexual acts. Although military criminal convictions for forcible sodomy declined, nearly 10,000 male soldiers were expelled administratively.

These events helped gay and lesbian soldiers forge a sense of solidarity and motivated many to fight discrimination on the basis of sexual orientation in the postwar years. Some of the gay and lesbian soldiers expelled from the military chose not to return to unwelcoming hometowns and instead stayed

---

[45]Michael Sibalis, "Homophobia, Vichy France, and the 'Crime of Homosexuality': The Origins of the Ordinance of 6 August 1942," *GLQ: A Journal of Lesbian and Gay Studies* 8:3 (2002): 301–18.

where they had been discharged, contributing to the emergence of strong and visible communities in port cities like Los Angeles, San Francisco, and New York.[46]

In the aftermath of World War II, new international organizations and protections for human rights arose. Shaped by their wartime experiences and inspired by the homosexual emancipation movement of the early twentieth century, a new wave of gay and lesbian rights activists mobilized and reestablished transnational connections. Despite intense Cold War repression and logistical challenges, the homophiles articulated dueling visions of gay rights: one that relied on heterosexual authorities for validation and another that defined homosexuals as a distinct minority deserving of civil rights. Although the gay liberation movement of the post-Stonewall era later overshadowed many of their achievements, the homophiles preserved and expanded gay rights rhetoric and strategies pioneered in the late nineteenth century.

[46]Allan Bérubé, *Coming Out under Fire: The History of Gay Men and Women in World War Two* (New York: Penguin Books, 1990); Margot Canaday, *The Straight State: Sexuality and Citizenship in Twentieth-Century America* (Princeton, NJ: Princeton University Press, 2009), 87–90.

CHAPTER THREE

The Global Homophile
Movement, 1945–65

Despite Nazi persecution of homosexuals, sexual minorities were not explicitly included in the new international protections for human rights that arose in the postwar era. Allied occupation authorities and then the West German government continued to prosecute men for violating Paragraph 175 through the 1960s. Dramatic shifts in culture and societal expectations also affected gays and lesbians. As wartime dislocations ended, many nations advocated a return to strict heterosexual norms. Postwar marriage and birth rates rose and nuclear families were extolled as bulwarks against the era's uncertainties. As US–Soviet relations degenerated, anticommunism intensified in many Western countries. In the United States, fears of communist subversion intersected with anxieties about gender and sexuality, triggering a Lavender Scare that defined gays and lesbians as national security risks, resulting in hundreds of gays and lesbians being expelled from federal and state jobs, the US armed forces, and many private occupations. Dependent on US economic and military aid and unwilling to alienate their powerful ally, Great Britain, Canada, Australia, and France adopted similar policies, as did international organizations like the United Nations (UN), the World Bank, and the International Monetary Fund.[1]

But this repressive climate also inspired gay rights activists in Europe and the United States to organize. Taking cues from both prewar sexual reformers and newly emerging discourses and legal frameworks guarding human rights, they began building transnational relationships that provided

---

[1]David K. Johnson, "America's Cold War Empire: Exporting the Lavender Scare," in *Global Homophobia*, Meredith L. Weiss and Michael J. Bosia, eds. (Urbana: University of Illinois Press, 2013), 55–74.

a critical foundation for today's international LGBT rights movement. New homophile publications and organizations arose after the war, spreading from the Netherlands through Northern Europe to the United States, West Germany, Belgium, and France.[2] Activists denounced government crackdowns on gay public culture and state-sponsored antigay persecution. In the late 1950s, the Wolfenden Report in Great Britain and the erosion of obscenity laws in the United States offered homophiles hope. They fiercely debated whether assimilationist strategies or direct-action tactics inspired by the civil rights movement were the best means of securing significant victories. By 1965, activists proved unable to reconcile these internal debates and the movement was poised for a more visible and confrontational phase of gay and lesbian advocacy.

The story of the Nazis' antigay oppression did not receive wide attention or generate much public sympathy for several decades. In the 1970s, a transnational network of LGBT activists transformed the pink triangle into a global symbol of gay liberation. Attempting to fill a void in historical scholarship and suffused with activist fervor, they crafted a narrative that made little attempt to distinguish the Nazis' persecution of homosexuals from the genocidal campaign to exterminate the Jews. But the "Homocaust" argument did not withstand the later scrutiny of professional historians who found no evidence of a systematic Nazi plan to eradicate homosexuals.[3]

These historians helped to recover the stories of the courageous homosexuals who fought for justice after being convicted of violating Paragraph 175 during the twelve years of Nazi rule. Of the 100,000 men who were arrested between 1933 and 1945, about 50,000 were sentenced. Of these, between 5,000 and 15,000 were sent to concentration camps. But while most of the German gay men arrested for violating Paragraph 175 escaped the camps, few escaped the stigma generated by the Nazis' persecution of homosexuals and the subsequent antigay policies of the Allied and West German governments. The Nazis crushed the thriving German homosexual emancipation movement and shut down gay bars and publications.[4]

After hostilities ended in Europe in May 1945, the Allies divided Germany into four zones of occupation. Soviet authorities assumed control of the east. British, French, and American officials governed the west. As military units began liberating concentration camps during the last weeks of the European campaign, gay prisoners assumed that their persecution would soon end. But such hopes were shattered when it became evident that the Allies had

---

[2]Craig Loftin, *Masked Voices: Gay Men and Lesbians in Cold War America* (Albany: State University of New York Press, 2012), 68; Heike Bauer and Matt Cook, eds. *Queer 1950s: Rethinking Sexuality in the Postwar Years* (London: Palgrave Macmillan, 2012).

[3]On the origins and evolution of these debates, see Newsome, "Homosexuals after the Holocaust."

[4]Newsome, "Homosexuals after the Holocaust," 21–64.

little sympathy for the Nazis' gay victims. Under the auspices of the War Department's handbook on military government in Germany, US officials continued to incarcerate anyone held in the camps on the basis of a criminal conviction. Accordingly, men who had not yet completed sentences imposed for violations of Paragraph 175 were transferred from the concentration camps to Allied military prisons. Despite the fact that Nazi ideology played a central role in the 1935 expansion of Paragraph 175, US officials did not include the law among those purged in their denazification of the German legal code. With sodomy defined as a criminal offense under their own military regulations, US occupation authorities were untroubled by their decision to uphold Paragraph 175. US military police arrested between 1,100 and 1,800 men for "indecency" during each of the four years of the American occupation. In many cases, these men faced judges allowed to remain on the bench even after serving in the Nazi judiciary.[5]

Following the Allies' merger of their three zones into a single nation, the Federal Republic of Germany (FRG) was founded in May 1949. Three months later, West Germans elected a new government and the newly established Christian Democratic Union (CDU) won the majority in the Bundestag, West Germany's federal parliament. Under Chancellor Konrad Adenauer, the conservative and mostly Catholic CDU pursued policies aimed at protecting and promoting Christian morality, traditional gender roles, and the nuclear family. In contrast to the "Aryan" warrior celebrated in the Nazi era, the ideal man in postwar West Germany was a dedicated husband and father.

In this political climate, gay men were seen as a threat to the German nation. The new West German government thus retained the more expansive version of Paragraph 175 in order to combat male homosexuality. Echoing their predecessors in the imperial, Weimar, and Nazi eras, officials in the FRG did not criminalize lesbian sexual activity. But in 1953, officials instituted the Law against the Distribution of Written Material Endangering Youth. Like an earlier "trash and smut" law imposed by the Weimar regime in the 1920s, the statute outlawed the distribution of homosexual publications, suppressing nascent efforts to resurrect a public lesbian and gay culture in West Germany. As activists attempted to rebuild the German homophile movement, they saw the continued enforcement of Paragraph 175 as a potent symbol of the endurance of Nazi ideology under the veneer of democracy.[6]

These formidable obstacles did not, however, deter a few German gay men from challenging the legality of Paragraph 175. After being convicted

---

[5]Newsome, "Homosexuals after the Holocaust," 69–75.

[6]Newsome, "Homosexuals after the Holocaust," 75–84; Benno Gammerl, "Affecting Legal Change: Law and Same-Sex Feelings in West Germany since the 1950s," *From Sodomy Laws to Same-Sex Marriage*, 109–14.

of having sex with a man in late 1949, an appellant, identified only as "N," appealed his conviction. But on March 13, 1951, when the Federal High Court considered his case, it upheld the constitutionality of Paragraph 175. Three months later, in a second challenge to the sodomy law, the High Court rejected the idea that Paragraph 175 violated the gender equality provision in Article 3 of the West German constitution.

In 1957, two men each sentenced to a year in prison after separate convictions for Paragraph 175 violations appealed their cases all the way to the Federal Constitutional Court, Germany's highest judicial body on matters related to administrative and legislative matters. Like the High Court, the judges argued that the biological differences between men and women justified Paragraph 175's different treatment of the sexes. Because some states had criminalized male homosexuality prior to German unification and the original version of Paragraph 175 was enshrined in the penal code adopted in 1871, courts consistently interpreted it as a *national* law, not an anomaly imposed by the Nazis. Between 1949 and 1969, over 100,000 men were arrested for indecency, 59,000 of whom were found guilty.[7] When West German men jailed for such offenses petitioned the European Court of Human Rights established in 1959, the Court ruled that their convictions were justified under the "health and morals" exceptions of the European Convention on Human Rights.[8] Like their Nazi predecessors, authorities in the FRG kept *Rosa Listen* (pink lists), registries of "convicted, known, or even suspected homosexuals." Gay men on these lists could face serious consequences, including public exposure, job loss, or withdrawal of licenses or credentials.

The fact that male homosexuality remained illegal in postwar Germany deterred most of the men arrested and imprisoned by the Nazis from speaking publicly about their experiences for decades. But the parallels between the techniques used by the Nazis and the Federal Republic to surveil, harass, and prosecute gay men did not escape the attention of the homophile publications that began appearing in West Germany in the early 1950s. After the 1953 "trash and smut" law barred the public displays of these magazines, people smuggled copies of homophile magazines from other nations to keep apprised of nascent efforts to challenge antigay laws and attitudes.[9]

---

[7] In June 2017, the German Parliament voted unanimously to vacate these convictions and awarded the 5,000 surviving men convicted of Paragraph 175 offenses 3,000 euros ($3,400), plus an additional €1,500 ($1,700) for each year of incarceration. David Shimer, "Germany Wipes Slate Clean for 50,000 Men Convicted under Anti-Gay Law," *New York Times*, June 23, 2017, https://www.nytimes.com/2017/06/23/world/europe/germany-anti-gay-law.html.

[8] Nicole LaViolette and Sandra Whitworth, "No Safe Haven: Sexuality as a Universal Human Right and Gay and Lesbian Activism in International Politics," *Millennium: Journal of International Studies* 23:3 (1994): 567.

[9] Newsome, "Homosexuals after the Holocaust," 84–97.

The illegality of homosexuality also prevented gay victims of Nazism from receiving reparations from postwar authorities. Under the terms of the Federal Compensation Law passed by the Bundestag in 1956, only those persecuted by the Nazis on the bases of race, religion, or political belief qualified for compensation from the state. The 50,000 gay men arrested by the Nazis—even those sent to concentration camps—therefore did not qualify for assistance. The following year, when the Bundestag passed a law permitting concentration camp survivors excluded from the 1956 legislation to apply for aid, "only fourteen men (out of the estimated 1,750–3,500 pink triangle survivors) risked prosecution by revealing that they had been persecuted because of their homosexuality. All fourteen petitions were denied."[10]

Despite communist associations of homosexuality with bourgeois degeneracy, the German Democratic Republic (GDR) adopted less harsh policies on homosexuality than its Western counterpart.[11] In the aftermath of World War II, authorities in the Soviet Occupation Zone took steps toward repeal of the 1935 version of Paragraph 175. On September 20, 1948, the Superior State Court in Halle struck down the law specifically because of its Nazi origins. But on March 13, 1951, the East German Supreme Court retained Paragraph 175a, the provision of the Nazi version of the law that set twenty-one as the age of consent for same-sex sexual activities between men, while leaving it at sixteen for heterosexual relations. In 1954, the same court declared that documentation of intercourse-like activities was not necessary for a Paragraph 175 conviction. Lesser displays of male same-sex physical intimacy could be construed as sodomy.[12]

But throughout the Cold War, antigay laws varied among countries in the Eastern Bloc. For example, the GDR's policies were more liberal than those of Romania. Having already criminalized male and female same-sex activities associated with "public scandal" in 1937, Romania adopted even more stringent laws under its post-WWII communist government. In 1948, the state outlawed public displays of homosexuality, mandating between two to five years of imprisonment as punishment. Nine years later, the government broadened the statute to encompass private as well as public displays of same-sex intimacy and increased the range of prison sentences to three to ten years.[13]

---

[10]Newsome, "Homosexuals after the Holocaust," 100–5.

[11]Josie McLellan, *Love in the Time of Communism: Intimacy and Sexuality in the GDR* (New York: Cambridge University Press, 2011), 114–43.

[12]Erik G. Huneke, "Morality, Law, and the Socialist Sexual Self in the German Democratic Republic, 1945–1972" (PhD diss., University of Michigan, 2013), 141–3.

[13]Lukasz Szulc, "Was Homosexuality Illegal in Communist Europe?" *Public Seminar*, April 22, 2018, http://www.publicseminar.org/2018/04/was-homosexuality-illegal-in-communist-europe/.

While Romania intensified its antigay policies, activist Rudolf Klimmer worked for LGBT rights in East Germany. A psychiatrist who got his medical degree from the University of Leipzig, Klimmer joined the Communist Party of Germany in 1926. After the Nazis took power, he was imprisoned twice because of his political affiliations and barred from practicing medicine. Fearful that exposure of his homosexuality would result in further Nazi persecution, he married a lesbian friend to cloak his true sexual identity. Despite these obstacles, Klimmer conducted medical research for a pharmaceutical company during World War II.

Once hostilities ended, Klimmer established a psychiatric practice in Dresden and joined the Socialist Unity Party, the governing party of the German Democratic Republic. He soon met Armin Schreier, the man who became his life partner. While trying to keep their romantic relationship and his criminal convictions secret, Klimmer advocated repeal of Paragraph 175. Drawing on the work of sexologists, Klimmer emphasized the congenital nature of homosexuality and described Paragraph 175 as a legacy of fascism that violated communist ideals of fairness and non-intervention into citizens' private lives by the state. Although he did not succeed in getting the East German government to repeal Paragraph 175 in the 1950s, his writings calling for reform of laws that criminalized consensual same-sex relations influenced a number of public officials and Protestant authorities. After 1957, the state stopped convicting men for Paragraph 175 violations. Throughout this era, Klimmer read and wrote articles for international homophile publications like Switzerland's *Der Kreis*, one of the only prewar homophile publications to survive World War II. Neither the Iron Curtain nor the absence of an East German homophile organization precluded Klimmer from forging connections with the transnational network of LGBT activists that began cohering in the early Cold War.[14]

In Western Europe, the Dutch took the lead in rebuilding the gay rights movement. Popular outrage at the Nazis' imposition of Paragraph 175 and other antigay laws during the wartime occupation of the Netherlands gave momentum to calls for decriminalizing sodomy in the postwar era. Although many conservative Catholics and Protestants remained opposed to homosexuality, there was rising popular sentiment that the state should not interfere in private behavior. Dutch gay activists capitalized on these views and began organizing at a level unparalleled anywhere in the world at the time.

In 1946, members of the Dutch chapter of the Scientific Humanitarian Committee joined forces with the editors of the prewar magazine *Levensrecht* and founded the Cultuur-en Ontspannings Centrum (Cultural and Recreational Center), better known as COC. Led by Nico Engelschman

---

[14]Huneke, "Morality, Law, and the Socialist Sexual Self in the German Democratic Republic," 67–141.

(using the pseudonym Bob Angelo), COC was a public space that hosted discussion groups and social events for gays and that attempted to build alliances with ministers, public officials, and law enforcement.[15]

Gay politics and culture in post-WWII Denmark also changed dramatically. Prior to the mid-nineteenth century, civil authorities banished suspected and known sodomites. Nonetheless, by 1860, urbanization fostered an increasingly visible gay subculture in Copenhagen. Beginning in 1906, a series of homosexual scandals drew widespread press attention and a number of men were convicted of sodomy and imprisoned. Dismayed by the furor, medical and legal experts called for the decriminalization of sodomy, then punishable by a year's imprisonment for consenting adults and up to four years if it involved boys under the age of fifteen. In 1912, a royal commission recommended the decriminalization of sodomy, but the civil code was not changed until 1933. Under the new law (which also applied to Iceland), consensual homosexual relations between men eighteen or older were legal, while the age of consent for heterosexual activities was set at fifteen. The new statute was vigorously enforced and men convicted of having sex with male minors faced harsh penalties including aversion therapy and castration. In 1948, as antigay repression intensified, Danish gays formed a new homophile organization called Forbundet af 1948 (the League of 1948).[16]

Like their counterparts in the Netherlands and Denmark, Swedish gays also began organizing in the early postwar era. Although the Swedish government had decriminalized consensual same-sex sexual acts between men over age eighteen in 1944, most Swedes still considered homosexuality immoral. The depth of popular animosity became evident after Reverend Karl-Erik Kejne began campaigning to end gay prostitution in Stockholm. In 1948, he publicly alleged that gangs of gay men were now threatening his life. Swedish newspapers widely circulated his claims about a "homosexual mafia" that was protected by the police.[17]

In October 1950, in response to the hysteria, about three dozen gay men and a lesbian who belonged to Forbundet af 1948 gathered in Solna to discuss how they could better educate the public and refute Kejne's false accusations. Two years later, they created an independent organization called Riksförbundet för sexuellt likaberättigande—RFSL (National Organization for Sexual Organization). Like COC, it combined political advocacy with social activities. In 1951, it began lobbying for lowering the age of consent for homosexual relations. The following year, RFSL called on the Swedish delegate to the UN to advocate for gay rights. In 1953, RFSL petitioned the Swedish Ministry of Health and Social Affairs for the legalization of

---

[15]Tielman, "Dutch Gay Emancipation History," 9–13.
[16]Dag Heede, "Denmark," GLBTQ Archive, http://www.glbtqarchive.com/ssh/denmark_S.pdf.
[17]RFSL History, https://www.rfsl.se/en/about-us/history/.

same-sex marriage. None of these campaigns succeeded and all generated controversy among RFSL members.[18]

The increasingly negative views of homosexuality being medical authorities in several countries posed a major obstacle to homophile activists everywhere. During and after World War II, many psychologists characterized homosexuals as antisocial and incapable of lasting love. Deviating from subtleties in Freud's original views, these psychoanalysts made sweeping generalizations based on their observations of a very narrow subset of homosexuals who were imprisoned or institutionalized. Gays who were well adjusted and well integrated into society were not included among the subjects studied. The ill-informed stereotype of the unhappy, unstable homosexual began filtering into postwar culture with pernicious legal, medical, and societal consequences. Psychiatrists like Edward Bergler, a student of Freud's who emigrated to the United States in 1938, espoused extreme views suggesting that homosexuals posed a threat to others and were intent on seducing unsuspecting youth. In 1952, the American Psychiatric Association added homosexuality to the list of personality disorders included in its *Diagnostic and Statistical Manual*, further fueling the idea that homosexuals were mentally unbalanced and helping to corrode gays' and lesbians' views of themselves.[19]

There were, however, doctors and psychiatrists who challenged these views. In 1948, Dr. William Meninger, chief consultant on neuropsychiatry to the US Army Surgeon General during World War II, published a study of wartime homosexuality. Although he shared the majority view that homosexuality was a pathology caused by arrested psychological development, he expressed compassion when describing his own experiences working with gay soldiers. He stressed that most gay soldiers served honorably without drawing notice and emphatically rejected blanket societal condemnation of homosexuals.[20] Under the leadership of Karl Bowman, the Porter Psychiatric Clinic at the University of California at San Francisco emerged as a research center on gender identity and transsexuality.[21]

The era's most famous (and infamous) sex researcher was undoubtedly Alfred Kinsey. His landmark studies of male and female sexual behavior, published in 1948 and 1953, shattered many prevailing assumptions and became unlikely international bestsellers. Although critics attacked his sampling techniques and accused him of skewing his findings, Kinsey revolutionized the study of sex through the use of questionnaires and interviews given to a broad sample of ordinary people. Kinsey found that

---

[18]RFSL History, https://www.rfsl.se/en/about-us/history/.
[19]Edsall, *Toward Stonewall*, 243–8.
[20]Edsall, *Toward Stonewall*, 264–5.
[21]Stryker, *Transgender History*, 58–9.

incidences of premarital sex and masturbation were much higher than the era's traditional mores suggested.

Kinsey's discoveries on homosexual behavior were even more shocking. He claimed that 37 percent of American men had reached orgasm during homosexual sex at least once. He also concluded that 10 percent of men were exclusively homosexual for at least three years and 4 percent were exclusively homosexual for their entire lives. Among his female subjects, Kinsey reported that 13 percent had experienced orgasm with another woman and approximately 2 percent were primarily lesbian. Kinsey urged his readers not to cast moral judgment on sexual behavior, but to form their opinions based on objectively gathered scientific data. Using a scale of 0–6, Kinsey described people's sexual orientation based on their experiences and responses at specific times, ranging from exclusive heterosexuality on the low end to exclusive homosexuality on the high end. Most people fell somewhere in between.

Kinsey's findings intensified an already-fraught debate on homosexuality in postwar America. Some gays and lesbians felt empowered by the discovery that same-sex activities were not uncommon. But the same data alarmed legal, medical, and religious authorities fearful of increasing visibility and occurrence of homosexuality. While experts disagreed over whether Kinsey had overestimated the extent of same-sex sexual activities, a flood of studies and commentary on the dangers posed by homosexuals entered American culture.[22]

European homophiles quickly grasped the global implications of Kinsey's findings. In December 1948, COC's Bob Angelo celebrated their potential to liberate society from "the hypocritical standards of our sexual morality." In its magazine *Vriendschap (Friendship)*, COC drew on Kinsey's statistics to extrapolate that 500,000 homosexuals were among the Dutch population. In Switzerland, the editors of *Der Kreis (The Circle)* used information gleaned from *Time* magazine for a series on the Kinsey report published over four months in 1949.[23] Although paper shortages made it extremely difficult to obtain *Sexual Behavior in the Human Male* in economically depressed Great Britain, summaries and differing assessments of Kinsey's work were featured in many British newspapers and magazines.[24]

---

[22]Miriam G. Reumann, *American Sexual Character: Sex, Gender, and National Identity in the Kinsey Reports* (Berkeley: University of California Press, 2005), 165–98.

[23]*Der Kreis* was one of the only gay publications in the world founded in the interwar years that endured after World War II. Launched in 1932 as *Menschenrecht (Human Rights)*, the magazine was initially edited by Anna Vock, who managed to keep the publication going during the Depression and clashes with police. In 1942, after Switzerland legalized consensual private homosexual acts, Karl Meier took over as editor and, under the pseudonym Rolf, ran the magazine until it ceased publication in 1967.

[24]Minto, "Special Relationships," 28–55.

While Kinsey's work on sexuality drew global attention, he entered emerging debates over gender identity among a small group of US physicians. After forging an alliance with San Francisco-based transgender activist Louise Lawrence, Bowman was introduced to transgender Americans connected to Lawrence through personal acquaintance and written correspondence. In 1944, Bowman introduced Kinsey to Harry Benjamin, a German émigré and pioneering endocrinologist who had studied the rejuvenating impact of hormones under the guidance of Magnus Hirschfeld and Eugen Steinach during visits to Berlin and Vienna in the 1920s and 1930s. Unlike most American doctors at the time, Benjamin believed that transgender identity had biological origins and therefore merited medical intervention.

In 1949, Kinsey referred a patient seeking sexual reassignment to Benjamin. After reading her medical history, Benjamin concluded that Val Berry (a pseudonym) was "a woman [who] accidentally possesses the body of a man" and began administering hormone treatment in his San Francisco office. He then contacted California's Attorney General Edward G. (Pat) Brown to inquire whether castration was legal in the state. Brown was initially encouraging, but, after consulting with another attorney, informed Benjamin that "transsexual genital modification would constitute 'mayhem' (the willful destruction of healthy tissue) and would expose any surgeon who performed such an operation to possible criminal prosecution." Alarmed by the possible legal risks of ignoring Brown's assessment, virtually no US physician would perform sexual reassignment surgery openly for several years, though Los Angeles urologist Eugene Belt secretly performed a few.[25]

These obstacles compelled Christine Jorgensen, assigned a male identity at birth and raised by a Danish-American family, to seek a sex change in Copenhagen, Denmark. Although she was far from the first individual to undergo such a procedure, Jorgenson sparked a worldwide sensation after she leaked news of her transformation to the media in December 1952, her story encapsulating the era's gender anxieties and fixation on scientific innovation. She successfully parlayed her fame into public appearances, a best-selling book, and a brief acting career. A flood of stories about individuals undergoing sex change entered American popular culture through tabloids, newspapers, magazines, pulp novels, and B-movies like Edward Wood Jr.'s *Glen or Glenda?* (1953). By the mid-1950s, US physicians and scientists were adopting the term *transsexual*, hotly debating sexual reassignment, and engaging older European scientific literature on sexology.[26]

---

[25]Val Berry underwent gender reassignment surgery in 1953. Stryker, *Transgender History*, 62; Meyerowitz, *How Sex Changed*, 45–8.

[26]Stryker, *Transgender History*, 65–7; Meyerowitz, *How Sex Changed*, 51–97.

IMAGE 3.1 After undergoing gender reassignment surgery in Denmark in 1952, Christine Jorgenson returned to the United States and shared her story with the *New York Daily News*. She quickly gained widespread attention and parleyed her fame into a best-selling book and brief career as an actress and singer.

The rise of anticommunism in the postwar era underscored transnational discussions about sexuality and both triggered and imperiled gay activism. In the immediate aftermath of World War II, the political climate in the United States shifted away from bipartisanship and grew more polarized as US–Soviet relations deteriorated and a strong societal emphasis on the reestablishment of traditional gender roles and the nuclear family arose. In early 1950, Republicans began to fuse anticommunism and antigay sentiments, igniting a Lavender Scare that had transnational ramifications. In December 1950, a US Senate committee charged with investigating the employment of "homosexuals and other sex perverts" by the federal government released a sensationalized report. It claimed that homosexuals were emotionally unstable, had weak moral fiber, and tried to seduce impressionable co-workers.

More alarmingly, the report claimed that gay and lesbian federal employees jeopardized national security. They were portrayed as easy targets for blackmailers and foreign agents who could threaten to expose their identities unless provided with sensitive government information. The reports' authors cited the case of Alfred Redl, the homosexual Austrian counterintelligence operative who became a double agent for Russia decades earlier. The fact that the "sex perverts" report appeared just six months after US troops joined a multinational force fighting off North Korea's invasion of its southern neighbor accentuated the real risks of government employees susceptible to extortion.

To root out potential subversives and to undercut political opponents who alleged they were "soft on communism," the Truman administration launched a government loyalty program in early 1947. Shrouded in secrecy and failing to specify the exact meaning of "loyalty," the operation targeted a broad array of employees and was soon emulated by state and local employees. The FBI and local police departments compiled lists of suspected homosexuals. Threatening images of gays helped to fuel passage of "sexual psychopath" laws in several states. The US post office tracked the recipients of "obscene" material. By early 1953, the US Department of State had dismissed 425 employees said to have "homosexual proclivities," twice as many as were fired for suspected or proven communist sympathies.[27]

Gays who were not federal employees also faced new dangers. Vice squads routinely raided gay bars and newspapers published the names and employers of those arrested. Because many cities had outlawed serving alcohol to known homosexuals, gay bars were often closed or survived only after owners paid off corrupt police or mobsters promising protection. In 1955, the discovery of gay cruising areas in Boise, Idaho plunged the city into a wave of hysteria leading to the arrests of dozens of men, many of whom lost jobs, had their reputations destroyed, or were sent to prison.[28]

But the Lavender Scare coexisted with the appearance of more positive portrayals written by gays themselves. Gore Vidal's *The City and The Pillar* (1948) signaled a major shift in fictional depictions of homosexual characters. Its gay characters are given centrality in a story with World War II as its backdrop. Society's hostility, not homosexuality, is the driving force behind the protagonist's unhappiness and violent behavior. Although US newspapers and magazines refused to publish reviews of his work for several years after the novel's release, it sold well and Vidal continued to publish under pseudonyms. Vidal, Tennessee Williams, James Baldwin, and Truman Capote were only a few of the gay authors who flourished in postwar New York City.

In 1951, Edward Sagarin, using the pen name Donald Webster Cory, published *The Homosexual in America*, a pioneering examination of gay life in the United States written by a gay man. Cory defined gays as a minority deserving of civil rights. He challenged gays to accept themselves and to forge collective solidarity. He urged them to reveal their sexual identity to trusted relatives, friends, and colleagues.

Cory was not alone in envisioning collective action for homosexual equality. In November 1950, Harry Hay, Rudi Gernreich, Bob Hull, Charles Rowland, and Dale Jennings gathered at Hay's Los Angeles home and

---

[27]David K. Johnson, *The Lavender Scare: The Cold War Persecution of Gays and Lesbians in the Federal Government* (Chicago: University of Chicago, 2004).
[28]D'Emilio, *Sexual Politics, Sexual Communities*, 40–56; John Gerassi, *The Boys of Boise: Furor, Vice, and Folly in an American City* (New York: Macmillan, 1966).

founded the Mattachine Society, the first enduring homophile organization in the United States. Hay and two others had been active Communist Party members, but had been expelled due to the party's conflation of homosexuality with bourgeois decadence, ironic given anticommunists' close association of homosexuality with communist subversion. Reflecting Marxist doctrine, Mattachine defined homosexuals as a distinct minority that needed to raise gays' consciousness in order to create solidarity that would be translated into political and social action. Distancing themselves from the negative connotations of "homosexual," they adopted the term "homophile," embracing the language used by the homosexual equality movement in pre-WWII Germany. In January 1953, Jennings and Rowland founded *ONE*, the first successful US magazine targeted at a gay audience.[29]

At the same time, the US government pressured international organizations and allied governments to adopt antigay policies. At US insistence, the UN agreed to expel employees found to be "disloyal" to member nations. But the new International Employees Loyalty Board created to conduct background checks lacked enforcement powers. In 1953, the UN dismissed fewer than a quarter of the 200 employees flagged as morally unsuitable by investigators working for the US Department of State. Exasperated, US officials escalated their efforts to persuade international organizations to purge their homosexual employees. In 1955, Henry Cabot Lodge, the US ambassador to the UN, warned UN Secretary General Trygve Lie that the United States would cut its financial support if the UN did not fire any of its American employees found to be homosexual by State Department security agents. Although the United States did not have the legal authority to dictate who was a suitable employee for international organizations, US officials continued to do so until 1972.[30]

Using US policies as a model, Great Britain, Australia, and Canada also instituted screening procedures and policies aimed at homosexuals working in sensitive government posts. The British Labour government was initially no more supportive of homosexuals than the Democrats of the Truman administration. Facing crushing economic problems and focused on building a social welfare state, the Labour government emulated its American ally in linking homosexuality to the international communist conspiracy.

Such fears seemed far less paranoid after Guy Burgess and Donald Maclean, two British spies, defected to the Soviet Union in 1951. Both men exemplified some of the era's most malevolent antigay stereotypes. Each came from a privileged background: Maclean's father a lawyer and member of Parliament; Burgess's a commander in the British Royal Navy. After each attended elite boarding schools and matriculated at the University of Cambridge, the two struck up a friendship and became active in radical leftist

---

[29]Edsall, *Toward Stonewall*, 268–75.
[30]Johnson, "America's Cold War Empire," 63–5.

causes popular during the Great Depression. While at Cambridge, the Soviets recruited Burgess and Maclean as undercover spies. Upon graduation, the pair entered the British Foreign Service and rose through the ranks, despite being known as heavy drinkers and active homosexuals (though Maclean married a woman in his late twenties, Burgess remained exclusively gay). After their defections, their whereabouts remained unknown until 1956, when the pair were spotted in Moscow.[31]

Although mortified by the Burgess–Maclean episode and indebted to their powerful American allies, British authorities did not institute sweeping security measures that targeted civil servants and diplomats suspected of subversion or homosexuality. There was no British counterpart to President Dwight Eisenhower's Executive Order 10450, an April 1953 directive that resulted in the investigation and dismissal of thousands of gay and lesbian federal employees on the grounds that "sexual perversion" in and of itself posed a national security risk.[32] By contrast, the Foreign Office adopted a security code in 1956 that called for gay diplomats to be discreet and for their supervisors to be apprised of the potential blackmail of these employees because of the criminality of "some forms of homosexuality" in Great Britain and many other countries. Unwilling to jeopardize *esprit de corps* by ordering diplomats to surveil one another, the Foreign Office steadfastly refused to define its gay and lesbian employees as security risks on the basis of their sexual orientation alone and recommended their dismissal only in cases of public exposure.[33] At a time when the British were adjusting to the erosion of their global power, their rejection of McCarthyism proved a potent way to preserve national autonomy.

Australian officials adopted a similar posture on national security. In the late 1940s, in response to police data showing an increase in arrests for "unnatural" sexual crimes like sodomy, the Australian media noted an apparent rise in "sexual perversion" and public anxieties about homosexuality rose. In the aftermath of the Burgess and Maclean defections, the government directed the Australian Security Intelligence Organisation to ensure that gay and lesbian civil servants did not have access to classified documents related to the national security. But while the Cabinet worried that homosexuals were prone to treasonous behavior because of their "instability, willing self-deceit, [and] defiance toward society," they rejected a complete ban on gay and lesbian civil servants. The Australian government did, however, escalate prosecutions for "unnatural offenses." Between

[31]Minto, "Special Relationships," 110–36.

[32]In August 2017, the US District Court for the District of Columbia ordered the US Department of Justice to release its records on Executive Order 10450 and its ramifications. Brooke Sopelsa, "Justice Department Ordered to Release 1950s Gay 'Purge' Documents," NBC News, August 3, 2017, https://www.nbcnews.com/feature/nbc-out/court-tells-justice-department-release-1950s-gay-purge-documents-n789056.

[33]Minto, "Special Relationships," 110–36.

1945 and 1960, over 3,000 people were convicted in antigay crackdowns targeting parks, lavatories, and other public places. It also maintained strict censorship of fictional and academic examinations of homosexuality. This did not mean that discreet Australian gays could not live their lives without harassment, but the political climate greatly restricted gay activism and public manifestations of a gay and lesbian subculture.[34]

Although public fears of homosexual subversion did not pervade Canadian society on the scale seen in the US Lavender Scare, Canadian officials adopted antigay security policies to appease their powerful American ally. Lacking intelligence agencies of its own, the Canadian government depended on shared information provided by American operatives at the Federal Bureau of Investigation (FBI) and the Central Intelligence Agency (CIA). To preserve that partnership, Canadian officials adopted rigorous standards for vetting government employees and uncovering espionage. In response to US concerns about the vulnerability of the "world's longest undefended border," Canadian lawmakers passed immigration legislation barring homosexuals from visiting or emigrating, a provision that remained law from 1952 until 1977.[35] The legislation closely resembled the Immigration Act of 1952, US legislation permitting the exclusion or deportation of anyone demonstrating a "psychopathic personality," a category widely presumed by the Immigration and Naturalization Service and courts to encompass homosexuals.[36]

Like their American counterparts, Canadian officials took aggressive steps to purge the civil service and the armed forces of suspected and known homosexuals. In the late 1940s, the Royal Canadian Mounted Police (RCMP) and a panel from National Defense and External Affairs began screening government employees for political views, "moral failings," and "character weakness" that could make them susceptible to extortion. By 1952, after a cabinet directive formally defined "character defects" as a danger to national security, a special "A-3" unit of the RCMP investigated homosexuals and created a classification system using pink forms to report those with politically subversive views, yellow forms to document those deemed morally deficient. The investigations soon spread throughout the entire Canadian government. Suspected gay and lesbian federal employees were surveilled and interrogated. The results were reported to the Security

---

[34]Kate Davison, "The Sexual (Geo)Politics of Loyalty: Homosexuality and Emotion in Cold War Security Policy," *From Sodomy Laws to Same-Sex Marriage*, 123–40; Garry Wotherspoon, "'The Greatest Menace Facing Australia': Homosexuality and the State in NSW During the Cold War," *Labour History* 56 (May 1989): 17; Graham Willett, "The Darkest Decade: Homophobia in 1950s Australia," *Australian Historical Studies* 27 (1997): 120–32.

[35]Johnson, "America's Cold War Empire," 67–9; Philip Girard, "From Subversives to Liberation: Homosexuals and the Immigration Act, 1952–1972," *Canadian Journal of Law & Society* 2 (1987): 1–27.

[36]Canady, *The Straight State*, 215–50.

Panel, a board comprised of representatives from RCMP, the civil service, the Privy Council, External Affairs, and National Defence. They imposed punishments on suspected and admitted homosexuals including dismissal, transfer, demotion, and denial of benefits and pensions. It was common for gay and lesbian civil servants who acknowledged their homosexuality to be forced to undergo psychiatric treatment as a condition for keeping their government jobs. The Security Panel's proceedings were conducted in secret. Those accused of jeopardizing national security were not given the ability to defend themselves against allegations or the right to appeal any sanctions imposed upon them.

Britain's Lavender Scare had a trajectory quite different than that of its Canadian and US equivalents. Rather than attempt to purge its own ranks of the politically and sexually suspect, the British government escalated crackdowns on public immorality. In October 1951, after the Conservative party won power just four months after the Burgess–Maclean defections were revealed, R.A. Butler, the new home minister, announced in Parliament that he would take steps to protect the general public from homosexuals, whom he described as "exhibitionists and proselytizers, and a danger to others, especially the young." Almost immediately, arrests and prosecutions for sodomy, solicitation, and gross indecency hit levels five times higher than before the war. Many cases involved police entrapment and coerced testimony. Authorities pressured offenders to name others, sometimes in exchange for immunity or lesser charges. Inevitably, prominent members of British society were soon engulfed in sensationalized cases.[37]

Alan Turing was one of the most notable and tragic of these figures. A brilliant mathematician trained at the University of Cambridge, King's College, and Princeton University, Turing became a pioneer in computer science and theoretical biology. During World War II, his highly classified codebreaking work at the Government Code and Cypher School in Bletchley Park was pivotal in decoding efforts that helped the Allies defeat the Nazis in critical battles in the later stages of World War II. In 1946, George VI secretly appointed Turing an Officer of the Order of the British Empire for his immense contributions to the Allied victory.

But neither his genius nor his patriotism saved Turing from the consequences of an arrest for gross indecency. In December 1951, Turing, thirty-nine, met Arnold Murray, an unemployed nineteen-year-old man, while walking in Manchester. He invited Murray to lunch and the two began seeing each other. Three weeks later, Turing's apartment was robbed. When Murray admitted that the thief was a friend of his, Turing reported the incident to the police. Long comfortable with his homosexuality but quite naïve about the grave risks its public exposure could create, Turing told the investigators about his sexual relationship with Murray. Both men

---

[37]Edsall, *Toward Stonewall*, 291–3.

were then charged with gross indecency under Section 11 of the Criminal Law Amendment Act of 1885. On the advice of his solicitor and his brother, Turing pled guilty. On March 31, 1952, he was convicted and given a choice between imprisonment and a year's probation paired with hormonal treatment. Turing opted for the latter and received injections of synthetic estrogen designed to suppress his sex drive.

Turing's career was unquestionably affected by the loss of his security clearance in the wake of his conviction. Although no longer able to work as a cryptographic consultant for the British government and barred from travel to the United States due to recent changes in US immigration law that precluded the entry of known homosexuals, Turing kept his academic position at what is now the University of Manchester and continued writing and working on one of the only computers in the world at the time. On June 8, 1954, Turing's housekeeper found him dead. An autopsy revealed the cause of death as cyanide poisoning and an inquest ruled it a suicide—a conclusion disputed by acquaintances and later scholars. Whether or not Turing intentionally took his own life, his experience encapsulated the shattering impact of the postwar antigay prosecutions.[38]

While Turing's conviction drew little public notice at the time, author and critic Rupert Croft-Cooke's sparked a media firestorm. In 1953, Croft-Cooke's secretary and companion Joseph Alexander met two sailors at a London tavern. He invited them to spend the weekend at Croft-Cooke's home in East Sussex. The four ate and drank together and had sex. On their way back to London, the two sailors physically attacked two men, one of whom was a police officer. They agreed to testify in a gross indecency case against Croft-Cooke in exchange for immunity from prosecution on assault charges. Although no other witnesses could corroborate their claims and they recanted their statements (and then reversed their disavowals), the sailors' allegations stood and Croft-Cooke received a six-month jail sentence spent in Wormwood Scrubs and Brixton Prison. Upon his release, Croft-Cooke announced his intent to write a book about his experiences. He soon received an ominous visit from a plainclothes police officer who warned that "a second conviction" could be "very much more easily obtained" and would have even more severe consequences. Croft-Cooke moved to Tangier to join the many gay expatriates living there and published *The Verdict of*

---

[38]Andrew Hodges, *Alan Turing: The Enigma* (Princeton: Princeton University Press, 2012). Turing's death might have been the result of exposure to improper usage and storage of chemicals in his home. See Roland Pease, "Alan Turing: Inquest's Suicide Verdict 'Not Supportable,'" *BBC News*, June 26, 2012, https://www.bbc.com/news/science-environment-18561092. In 2013, Turning received a posthumous royal pardon. In January 2017, the British government enacted the so-called Alan Turing law and cleared the convictions of approximately 49,000 living men convicted of consensual homosexual offenses. See "Thousands of Gay Men Pardoned for Past Convictions," *BBC News*, January 31, 2017, https://www.bbc.com/news/uk-38814338.

You All (1955), a blistering attack on the British penal system. Under the name Leo Bruce, he went on to write dozens of detective stories.[39]

Celebrated actor John Gielgud was also caught up in the frenzy. On October 21, 1953, after rehearsing for the play "A Day by the Sea," Gielgud had a few drinks and then stopped by a Chelsea lavatory known to be a site of homosexual encounters. After he made eye contact with a man who turned out to be an undercover police officer, Gielgud was arrested for "importuning for immoral purposes." Cognizant of the dangers he now faced, Gielgud attempted to hide his identity by saying he was a clerk and giving the officer his real name, Arthur. When he appeared in court the next day, the magistrate imposed a £10 fine and ordered Gielgud to seek immediate medical attention. The affair might have ended there, but a reporter from the *Evening Standard* recognized Gielgud and news of his arrest became a national scandal.

Much to Gielgud's surprise, his theater company stood by him through the humiliating (and potentially career-ending) ordeal. The show's producer, Binkie Beaumont, was rattled by the newspaper coverage and hate mail, but opted not to fire Gielgud after the actor's brother, Val, not-so subtly warned Beaumont that his own sexual escapades could be exposed too. Gielgud soon recovered professionally and went on to an illustrious career culminating in a knighthood. He never publicly acknowledged the incident or the nervous breakdown it triggered six months after his arrest.[40]

The antigay crackdown even hit the pinnacle of the British aristocracy. Like the Oscar Wilde trials of 1895, the arrests of Lord Edward Douglas-Scott-Montagu, a peer of the realm, inflamed popular prejudices when prosecutors highlighted the age and class differences between the men implicated. Unlike the Wilde trials, however, the Montagu scandal became a catalyst for an organized LGBT rights movement in Britain and a government commission that called for the decriminalization of homosexuality.

Aware of his bisexuality from an early age and discreet in his sexual affairs, Lord Montagu's world was forever changed when he was arrested in 1953. Charged with unnatural acts and indecent assault of a fourteen-year-old Boy Scout at his Beaulieu estate, Montagu narrowly escaped imprisonment after prosecutors failed to secure a conviction on either charge. But Montagu's acquittal incensed prosecutors supporting Home Secretary Sir David Maxwell Fyfe's recent call to purge England of the "plague" of homosexuality, a declaration that prompted a widespread crackdown on "male vice" yielding as many as 1,000 arrests per year. Determined to score a high-profile conviction, authorities widened their

---

[39]Edsall, *Toward Stonewall*, 293.
[40]Rhoda Koenig, "John Gielgud: When England Hounded a Hero," *Independent*, February 28, 2008, https://www.independent.co.uk/arts-entertainment/theatre-dance/features/john-gielgud-when-england-hounded-a-hero-788459.html.

investigation of Montagu and in January 1954 charged him, his cousin Michael Pitt-Rivers, and his friend journalist Peter Wildeblood with "gross offenses" and "conspiracy to incite certain male persons to commit serious offences with male persons." Turning Queen's Evidence to escape criminal prosecution themselves, Edward McNally and John Reynolds, both servicemen in the Royal Air Force, testified to engaging in "abandoned behavior" with the three accused and identified twenty other men as their sexual partners (none of whom were prosecuted). During the eight-day, highly publicized trial, prosecutors read aloud incriminating love letters exchanged by Wildeblood and McNally. Although Montagu insisted he was innocent and that the men had only danced, drunk, and kissed, he was sentenced to twelve months' imprisonment—the first time in British history that a peer of the realm had been publicly convicted of a crime. By contrast, Pitt-Rivers and Wildeblood both admitted their homosexuality and received eighteen-month jail sentences.[41]

Although there was no gay rights organization in Great Britain comparable to America's Mattachine Society or the Netherlands's COC, the Montagu–Wildeblood trials proved critical in turning public opinion against the wave of antigay prosecutions that had swept Great Britain during the early Cold War. In 1955, British psychiatrist and criminologist D.J. West published *Homosexuality*, a sympathetic overview of the medical, social, and legal aspects of homosexuality. The same year, Wildeblood published *Against the Law*, a searing indictment of his persecution and incarceration in Wormwood Scrubs. He became an impassioned advocate of prison reform and overhauling laws on homosexuality. In 1956, inspired by the letters he received from people thanking him for his openness about his homosexuality, Wildeblood published *A Way of Life*, a collection of twelve essays detailing the lives of gays and lesbians. He went on to a successful career as a writer and television producer, and campaigned publicly for gay rights.[42]

Recoiling at prosecutorial abuses and public smear campaigns that evoked American McCarthyism, politicians, journalists, and ministers began demanding legal reforms. In February 1954, after publicly urging suppression of vice for months, Home Secretary David Maxwell Fyfe privately told the Cabinet it was evident that many "responsible people"

---

[41]"Lord Montagu on the Court Case Which Ended the Legal Persecution of Homosexuals," *London Evening Standard*, July 14, 2007, https://www.standard.co.uk/news/lord-montagu-on-the-court-case-which-ended-the-legal-persecution-of-homosexuals-6597923.html.

[42]Wildeblood's solicitor, Arthur Prothero, was the son of the Scotland Yard detective who was the only prosecution witness in the 1928 obscenity trial on *The Well of Loneliness*. His remarks resulted in the magistrate ordering the destruction of all copies of the novel. See William H. Honan, "Peter Wildeblood, 76, Writer Who Fought Britain's Laws against Homosexuality," *New York Times*, November 21, 1999, https://www.nytimes.com/1999/11/21/nyregion/peter-wildeblood-76-writer-who-fought-britain-s-laws-against-homosexuality.html; Adam Mars-Jones, "The Wildeblood Scandal: The Trial That Rocked 1950s Britain—and Changed Gay Rights." *The Guardian*, July 14, 2017, https://www.theguardian.com/books/2017/jul/14/against-the-law-the-wildeblood-scandal-the-case-that-rocked-1950s-britain-and-changed-gay-rights.

did not believe that consensual homosexual sex should be criminalized. For reasons that remain unclear, the puritanical Maxwell Fyfe recommended the creation of an inquiry on anti-vice laws. The following month, he stood in the House of Commons to defend the civil rights of those accused of public immorality and extolled the rule of law as a cherished precept of British life, a rather stunning declaration from the man who had described gays as "a danger to others" in December 1953. In July 1954, he announced the creation of the Wolfenden Committee to examine "the law and practice relating to homosexual offenses and the treatment of persons convicted of such offenses by the courts."[43]

Facing a rapidly shifting political landscape rife with antigay prejudices and rising Cold War tensions, homosexual rights activists in a few European countries established new organizations and began reestablishing transnational connections. In 1951, consciously emulating Hirschfeld's World League for Sexual Reform, COC organized the first International Congress for Sexuality Equality. Advocates from Denmark, Norway, Sweden, West Germany, Great Britain, Italy, France, and Switzerland gathered in Amsterdam. Inspired by the articulation of rights to all people "without distinction of any kind, such as race, colour, sex, language, religion, etc." in Article 2 of the Universal Declaration of Human Rights,[44] they sent the UN a telegram requesting "steps towards granting [the] status of human, social, and legal equality to homosexual minorities throughout the world." They also created the International Committee for Sexual Equality (ICSE) to continue their efforts to connect homophile organizations seeking civil rights in a time of Cold War hostilities.

Over the next decade, ICSE linked homophile organizations in Europe and the United States through publications and international congresses. Its members included the Scandinavian group Forbundet af 1948, the French group Arcadie, the Swiss journal Der Kreis, several German organizations including the Society for Human Rights, and the US groups ONE and the Mattachine Society. US homophile publications like ONE magazine republished articles from European homophile publications and closely followed European gay culture and legal developments affecting European homosexuals. European homophile publications like Germany's Die Insel (The Island), Der Ring, and Hellas referenced articles published in Der Kreis, the various Scandinavian magazines of Forbundet af 1948, and the French homophile magazine Arcadie.[45]

---

[43]Minto, "Special Relationships," 145–51.
[44]On the homophile response to the Universal Declaration of Human Rights, see David S. Churchill, "Transnationalism and Homophile Political Cultural in the Postwar Decades," GLQ: A Journal of Gay and Lesbian Studies 15:1 (2009): 33–4.
[45]Domenico Rizzo, "Public Spheres and Gay Politics since the Second World War," in Gay Life & Culture: A World History, Robert Aldrich, ed. (New York: Universe Publishing, 2006), 209–11.

Beginning with the Danish group Alle for Een Klubben (All for One Club) in 1954, lesbian organizations also participated in ICSE. The following year, the newly created US-based Daughters of Bilitis (DOB) became members and the male-dominated leadership of ICSE connected DOB with other women's groups in England and Sweden. Individuals whose nations had no official homophile organizations also joined, and throughout the 1950s, people from Australia, Austria, Greece, Indonesia, Italy, New Zealand, Portugal, Spain, and Syria attended ICSE congresses and social events.[46]

Many homophile organizations facilitated social connections among their members. Such activities were most visible in nations like the Netherlands, Belgium, Sweden, Denmark, and France where homosexual acts were legal. In Amsterdam, COC hosted parties and events at its headquarters. In Zurich, *Der Kreis* presented lectures, plays, and discussions and threw a huge party called Herbstfest every October.[47]

By contrast, although Mexico had decriminalized sodomy when it adopted the Napoleonic Code in the nineteenth century and did not participate in the Lavender Scare, Mexican gays did not formally organize or forge ties with the transnational homophile movement until the 1970s. Constrained by heteronormative cultural norms, upper- and middle-class gay men became familiar with homosexual life abroad through travel and local interactions with foreign tourists and expatriates. They read foreign homophile magazines purchased at newsstands and bookstores. But in the summer of 1954, when Jim Kepner and others affiliated with the US homophile magazine *ONE* traveled to Mexico City to investigate why the periodical sold so well there, they failed to make any professional contacts during their entire two-week trip. Unwilling to risk exposure, police harassment, or extortion, most economically privileged Mexican gay men socialized in private homes.[48]

In the United States, the Lavender Scare and antigay harassment by police and postal authorities forced US homophiles to be similarly cautious. Unlike their European counterparts, American homophile magazines did not include the pen-pal listings, male physique photographs, travel guides, and directories of gay-friendly establishments found in European publications like Germany's *Der Ring* and *Der Weg* (*The Way*) and the Dutch magazine *Eos* (*The Others*). However, unlike *ONE*, these publications were not usually sold on public newsstands and were only available to paying members who joined a club and bought a subscription. These restrictions

---

[46]On the origins and evolution of the ICSE, see Rupp, "The Persistence of Transnational Organizing," 1014–39.

[47]Loftin, *Masked Voices*, 64, 69–71.

[48]Alessio Ponzio is examining how a comparable domestic culture inhibited homophile organizing in Italy. On Mexico, see Victor M. Macías-González, "The Transnational Homophile Movement and the Development of Domesticity in Mexico City's Homosexual Community, 1930–70," *Gender & History* 26:3 (November 2014): 519–25.

kept circulation numbers low, but also fostered good relationships with state authorities. *Vennen* (*His Friend*), a Danish magazine that included full-frontal male nudity, was a notable exception. Condemned by other European homophiles for its risqué imagery, *Vennen* was also subject to a government crackdown in 1955. To avoid such prosecution, *Der Kreis* submitted every issue to the Zurich Sittenpolizei (vice squad) for inspection prior to publication.[49]

Homophiles in the United States and several other countries communicated and drew inspiration from one another. *ONE* routinely received letters from foreign readers. Most originated in Canada and Western Europe, but individuals in Latin America, Africa, the Middle East, Asia, and Australia also wrote. Foreigners could buy *ONE* at bookstores and newsstands in several international locations including Amsterdam, Buenos Aires, Vienna, and Mexico City. The *ONE* editorial board often highlighted its global reach, publishing foreigners' letters, international homophile news, and stories about homosexuality in other cultures (some with a decidedly Orientalist view of non-Europeans). *ONE* amassed an enormous collection of material about homosexuality around the world and throughout history. Nation-based activists did not operate in a vacuum. They were connected to other advocates in several countries who were resisting state-sponsored antigay repression and mobilizing for gay civil rights.[50]

André Baudry was one such activist. Born in Rethonde, France in 1922, Baudry received a Jesuit education and entered a Roman Catholic seminary in 1943. Unable to reconcile the dictates of the priesthood with his homosexuality, Baudry left the seminary two years later and began teaching philosophy at a private Catholic school in Paris. Count Jacques de Ricaumont introduced Baudry to the city's gay life. With Ricaumont's encouragement, Baudry began submitting articles to *Der Kreis* in 1952. Using the pseudonym André Romane, he kept the content apolitical and emphasized culture and the arts. The following year, Baudry joined the executive committee of the International Committee for Sexual Equality and began presiding over meetings of the 200 French subscribers of *Der Kreis*. With a divisive personality and a penchant for moralizing, Baudry argued that homophiles could gain acceptance from political and intellectual elites if they conducted themselves with discretion and dignity.

Although consensual private homosexual acts remained legal in France and a number of French writers were openly gay, the political climate was fraught. During World War II, the Vichy regime had raised the age of consent for gay and lesbian sex to twenty-one, reflecting a conservativism that continued into the post-WWII era. Trying to restore national honor and strength after suffering the indignity of Nazi defeat and occupation, President Charles de Gaulle and the Catholic Church opposed communism and called

---

[49]Loftin, *Masked Voices*, 64, 69–71.
[50]Loftin, *Masked Voices*, 63–4.

for a return of traditional morality and greater emphasis on family life. In 1949, the state tightened laws on public solicitation. Conservative doctors, politicians, and journalists called for barring homosexuals from the civil service and the armed forces.[51]

In January 1954, Baudry, de Ricaumont, and writers André du Dognon and Roger Peyrefitte founded *Arcadie*, a monthly homophile magazine. In hopes of challenging negative attitudes about homosexuality, Baudry, Peyrefitte, and artist and filmmaker Jean Cocteau heavily promoted *Arcadie* on French radio and television and the review's editors distributed free copies to influential physicians, religious leaders, and politicians. Published continuously until 1982, *Arcadie* published scientific information about homosexuality, news about homosexuals in France and other countries, reviews of films and plays, and short fiction. Although the review was serious and dry, it also included an insert featuring personal ads and suggestive photographs.

In keeping with his assimilationist views, Baudry encouraged homosexuals to exercise moderation and to integrate themselves into larger society. But Baudry's moralism and refusal to print salacious material did not protect *Arcadie* from legal harassment. In May 1954, French authorities outlawed its public sale and sale to minors—a ban that remained in place for the next thirty-one years. In 1956, a court ruling declared *Arcadie* "a danger to youth," ordered the destruction of the magazine's proofs, and fined Baudry 40,000 francs. Undeterred, Baudry continued publishing *Arcadie* and the review had 10,000 subscribers at its peak. In 1957, Baudry founded the Club Littéraire et Scientifique des Pays Latins (CLESPALA), a private club in Paris that offered *Arcadie* subscribers an alternative to gay bars and public cruising. Modeled on COC in the Netherlands, CLESPALA had strict rules of decorum and hosted dances, lectures, symposia, and an annual banquet. Baudry gave regular "Word of the Month" addresses in which he advocated conformity and castigated effeminacy, conspicuous public behavior, and promiscuity. Some members derided Baudry's moralizing "sermons" and called him "His Holiness" and "the Pope." But others admired his courage and visibility in a very conservative age.[52]

Homophiles on both sides of the Atlantic celebrated the Wolfenden Report.[53] Released in the UK in September 1957, the treatise, formally titled the Report of the Departmental Committee on Homosexual Offenses and Prostitution, was commissioned by the Conservative Government three years

---

[51]Edsall, *Toward Stonewall*, 286–9.

[52]Olivier Jablonski, "The Birth of a French Homosexual Press in the 1950s," *Journal of Homosexuality* 41:3–4 (2002): 235–40. See also Jackson, *Living in Arcadia*, 58–97; Michael D. Sibalis, "Baudry, André Émile," http://www.glbtqarchive.com/ssh/baudry_a_S.pdf.

[53]On the Wolfenden Report's impact in Australia, New Zealand, and Canada, see Graham Willett, "Homosexual Politics in the British World: Toward a Transnational Understanding," *From Sodomy Laws to Same-Sex Marriage*, 141–53.

earlier as a response to a postwar spike in convictions for prostitution and several highly publicized arrests of prominent men charged with homosexual offenses. Chaired by Sir John Wolfenden, the committee of fifteen met sixty times and interviewed about 200 people, including police and probation officers, religious leaders, and psychiatrists. Although it proved difficult to find gay men willing to provide evidence, Peter Wildeblood, Carl Winter, and Patrick Trevor-Roper privately attested to the pernicious impact of the Criminal Law Amendment Act of 1885 on their personal lives.[54]

Swayed by such testimonials, the Wolfenden Committee called for the legalization of "homosexual behavior between consenting adults in private." While defending laws designed to prevent sexual abuse and to protect minors, the committee asserted:

The law's function is to preserve public order and decency, to protect the citizen from what is offensive or injurious, and to provide sufficient safeguards against exploitation and corruption of others ... Unless a deliberate attempt is to be made by society, acting through the agency of the law, to equate the sphere of crime with that of sin, there must remain a realm of private morality and immorality which is, in brief and crude terms, not the law's business.

Defying some of the era's medical and psychiatric authorities, the committee also concluded that "homosexuality cannot legitimately be regarded as a disease, because in many cases it is the only symptom and is compatible with full mental health in other respects."[55]

But the Wolfenden Report stopped far short of full acceptance of homosexuality. The committee supported the continued criminalization of "homosexual importuning," explaining that its call for reforms was not "a general license to adult homosexuals to behave as they please." Wolfenden personally found homosexuality "morally repugnant." He not only proposed an age of consent set at twenty-one for same-sex sexual acts—five years higher than the law dictated for consensual heterosexual relations—but also called for a three-year increase of the current two-year maximum penalty imposed on men aged twenty-one or older who were convicted of oral

---

[54]As described earlier in this chapter, Peter Wildeblood had been imprisoned for homosexual offenses after a January 1954 arrest. Carl Winter was the director of the Fitzwilliam Museum. Patrick Trevor-Roper was a noted eye surgeon and brother of renowned historian Hugh Trevor-Roper. See Patrick Higgins, *Heterosexual Dictatorship: Male Homosexuality in Postwar Britain* (London: Fourth Estate, 1996), 41–2. For an annotated collection of the testimony presented to the Wolfenden Committee, see Brian Lewis, *Wolfenden's Witnesses: Homosexuality in Postwar Britain* (London: Palgrave Macmillan, 2016).

[55]On the committee's private deliberations, see Minto, "Special Relationships," 181–203. For the full text of the Wolfenden Report, see https://www.ncbi.nlm.nih.gov/pmc/articles/PMC1962139/.

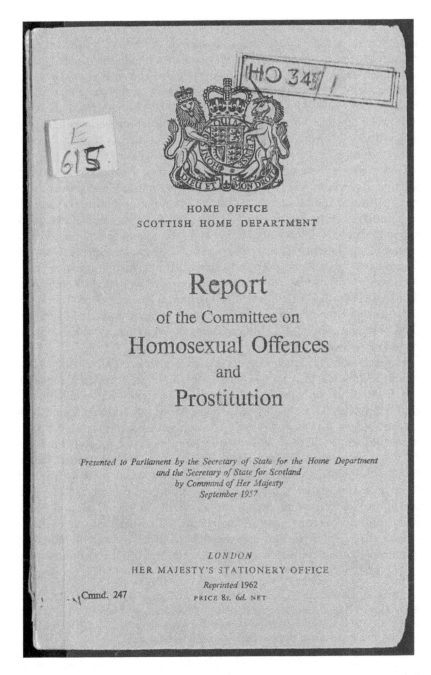

IMAGE 3.2 Formed in 1954 after several high-profile men were arrested for homosexual offenses, the Wolfenden Committee called for the decriminalization of consensual sexual relations between adult men in private. Its 1957 report generated international attention and inspired homophile activists in many countries.

sex or masturbation with men aged sixteen to twenty. The majority of the committee favored setting the age of consent for consensual same-sex sexual acts at eighteen or seventeen, but Wolfenden overrode them. Furthermore, Wolfenden supported the continued illegality of consensual anal sex in all circumstances, regardless of the ages or genders of the participants. Over the objections of some committee members, he also defended the use of undercover agents who targeted men seeking or having sex in public places like parks or lavatories, despite ample evidence of police entrapment in many such arrests.[56]

Under intensive scrutiny by the British press, Parliament had starkly different responses to the Wolfenden Committee's recommendations on prostitution and homosexuality. Sharing the committee's view that prostitution undermined families and community stability, Parliament quickly passed the Street Offenses Act (1959) and police launched a crackdown on streetwalkers. But British lawmakers refused to implement the Wolfenden Committee's call for the partial decriminalization of homosexual acts. In December 1957, during a brief discussion of the Wolfenden Report in the House of Lords, the Lord Chancellor Viscount Kilmuir declared that neither Parliament nor the British people were ready for even a limited legalization of homosexual conduct.[57] "I am not going down in history as the man who made sodomy legal," he avowed.[58]

To persuade Parliament to act on decriminalization, Arthur "Tony" Dyson, a literature professor in Wales, organized an open letter sent to the *Times*. Published on March 5, 1958, the letter had thirty-one signatories including former Prime Minister Clement Attlee, philosopher Isaiah Berlin, and sociologist Barbara Wooten. The letter inspired several supporters of the Wolfenden Report to form the Homosexual Law Reform Society (HLRS) two months later. Its founders included Dyson, psychiatrist Kenneth Younger, MP Kenneth Walker, and the poet and journalist Stephen Spender. To increase the advocacy organization's visibility and respectability, HLRS named an honorary committee of notable religious, political, and cultural figures and an executive committee comprised of heterosexuals who met periodically to plan the group's strategy. A small group of mostly gay volunteers handled daily operations. The founders of HLRS simultaneously

---

[56]Peter Tatchell, "Wolfenden: Not So Liberal on Homosexuality After All," *The Guardian*, August 17, 2017, https://www.theguardian.com/commentisfree/2017/aug/20/wolfenden-not-so-liberal-on-homosexuality-peter-tatchell.

[57]Although their coverage was more subdued than that of their British counterparts, US newspapers also recognized the importance of the Wolfenden Report. The *New York Times* ran its entire text, adding commentary on the implications of the report's distinction between public nuisance and private behavior. Jeffery Weeks, *Sex, Politics, and Society: The Regulation of Sexuality since 1800* (London: Longman, 1981), 240; Edsall, *Toward Stonewall*, 316.

[58]"No Early Vice Law Change: 'Further Study of Report Needed', Lord Chancellor's Statement," *The Times*, December 12, 1957, 10.

established the Albany Trust, a parallel organization focused on research and public education. By the fall of 1958, the groups shared an office.[59]

While these activists were prepared for a long struggle, they greatly underestimated the hostility with which their efforts would be met. In late 1958, as the House of Commons prepared to debate the Wolfenden Report more than a year after its initial release, HLRS supporter Peter Wildeblood wrote the pamphlet *Homosexuals and the Law* and distributed copies to every member of Parliament. Opponents of reform recoiled at the outside pressure. The HLRS retreated and regrouped, embarking on letter writing campaigns aimed at alerting the press and British politicians to police harassment and entrapment of suspected homosexuals and the tragic personal consequences resulting from arrests for homosexual offenses.[60]

Although homophiles recognized its limitations, they hailed the Wolfenden Report as a significant milestone. ICSE monitored related political and legal developments and distributed information to its international network. In France, *Arcadie* ran a six-part series on the report from October 1957 to March 1958, followed by pieces on the creation of HLRS and an assessment of the post-Wolfenden legal landscape in Great Britain in its October 1958 issue.[61]

In the United States, the editors of the December 1957 issue of the *Mattachine Review* heartily endorsed the Wolfenden Committee's call for the legalization of private consensual sexual acts between adults, but rejected its characterization of homosexuality as immoral. In February 1958, a *ONE* editorial emphasized the eventual impact of the report on US state laws. "In the long run, we will find Wolfenden's work to have as much significance for this country as for England." Four years later, the prediction proved accurate when Illinois adopted the Model Penal Code and became the first state to repeal its sodomy law, its lawmakers influenced by the recommendations of the Wolfenden Report as well as of those in a 1955 report drafted by the American Law Institute.[62] Legal commentary and philosophical debates inspired by the Wolfenden Report also played an important role in shaping the context for the Supreme Court's landmark ruling in *Griswold v. Connecticut* (1965). By a vote of 7–2, the justices struck down a Connecticut law barring married couples from using contraception, citing a "right to marital privacy." The case's legal protection of private intimate behavior had sweeping ramifications.[63]

---

[59]Edsall, *Toward Stonewall*, 316–17.
[60]Edsall, *Toward Stonewall*, 317.
[61]Minto, "Special Relationships," 206–7.
[62]Minto, "Special Relationships," 212–13; William N. Eskridge, *Dishonorable Passions: Sodomy Laws in America: 1861–2003* (New York: Viking, 2008), 123–7.
[63]David Minto, "Perversion by Penumbras: Wolfenden, Griswold, and the Transatlantic Trajectory of Sexual Privacy," *American Historical Review* 123:4 (October 2018): 1093–121.

An earlier Supreme Court ruling in *ONE, Inc. v. Olesen* had equally important implications for LGBT advocacy and free expression. Like many of their counterparts in Europe, the editors of American homophile publications faced intense scrutiny from legal authorities. Published in August 1953, the first issue of *ONE* magazine was confiscated by postal inspectors who objected to its cover story, "Homosexual Marriage?" Such harassment escalated after Los Angeles Postmaster Otto Olesen seized the October 1954 issue, declaring it "obscene, lewd, lascivious, and filthy" and thus illegal to mail under the Comstock Act of 1873. Ironically, the issue's cover story was "You Can't Print That," an article about the threat of government censorship.[64]

Eric Julber, the straight, thirty-year-old attorney who wrote the piece, agreed to represent ONE, Inc. pro bono in fighting Olesen's actions. He sued Olesen on the grounds that the seizure of the magazine was an unconstitutional breach of free speech rights and equal protection under the law. In March 1956, US District Judge Thurmond Clarke rejected Julber's arguments and ruled on behalf of the United States Postal Office (the service's name at the time). As evidence of the magazine's obscenity, he mentioned "Sappho Remembered," a fictional story about a lesbian who wistfully recalls how her girlfriend rejected a marriage proposal from an old boyfriend in favor of living with her. The story, Clarke explained, was "obviously calculated to stimulate the lust of the homosexual reader." He also cited the "filthy" poem "Lord Samuel and Lord Montagu" and an advertisement from the Swiss magazine *Der Kreis* that could "lead to the obtaining of obscene material." He emphatically concluded: "The suggestion advanced that homosexuals should be recognized as a segment of our people and be accorded special privilege as a class is rejected." In February 1957, a three-judge panel of the Ninth Circuit of Appeals unanimously upheld Clarke's decision.[65]

Cognizant that the ruling would greatly inhibit their efforts to circulate *ONE* to its 2,000 current subscribers, the magazine's founding editors Dale Jennings and Don Slater agreed to pay Julber's expenses while he appealed the decision to the Supreme Court. On June 13, 1957, Julber filed the first-ever petition asking the high court to consider whether discussion of homosexuality, in and of itself, constituted obscenity and could therefore be legally banned. The Supreme Court was simultaneously considering an appeal from Samuel Roth, a New York book vendor convicted of selling

---

[64]Jonathan Rauch, "The Unknown Supreme Court Decision That Changed Everything for Gays," *Washington Post*, February 5, 2014, https://www.washingtonpost.com/news/volokh-conspiracy/wp/2014/02/05/the-unknown-supreme-court-decision-that-changed-everything-for-gays/?utm_term=.6fbbe5ce2b1b.

[65]David G. Savage, "Supreme Court Faced Gay Rights Decision in 1958 over 'Obscene' Magazine," *Los Angeles Times*, January 11, 2015, https://www.latimes.com/nation/la-na-court-gay-magazine-20150111-story.html.

sexually explicit material. Eleven days later, the justices released their 6–3 decision on *Roth v. United States*, upholding the bookseller's conviction, but also significantly restricting the legal definition of obscenity. Justice William Brennan wrote: "All ideas having even the slightest redeeming social importance—unorthodox ideas, controversial ideas, even ideas hateful to the prevailing climate of opinion—have the full protection" of the First Amendment. "Sex and obscenity are not synonymous," Brennan added.[66]

The *Roth* decision had a profound impact on gay rights in the United States. On January 13, 1958, citing *Roth*, the Supreme Court granted

IMAGE 3.3 Published from January 1953 until December 1969, *ONE* was a vitally important publication for the homophile movement. In 1958, its editors prevailed in an obscenity case that reached the Supreme Court, a ruling that had dramatic ramifications for freedom of speech and expression across the United States.

---

[66]Savage, "Supreme Court Faced Gay Rights Decision in 1958 over 'Obscene' Magazine."

the *ONE* case certiorari, opted not to hear oral arguments, and issued a one-sentence ruling reversing the lower court decisions. Celebrating the "electrifying news" of their victory, the editors of *ONE* declared, "For the first time in American publishing history, a decision binding on every court now stands ... affirming in effect that it is in no way proper to describe a love affair between two homosexuals as constitut(ing) obscenity." The *ONE, Inc. v. Olesen* decision not only facilitated the growth of gay and lesbian publications, but also fostered a sense of solidarity in an era when police harassment, loss of employment, and involuntary commitment remained omnipresent threats for many LGBT people.[67] Nonetheless, in the years immediately following the Wolfenden Report and the *ONE, Inc. v. Olesen* decision, gays and lesbians were still prosecuted under vagrancy, solicitation, and public indecency laws.

As the 1960s began, anti-LGBT policies intensified in some countries, but a few nations made significant reforms that benefited their LGBT citizens. In France, the reelection of De Gaulle in 1959 ushered in renewed hostility toward gays. In July 1960, a time of widespread anxieties about juvenile delinquency and the Franco-Algerian War, the National Assembly passed the Mirguet Amendment, listing homosexuality, alcoholism, and prostitution among "social plagues" meriting special attention. It made fines for public indecency higher for homosexuals than heterosexuals and authorities launched raids on establishments with gay clientele. In response to the repressive climate, Baudry stopped including photographs in *Arcadie* and emphasized material of a "scientific character" in the review.[68]

Canadian authorities also escalated antigay persecution. In 1961, Parliament adopted legislation designating anyone "likely to commit another sexual offense" as a "dangerous sexual offender." These expansive terms imperiled any homosexual arrested for gross indecency, which remained illegal under Canadian law.[69] Convinced that what it perceived as psychological abnormalities in gays and lesbians could be "scientifically" detected, the Canadian government sent Frank Robert Wake, a psychology professor who had conducted research on sexual psychopaths, to study homosexual detection methods being developed in the United States. In 1962, Wake received state funding to begin similar research in Canada. Wake's subjects were asked a series of questions and shown heteroerotic and homoerotic photographs while scientists using a "fruit machine" monitored a number of physiological variables. If, for example, a subject's pupils dilated upon viewing a person of the same sex, scientists presumed the individual was homosexual and therefore a potential threat to national security. But

---

[67]Savage, "Supreme Court Faced Gay Rights Decision in 1958 over 'Obscene' Magazine."
[68]Jackson, *Living in Arcadia*, 97–104.
[69]Gary Kinsman and Patrizia Gentile, *The Canadian War on Queers: National Security as Sexual Regulation* (Vancouver: University of British Columbia Press, 2010), 73.

IMAGE 3.4 Prototype of the "Fruit Machine," 1953. Convinced that electropsychometers could detect physiological traits associated with gays and lesbians, the Canadian government used the "Fruit Machine" in a failed effort to root out individuals viewed as dangerous sexual predators and national security risks.

the "fruit machine" never worked. Other factors, such as exposure to light, cause pupils to dilate. It had no mechanism for assessing bisexuality. Subjects' differing heights, pupil sizes, and distances between the eyes led to inconsistent results. Despite these serious flaws, the Canadian government poured tens of thousands of dollars into the project before officially ending it in 1967.[70]

The government harassment of gays in France and Canada was a stark contrast to the tolerance emerging in the Netherlands and Denmark. By the mid-1950s, Amsterdam was justifiably known as Europe's most gay friendly city and gay bars, clubs, and hotels flourished on the Leidsestraat. Dutch theologians, psychiatrists, and social workers began to advocate publicly for greater societal acceptance and support of gay and lesbian people. In

---

[70]Gary Kinsman, "'Character Weaknesses' and 'Fruit Machines': Towards an Analysis of the Anti-Homosexual Security Campaign in the Canadian Civil Service," *Labour/Le Travail* 35 (1995): 133–61.

1962, when he succeeded Bob Angelo as leader of COC, Benno Premsela worked under his own name, a potent illustration of Dutch gay activists' increasing willingness to be open and visible as they challenged unfair legal practices and social hostility.[71] In 1961, after Denmark passed a law aimed at curtailing a thriving male prostitution culture in Copenhagen, politicians, doctors, psychiatrists, and gay activists rose up in opposition to the "Ugly Law," denouncing it as discriminatory. The outcry shifted public opinion and prompted the law's repeal just four years later, a major turning point in popular support for Danish gay rights.[72]

Although such organized homophile advocacy did not exist behind the Iron Curtain, Nikita Khrushchev's de-Stalinization campaign prompted reevaluation of sodomy laws. In 1959, a panel of experts in the Soviet Union recommended sweeping changes to Article 154a, the 1934 law criminalizing both consensual and forcible sodomy. They called for reducing the maximum sentence for consensual sodomy from five to three years with no minimum sentence. They also proposed retaining the maximum sentence of eight years for forcible sodomy, but reducing the minimum sentence from five to three years. However, the final revision of the sodomy law adopted by the Supreme Soviet in 1960 abolished minimum sentences for both consensual and aggravated sodomy and increased the maximum sentence for consensual sodomy to five years.[73]

But two communist states lessened criminal penalties for homosexual behavior. In Hungary, a period of repression immediately following the Soviet suppression of the revolution of 1956 eventually gave way to "fridzsider szocializmus" ("refrigerator socialism"), an era when the populace gained greater access to consumer products and the government relaxed rigid authoritarianism. The political transformation led to positive changes for Hungarian homosexuals. Hungary had criminalized sex between men in 1878, declaring it an "unnatural fornication" punishable by up to a year of incarceration. Prosecutions escalated dramatically under the communist regime that took power in 1948. Over 800 homosexuals were convicted of sodomy and declared enemies of socialism before 1961 and many more were surveilled by the state. But in 1961, as the communist regime loosened its grip on daily life, consensual homosexual activity between men was decriminalized and there were only fifty-six criminal convictions for sodomy between 1961 and 1988. However, the move did not signal legal equality between homosexuals and heterosexuals since the age of consent for homosexual or lesbian sex was set at twenty, six years higher than it was

---

[71]Edsall, *Toward Stonewall*, 288–91.

[72]Peter Edelberg, "The Queer Road to Frisind: Copenhagen, 1945–2012," in *Queer Cities, Queer Cultures: Europe since 1945*, Matt Cook and Jennifer V. Evans, eds. (London: Bloomsbury, 2014), 55–74.

[73]Rustam Alexander, "Soviet Legal and Criminological Debates on the Decriminalization of Homosexuality (1965–1975)," *Slavic Review* 77:1 (Spring 2018): 30–5.

for heterosexual relations. The gender equality in the new law also made consensual sex between women illegal for the first time in Hungarian history. The state continued to compile "homosexual inventories" which police used to coerce gays and lesbians into becoming informers. In a society where a majority still considered homosexuality an illness or gender inversion, most Hungarian gays or lesbians remained extremely vulnerable.[74]

Gays and lesbians in Czechoslovakia experienced similar risks after their government struck down its sodomy law in 1961. In the 1950s, the Czech government commissioned Dr. Karl Freund to use penile plethysmography to determine whether army recruits were falsely claiming to be homosexual in order to evade compulsory military service. The first physician to measure penile blood flow as a means of determining sexual arousal, Freund initially thought he could convert homosexuals to heterosexuality. But after his experiments failed, he concluded homosexuality was immutable and then played a critical role in convincing the Czech government to decriminalize homosexuality in 1961.[75]

In Great Britain and the United States, although homophiles lamented Parliament's continued refusal to enact the Wolfenden Report's recommendation to legalize consensual private homosexual acts, there were other signs that popular attitudes on sexuality were shifting. In the 1940s and 1950s, British censors, like their American counterparts, targeted films and theatrical productions addressing "sex perversion." Clever screenwriters managed to evade the rules and inserted subtle homosexual themes in films like *Rope* (1948), *Tea and Sympathy* (1956), and *Pillow Talk* (1959).[76]

But British and American censors were now facing challenges from artists unabashedly tackling controversial material. Italian and French filmmakers shattered cinematic conventions and scored box office success with bold new work like *La Dolce Vita* (1960) and *Breathless* (1960). Aware that audience tastes were changing and outraged by political inaction on the Wolfenden Report, British screenwriter Janet Green wrote *Victim*, a film about a closeted gay man who risks losing his law practice and his marriage when he confronts a group of blackmailers exploiting gay men. Director Basil Dearden persuaded matinee idol Dirk Bogarde to take the lead role and the film premiered in London in August 1961. Although the film's depiction of homosexuality was quite chaste, the British Board of Film Censors gave it an "X" rating. In October 1961, with *Victim* scheduled to open in the United States in early 1962, the Motion Picture Association of America's Production Code Administration (PCA)

---

[74]Anita Kurimay and Judit Takács, "Emergence of the Hungarian Homosexual Movement in Late Refrigerator Socialism," *Sexualities* 20:5–6 (2017): 585–90.
[75]Karen Freeman, "Karl Freund Dies at 82; Studied Deviant Sexual Arousal," *New York Times*, October 27, 1996, https://www.nytimes.com/1996/10/27/us/kurt-freund-dies-at-82-studied-deviant-sexual-arousal.html.
[76]Russo, *The Celluloid Closet*; Minto, "Special Relationships," 271–2.

lifted its ban on films portraying homosexuality "provided any references are treated with care, discretion, and restraint." Although PCA concluded that *Victim* did not meet those vague criteria and did not grant the film its seal of approval, *Victim* nonetheless won critical acclaim. Soon after, PCA approved landmark gay-themed films like *A Taste of Honey* (1961), *The Children's Hour* (1961), *Advise and Consent* (1962), and *Walk on the Wild Side* (1962). *Victim* was thus a cultural milestone, as well as a powerful tool for homophiles seeking to educate the public and win political support.[77]

This wave of films was only one facet of a proliferation of representations of gay and lesbian life in the early 1960s. In 1960, British sociologist Gordon Westwood published *A Minority: A Report on the Male Homosexual in Great Britain*, a quantitative analysis that defined homosexuals as member of social minority, not pathologized individuals—echoing the argument that Donald Webster Cory made nine years earlier in *The Homosexual in America*.[78] Dozens of pulp novels featuring LGBT themes and salacious cover art were published and readily available in drugstores.[79] After the Supreme Court ruled in *Manual Enterprises, Inc. v. Day* (1962) that nude male photographs in physique magazines were not obscene, monthly sales of these publications to mostly gay readers soared to over 750,000 by 1965. With circulation numbers far higher than any politically oriented gay publication, the physique magazines played an important role in shaping gay male culture and their publishers' successful legal challenges to censorship laws were significant victories for freedom of speech and expression in the United States.[80] Novels like James Baldwin's *Another Country* (1962), Mary McCarthy's *The Group* (1963), and Christopher Isherwood's *A Single Man* (1964) had fully realized gay or lesbian characters and garnered literary praise. Mainstream media outlets like the *New York Times*, *Life*, *Look*, and *Harper's* ran stories addressing urban gay subcultures, legal and medical views of homosexuality, and the homophile movement.[81]

A small number of psychologists, particularly Evelyn Hooker, began to challenge the prevailing medical consensus that homosexuality constituted psychopathology—the core argument of Irving Bieber's 1962 text *Homosexuality: A Psychoanalytic Study of Male Homosexuals*. Based on a comparative study of 106 homosexual and 100 heterosexual men undergoing psychiatric treatment, Bieber and his collaborators

---

[77]Minto, "Special Relationships," 273–9; D'Emilio, *Sexual Politics, Sexual Communities*, 137.
[78]Chris Waters, "The Homosexual as a Social Being in Britain, 1945–1968," *Journal of British Studies* 51:3 (July 2010): 702–5.
[79]Susan Stryker, *Queer Pulp: Perverted Passions from the Golden Age of the Paperback* (San Francisco: Chronicle Books, 2001).
[80]David K. Johnson, *Buying Gay: How Physique Entrepreneurs Sparked a Movement* (New York: Columbia University Press, 2019).
[81]D'Emilio, *Sexual Politics, Sexual Communities*, 134–44.

concluded that "a heterosexual shift is a possibility for all homosexuals who are strongly motivated to change." Although Hooker and other critics found the study's exclusive reliance on subjects undergoing psychiatric treatment profoundly flawed, Bieber's views nonetheless perpetuated the idea that homosexuality could be cured through reparative or conversion therapies—a position not fully rejected by the American Psychiatric Association until 2000.[82]

Despite the increasing visibility of homosexuality in popular culture, ICSE proved unable to draw a truly global membership. By the early 1960s, a lack of attendance, budgetary woes, and a failure to diversify its leadership killed the group. But in a difficult political climate, the ICSE and national homophile organizations "created a network across national borders, nurtured a transnational homophile identity, and engaged in activism designed to change both laws and minds, aimed at both national governments and supranational bodies such as the UN."[83] In keeping with what historian John D'Emilio called "the retreat to respectability" characterizing the homophile movement, most ICSE members adopted an assimilationist philosophy, and, while rejecting prevailing views of homosexuality as pathological, criminal, and immoral, still relied on outside medical, scientific, legal, and religious experts to validate their claims of normality.[84] Many homophiles also expressed discomfort with more flamboyant aspects of gay life such as drag shows.

Despite the disbanding of ICSE, transnational contacts among homophile activists endured. They exchanged personal correspondence. American homophile publications included ads for foreign gay books and magazines. Foreigners read, wrote letters to, and subscribed to US homophile publications like ONE, *Mattachine Review*, and *The Ladder*. Members of ONE, Mattachine, and the Daughters of Bilitis made trips to Europe and connected with homophile activists there. In 1958, Rudolf Burkhardt, an editor for the Swiss magazine *Der Kreis*, made the first of several trips to Los Angeles to lecture on the pre–World War II homosexual movement.[85] In 1963, a newly founded British lesbian organization called the Minorities Research Group began forging ties with the Daughters of Bilitis.[86]

But logistical challenges and strategic differences often undermined transnational solidarity. In both written and live communications, activists

---

[82]D'Emilio, *Sexual Politics, Sexual Communities*; American Psychiatry Association, Public Release "'Reparative' Therapy: Does It Work?" February 3, 2000, https://www.eurekalert.org/pub_releases/2000-02/APA-tdiw-0302100.php.
[83]Rupp, "The Persistence of Transnational Organizing," 1024.
[84]D'Emilio, *Sexual Politics, Sexual Communities*, 75–91.
[85]Churchill, "Transnationalism and Homophile Political Cultural," 43–8.
[86]David Minto, "Mr. Grey Goes to Washington: The Homophile Internationalism of Britain's Homosexual Law Reform Society," in *British Queer History: New Approaches and Perspectives*, Marie H. Loughlin, ed. (Manchester: Manchester University Press, 2013), 220.

struggled with language barriers. Many activists could not afford to travel internationally. While some homophiles wanted increased visibility and the creation of social spaces for gays, others feared more openness would trigger political backlash and intensified legal repression.

Similar tensions engulfed US homophile groups. Despite police repression and harassment by postal inspectors in many places, many homophiles clung to assimilationist strategies, distanced themselves from the gay and lesbian bar subcultures, and believed professional experts were gays' and lesbians' most effective advocates.[87]

But activists like Franklin Kameny, Randy Wicker, Barbara Gittings, and Clark Polak were pushing the movement in new directions. After earning a doctorate in astronomy from Harvard in 1956, Kameny taught for a year at Georgetown and then took a job with the US Army's map service. But he was fired after security investigators discovered he had been arrested for lewd conduct. Serving as his own counsel, Kameny appealed his dismissal through the civil service and then the courts, all while battling the crushing economic consequences of not being able to get a new job due to his lack of a security clearance. After the Supreme Court refused to hear his case, Kameny turned his prodigious energies toward establishing a chapter of the Mattachine Society in Washington, DC. He, co-founder Jack Nichols, and about ten other gays and lesbians began meeting in November 1961.[88]

Mattachine Washington focused on the US government's institutionalized discrimination. Protesting the bans on gays and lesbians in the Civil Service and the armed forces and the blanket denial of security clearances on the basis of sexual orientation alone, they wrote dozens of letters to the sitting justices of the US Supreme Court, officials in the Kennedy administration, and members of Congress. They joined forces with the Washington, DC chapter of the American Civil Liberties Union (ACLU) in a campaign against antigay government employment policies and in assisting gay men victimized by police harassment.[89]

At the same time, Randy Wicker adopted a bold new approach to homophile advocacy in New York. After leaders in New York Mattachine objected to his calls for increased visibility in the media, he formed a one-man organization called the Homosexual League of New York in 1962. Soon after, he began making radio appearances and successfully persuading major media outlets like *Newsweek*, the *New York Times*, and the *Village Voice* to publish features on gay rights and gay life. Kameny's and Wicker's insistence that gays and lesbians should advocate for themselves

[87]D'Emilio, *Sexual Politics, Sexual Communities*, 150–86; Marc Stein, *City of Sisterly and Brotherly Loves: Lesbian and Gay Philadelphia, 1945–1972* (Chicago: University of Chicago Press, 2000), 179–84.

[88]D'Emilio, *Sexual Politics, Sexual Communities*, 150–2.

[89]D'Emilio, *Sexual Politics, Sexual Communities*, 153–7; Johnson, *The Lavender Scare*, 203.

instead of relying on heterosexual elites and their willingness to expose all aspects of gay culture rankled more conservative homophiles. But both men continued pushing for more assertive stances and were instrumental in the creation of a regional coalition called the East Coast Homophile Organizations (ECHO).[90]

In the aftermath of World War II, activists in the Netherlands and Scandinavia founded new advocacy organizations that challenged persecution of gay and lesbian people and that invoked emerging discourses and laws on human rights. A renewed transnational network arose and activists from many countries shared news, publications, and correspondence. Such ties were powerful at a time when Cold War anxieties about sexuality and gender triggered fierce antigay crackdowns and the Lavender Scare. Medical claims that gays and lesbians were mentally unbalanced pervaded society and influenced public policy.

But by the late 1950s, there were also signs of positive changes for LGBT people. In Great Britain, the Wolfenden Committee called for the decriminalization of consensual sexual relations between adult men in private. Although the report did not lead to immediate legal reform, it electrified homophiles around the world and influenced legal conceptions of the right to privacy. In the United States, publishers of gay physique magazines successfully challenged laws restricting freedom of expression. More positive portrayals of LGBT people began to appear in popular culture.

By early 1965, homophiles across the United States and in other countries were poised for a more confrontational phase of gay and lesbian activism. With the rise of the civil rights movement, gays and lesbians were inspired by those working for social justice and challenging conventional norms. But they also experienced heterosexism and homophobia that made clear the limitations of alliances with straight people and highlighted the need to create a new gay liberation movement. Seizing on unexpected legal victories in Great Britain, East Germany, West Germany, and Canada and thrilled by the fearlessness demonstrated in the Stonewall uprising, gay and lesbian activists mobilized for political change and social acceptance in their own countries, formed new transnational alliances, and protested injustices against gay and lesbian people around the world.

---

[90]D'Emilio, *Sexual Politics, Sexual Communities*, 158–61.

CHAPTER FOUR

Liberation and Confrontation, 1965–81

In the mid-1960s, militant members of the homophile movement staged protests that garnered international attention and signaled a more confrontational phase of gay and lesbian advocacy. Unafraid of visibility and unwilling to defer to professional experts on matters of sexual identity, they rejected the accommodationist philosophy driving most homophile activism since World War II. The civil rights movement, the women's movement, the antiwar movement, student movements, and the counterculture showed the power of collective action and embodied the nonconformist spirit of the era. But persistent heterosexism and homophobia also made evident the need for a devoted gay liberation movement. In June 1969, the Stonewall uprising in New York exploded following years of tensions between police and LGBT youth and people of color who had long borne the worst of police abuse and been the most vulnerable members of the LGBT community. Their resistance became a rallying cry for activists across the world who were ready to launch new transnational forms of advocacy.

The ferment of the late 1960s also helped to inspire important advances for gay and lesbian rights in several countries. In Great Britain, East Germany, West Germany, and Canada, political leaders decriminalized consensual same-sex sexual activities. The swift legal changes inspired activists in many nations to push for similar changes, making important steps on the path to full equal rights for lesbian, gay, bisexual, and transgender people around the world.

The post-Stonewall wave of activism quickly cohered into a transnational LGBT movement more visible and geographically broader than preceding efforts. New NGOs focused on global LGBT equality arose and began holding international conferences, lobbying supranational bodies, and invoking human rights accords. Advocates around the world coordinated actions protesting injustices in individual countries. Although activists began scoring important victories, they faced new threats posed by an emerging international anti-LGBT movement.

The small Caribbean nation of Cuba exemplifies important trends of this era. For much of the 1950s, while some gays and lesbians working in industries catering to foreign tourists enjoyed a modicum of tolerance, most gay and lesbian Cubans led very closeted existences necessitated by the island's homophobic society. After leftist forces led by Fidel Castro overthrew dictator Fulgencio Batista in 1959, life for Cuba's gays and lesbians changed dramatically. Revolutionaries banned alcohol, closed all bars and nightclubs, and railed against vices associated with capitalism. Many affluent gays and lesbians emigrated to Miami, capitalizing on the US government's initial failure to enforce the provision of the Immigration Act of 1952 that barred "sexually deviant" aliens from entering the country. Gays and lesbians who remained in Cuba tried to adjust to the changing political realities, either by secretly joining counterrevolutionary activities or integrating themselves into the revolution.[1] Since both sides associated homosexuality with subversion and debauchery, gays and lesbians were forced to cloak their sexual identities, regardless of how they aligned themselves politically.[2]

After April 1961, when 1,500 CIA-backed commandos attempting to oust Castro launched an amphibious attack at the Bay of Pigs and were quickly killed or captured by Cuban troops, Castro's regime intensified its surveillance of the civilian population. Comités de Defensa de la Revolución (Committees for the Defense of the Revolution) policed personal lives in order to ensure internal security. Leaders of the Popular Socialist Party linked homosexuality to bourgeois decadence, parroting a long-standing trope of communist ideology. A special unit of the secret police, the El Escudrón de la Escoria ("the Scum Squad"), targeted "pederasts, prostitutes, and pimps." Although there were gay and lesbian members of the Cuban Writers' and Artists' Union, they did not publicly protest the government's official rhetoric on homosexuality for fear of possible reprisals.[3]

In early 1965, the situation grew dire when the Castro regime announced its intention to put homosexuals into forced labor camps as part of a larger campaign promoting revolutionary gender ideals, manual labor, and ideological purity. Self-acknowledged and presumed gays and lesbians,

---

[1]Lourdes Arguelles and B. Ruby Rich, "Homosexuality, Homophobia, and Revolution: Notes toward an Understanding of the Cuban Lesbian and Gay Male Experience," in *Hidden from History: Reclaiming the Gay and Lesbian Past*, Martin Duberman, Martha Vicinus, and George Chauncey, Jr., eds. (New York: Meridan, 1989), 443–6.
[2]Julio Capó, "It's Not Queer to Be Gay: Miami and the Emergence of the Gay Rights Movement, 1945–1995" (PhD diss., Florida International University, 2011), 96–100.
[3]Arguelles and Rich, "Homosexuality, Homophobia, and Revolution," 447–8.

Jehovah's Witnesses, Seventh Day Adventists, Catholic priests, youth, peasants, artists, and intellectuals were among the dissidents purged and sent to camps run by Unidades Militares de Ayuda a la Producción (Military Units for the Aid of Production) (UMAP). In late 1967, Castro closed the camps in the face of intense criticism from fellow revolutionaries.[4]

Militants in the US homophile movement seized on Castro's antigay policies as a pretext for attacking those of the American government. On April 17, 1965, the day after the *New York Times* reported Castro's plans to put gays in detention camps, Craig Rodwell of New York Mattachine and Jack Nichols of Washington Mattachine quickly organized demonstrations at the United Nations (UN), the Cuban consulate in New York, and the White House. Picketers carried signs reading: "Cuba's Government Persecutes Homosexuals. U.S. Government Beat Them to It," "Fifteen Million U.S. Homosexuals Protest Federal Treatment," and "Russia, Cuba, and the United States Unite to Persecute Homosexuals."[5] Determined to keep the momentum going, the militants convinced their colleagues in ECHO to support additional demonstrations. Over the next several weeks, Washington, DC activists picketed the US Civil Service Commission, the State Department, the Pentagon, and the White House. In Philadelphia, militants staged a 4th-of-July protest outside Independence Hall. Emboldened by the peaceful reception of their first demonstrations, they issued press releases announcing the second wave of protests and received media coverage from the Associated Press, UPI, Reuters, the French News Agency, and television stations in nine US cities and Rome, Italy.[6]

Canada's gays and lesbians were mobilizing too. In the early 1960s, police surveilled cruising areas, restaurants, and nightclubs in Montréal and Toronto and arrested dozens of men for gross indecency. In response, Vancouver activists formed the Association for Social Knowledge (ASK), Canada's first homophile organization. Bruce Somers, the first president of ASK, was inspired to create the group after meeting Hal Call during a visit to San Francisco Mattachine.[7]

The case of Everett George Klippert catapulted the Canadian homophile movement into national advocacy. In 1960, Klippert, a bus driver in Calgary, was investigated after the father of one of his male sexual partners reported him to the police. After Klippert admitted to engaging in mutual masturbation with eighteen men, he pled guilty to gross indecency (a crime under an 1892 Canadian law) and received a four-year jail sentence. He never consulted an attorney. Upon his release

---

[4]Lillian Guerra, "Gender Policing, Homosexuality, and the New Patriarchy of the Cuban Revolution, 1965–70," *Social History* 35:3 (August 2010): 268–89.
[5]D'Emilio, *Sexual Politics, Sexual Communities*, 164; Johnson, *The Lavender Scare*, 199.
[6]Don Teal, *The Gay Militants* (New York: Stein and Day, 1971), 101.
[7]Gary Kinsman, *The Regulation of Desire: Homo and Hetero Sexualities*, 2nd ed., rev (Montréal: Black Rose Books, 1996), 229–35.

IMAGE 4.1 Barbara Gittings in a picket line, 1965. A legendary LGBT activist, Gittings founded the New York chapter of the Daughters of Bilitis in 1958 and edited the organization's national magazine, *The Ladder*, from 1963 to 1966. Gittings was a leading figure among the militant homophiles who began protesting the US government's ban on gay and lesbian employees in the mid-1960s.

from prison, Klippert moved to the Northwest Territories and worked as a mechanic's helper. In August 1965, while being interviewed as part of an arson investigation in which he was not a suspect, Klippert admitted that he still had consensual sex with men. He was then arrested and charged with four counts of gross indecency. Once again failing to seek help from a lawyer, Klippert pled guilty and received a three-year sentence. But after the crown attorney of the territory discovered Klippert's previous conviction and concluded he was unlikely to stop having sex with men, he declared Klippert "a dangerous sexual offender." On March 9, 1966, a judge cited a provision of Canada's 1961 "sexual psychopath" law and sentenced Klippert to indefinite detention.[8]

In 1967, Brian Crane, an attorney enlisted by Klippert's sister Leah, appealed the ruling. Challenging the court's interpretation of "dangerous sexual offender," Crane emphasized Klippert's nonviolent behavior and disputed the testimony of two psychiatrists who had claimed that Klippert could not control his sexual impulses. After losing the case, Crane appealed to Canada's Supreme Court. On November 7, 1967, in a 3–2 decision, the Supreme Court rejected the appeal, ensuring that any gay man convicted of gross indecency could be declared a "dangerous sexual offender" and incarcerated for life, even in cases when same-sex sexual activities occurred between consenting adults in private. ASK publicized Klippert's case, and the popular outrage generated by intense media coverage of the court's ruling sparked immediate calls for homosexual law reform.

Justice Minister Pierre Trudeau, a member of the ruling Liberal Party, included such reforms in a seventy-two-page omnibus bill he introduced in the House of Commons on December 21, 1967. Aiming to secularize Canadian law and to maximize individual freedom, Bill C-150 fell far short of the complete decriminalization of homosexuality, legalizing only private, consensual same-sex sexual acts between adults aged twenty-one or older. "There's no place for the state in the bedrooms of the nation," Trudeau declared. Other sections decriminalized abortion in cases where the mental or physical well-being of the mother was endangered; legalized lotteries; instituted new restrictions on gun ownership; and authorized police use of breathalyzers on drivers reasonably assumed to be intoxicated. Over the next several months, Trudeau's omnibus bill was hotly debated, drawing opposition from many Conservatives and police officials.[9]

---

[8]Kinsman, *The Regulation of Desire*, 257–61.

[9]Kinsman, *The Regulation of Desire*, 261–4. Although the "bedrooms of the nation" statement is usually attributed to Trudeau, he was actually quoting Martin O'Malley of *The Globe and Mail*. See Trudeau, "There's No Place for the State in the Bedrooms of the Nation," CBC Archives, December 21, 1967, https://www.cbc.ca/archives/entry/omnibus-bill-theres-no-place-for-the-state-in-the-bedrooms-of-the-nation.

The Klippert decision was a stark contrast to the British Parliament's recent partial decriminalization of homosexual activities in England and Wales. Passage of the Sexual Offences Act of 1967 followed nearly a decade of lobbying efforts inspired by the Wolfenden Report. Following a crushing 213–99 parliamentary rejection of a homosexual law reform bill in 1960, the Homosexual Law Reform Society focused on public education efforts and collaborated with the Home Office in disseminating information on the numbers of men arrested, blackmailed, and assaulted for homosexual offenses. In 1962, the arrest and conviction of William Vassall helped to highlight the injustices of these laws. A clerk for the Foreign Office stationed in Moscow, Vassall was targeted by the KGB upon its discovery of his homosexuality. After entrapping him in a same-sex sexual encounter, Russian agents threatened to release incriminating photographs unless Vassall provided government secrets. While a few British newspapers emphasized old stereotypes about the treachery of homosexual civil servants, other media outlets saw the case as evidence of the need for legal reforms.[10]

Following the Labour Party's victory in the 1964 general election, the British government pursued several social reforms on capital punishment, divorce, and censorship. The political climate proved conducive to the legalization of consensual private sexual activities between men aged twenty-one or older. First introduced in the House of Lords in May 1965, the Sexual Offenses Act became law in July 1967, following months of spirited debate and difficult negotiations. But the law was limited in scope and, in some ways, more restrictive than the recommendations of the Wolfenden Report. Only applicable to England and Wales, it set the age of consent for homosexual relations at twenty-one (five years higher than for heterosexual relations), exempted the British armed services and merchant marine, and increased the legal penalty for adults convicted of gross indecency with young men aged sixteen to twenty to a five-year jail sentence. The law also narrowly construed the parameters of a "private" homosexual act and left in place vague language criminalizing "procuring." All homosexual activities in Scotland and Northern Ireland remained illegal. Neither of the bill's principal architects, Lord Arran or Leo Abse, consulted directly with HLRS on the law's contents and both rejected the organization's subsequent calls to amend the legislation. Frustrated with these results, Antony Grey, secretary of HLRS, rightly predicted the Act would "prolong social difficulties and cause some individual tragedies." Indeed, prosecutions of gay men increased in the years that followed, prompting future activists to excoriate the accommodationist strategy of the HLRS.[11]

---

[10]Stephen Jeffery-Poulter, *Peers, Queers, & Commons: The Struggle for Gay Law Reform from 1950 to the Present* (London: Routledge, 1991), 60–2.
[11]For a detailed overview of the legislative history of the Sexual Offenses Act of 1967, see Jeffery-Poulter, *Peers, Queers, & Commons*, 49–89.

Despite the limitations of the Sexual Offences Act of 1967, homophiles in the United States hailed it as a milestone. During the two years that the British legislation had wended its way through Parliament, they were often mired in heated disputes over tactics and organizational resources. In May 1965, New York Mattachine split after militants advocating direct action easily won chapter elections. The Daughters of Bilitis fractured after clashes between its San Francisco-based governing board and more militant rank-and-file members on the East Coast.[12]

As dispiriting as this infighting was, it also proved generative. To capitalize on their increasing numbers and to coordinate strategy, leaders of several US homophile groups convened in Kansas City in August 1966. Although many of the militants from the East Coast including Kameny, Barbara Gittings, and Clark Polak advocated the creation of a strong, unified national organization, San Francisco activists were wary of such centralization. The factions compromised by creating the North American Conference of Homophile Organizations (NACHO). NACHO established a national fund that financed legal challenges to antigay provisions of US immigration law and expulsions of gay and lesbian members of the US armed forces. To maximize press coverage, NACHO organized simultaneous protests in several cities. It also conducted and disseminated studies on employment discrimination and legal reform. At NACHO's regional meetings, militants emphatically rejected reliance on medical authorities who considered homosexuality an illness and called for self-acceptance and full legal equality. At the 1968 NACHO convention in Chicago, delegates adopted "Gay is Good" as the movement's slogan, a dramatic departure from the accommodationist philosophy guiding the homophiles only a few years earlier.[13]

But activists failed to overturn antigay US immigration and naturalization laws. The Immigration and Nationality Act of 1965 explicitly allowed for the exclusion and deportation of aliens with "sexual deviations." The legislation also left intact the provision of the 1952 US immigration law that mandated the exclusion and deportation of noncitizen immigrants "afflicted with psychopathic personality," a category that Congress interpreted to include gays and lesbians.

In a case that reached the US Supreme Court, Clive Michael Boutilier challenged the latter policy. Born in Nova Scotia in 1933, Boutilier migrated from Canada to the United States in 1955. He settled in Brooklyn and worked as a janitor and an attendant for a mentally ill man. He became a US permanent resident and formed an intimate partnership with a man

---

[12]D'Emilio, *Sexual Politics, Sexual Communities*, 165–73.
[13]D'Emilio, *Sexual Politics, Sexual Communities*, 193–9.

named Eugene O'Rourke. They lived near several of Boutilier's siblings who had also migrated to New York City.[14]

In 1963, Boutilier applied to become a US citizen. During the interview process the following year, he told officials from the Immigration and Naturalization Service (INS) that he had been arrested for sodomy in 1959, a charge later dropped when the seventeen-year-old "complainant" (likely a consenting sexual partner pressured by police to testify against Boutilier) refused to appear in court. Boutilier also discussed past opposite- and same-sex sexual activities and crossdressing.

Boutilier's honesty cost him dearly. Citing his testimony, INS officials not only denied his application for citizenship, but also ordered him deported on grounds of "psychopathic personality." Horrified at the prospect of leaving his partner and family, he sought legal counsel and his attorneys sued the INS. In building their case, they obtained statements from two different psychiatrists who proclaimed that Boutilier was not psychotic. Nonetheless, in 1966, the Second Circuit Court of Appeals voted 2–1 to uphold Boutilier's deportation. Appealing to the US Supreme Court, his legal team solicited amicus curiae briefs from the New York Civil Liberties Union and the Philadelphia-based Homosexual Law Reform Society, which also funded the legal team.

Although Boutilier's attorneys built a strong defense, the Supreme Court voted 6–3 on behalf of the INS. In the majority opinion issued in June 1967, Associate Justice Tom Clark argued that the deportation was merited because Boutilier was homosexual, the intent of the 1952 immigration law was clear, and the INS had not violated any procedures. Furthermore, citing the precedent of the 1889 *Chinese Exclusion Cases*, the majority asserted that Congress had the constitutional power to exclude and deport noncitizens who were homosexuals. The Court did not issue another ruling on gay rights until 1984 and the immigration law upheld in *Boutilier v. INS* was not struck down for another twenty-three years.

Twelve days before the Court released its decision, Boutilier was hit by a car and fell into a coma due to severe head injuries. Some family members speculated that he may have intended to kill himself. His lawyers successfully petitioned for a delay in his deportation. Following his deportation on November 10, he was cared for by his mother and sisters in Nova Scotia

---

[14]Marc Stein is the foremost authority on the case's fascinating history. See Marc Stein, *Sexual Injustice: Supreme Court Decisions from Griswold to Roe* (Chapel Hill: University of North Carolina Press, 2010); Marc Stein, "All the Immigrants Are Straight, All the Homosexuals Are Citizens, but Some of Us Are Queer Aliens: Genealogies of Legal Strategy in Boutilier v. INS," *Journal of American Ethnic History* 29:4 (Summer 2010): 45–77; Marc Stein, "Boutilier and the U.S. Supreme Court's Sexual Revolution," *Law and History Review* 23 (2005): 491–536; Marc Stein, Boutilier v. Immigration and Naturalization Service (1967), OutHistory.org, May 22, 2017, http://outhistory.org/exhibits/show/boutilier/intro.

and Ontario before relocating to a group home for the disabled, where he lived until his death in 2003.[15]

The *Boutilier* case reflected the deepening divisions appearing among homophiles on both sides of the Atlantic. While more militant activists were willing to challenge systemized injustices and refused to live in secret, more conservative advocates worried that more confrontational tactics and increased visibility of gay life would trigger an intense backlash. The demise of *Der Kreis* in Switzerland reflected the movement's discord. Losing readership and reluctantly acknowledging "our less restricted way of living today," the editors of the pathbreaking European homophile magazine ceased publication in December 1967.[16] As homophile periodicals like *Der Kreis* declined, bolder LGBT publications arose. In Los Angeles, following a January 1967 police raid on the Black Cat Tavern, a local LGBT bar, activists formed Personal Rights in Defense and Education (PRIDE) and began publishing a newsletter. Over the next two years, Richard Mitch (under the pseudonym Dick Michaels) and Bill Rau (under the pseudonym Bill Rand) transformed the publication into *The Advocate*, a nationally distributed LGBT magazine.[17] Accommodationist views were increasingly out of sync with the fierce anticolonialism and militancy among civil rights and antiwar activists whose views many homophiles supported. The protests and societal changes of the late 1960s unleashed forces that soon converged in a gay liberation movement with sweeping transnational ramifications.

Some of the era's most vociferous protests originated in France. In May 1968, students and workers demonstrated across the country, sparking often violent confrontations with police. They challenged social norms and traditional hierarchies. During an occupation of the Sorbonne, female students who asked to form a women's liberation committee were mocked by their male comrades. Guy Chevalier, a twenty-eight-year-old literature student, encountered similar derision when he and a friend formed a "Committee of Revolutionary Pederastic Action" (CAPR) and hung posters proclaiming "For each glorious Jean Genet, there are a hundred thousand shamed homosexuals, condemned to misery!" Members of the Student Occupation Committee tore down many of the posters and when CAPR hosted meetings, they met hostility. After encountering intolerance and intractability among their fellow leftists, radical feminists and gay liberationists would soon form their own revolutionary movements.[18]

Such protest activities were unfathomable in many countries governed by autocratic governments. Following the founding of the People's Republic of China in 1949, the communist regime often addressed sexuality, but in

---

[15]Stein, Boutilier v. Immigration and Naturalization Service, OutHistory.org, May 22, 2017, 1967, http://outhistory.org/exhibits/show/boutilier/intro.

[16]Rizzo, "Public Spheres and Gay Politics since the Second World War," 212.

[17]D'Emilio, *Sexual Politics, Sexual Communities*, 202–9, 219.

[18]Jackson, *Living in Arcadia*, 172–9.

exclusively heterosexual terms. The Maoists did not publicly denounce homosexuality and in 1957, the Chinese Supreme Court ruled that consensual sodomy between adults was not a crime. But the atmosphere for gay men changed dramatically with the onset of the Cultural Revolution in 1966. State policies became markedly hostile toward homosexuality, associating it with criminality, Western decadence, and ideological impurity. Red Guard brigades publicly humiliated and physically attacked perceived enemies of the revolution. Senior party officials were purged. Millions had their property seized, were imprisoned, or were forcibly relocated from cities to rural areas. Yet while some gay men endured brutal persecution, the chaos and disruption of traditional family life created freedom and space for some people to explore their same-sex attractions. It was not until 1979, four years after the Cultural Revolution ended, that the Chinese Supreme Court ruled that homosexuality was a criminal "destruction of the public order" that could be persecuted under the nation's hooliganism statute.[19]

By contrast, the East German government decriminalized consensual homosexual relations between adults earlier than most democratic nations. In July 1968, eleven years after a Berlin appeals court ruling led to the cessation of punishment for consensual same-sex sexual activities between adult men, the GDR adopted a criminal code that omitted Paragraphs 175 and 175a entirely. Although activists around the world praised the decision, it did not signal a new era for freedom for East Germany's LGBT citizens. The government simultaneously instituted Paragraph 151, a law that criminalized same-sex sexual activities between adults over eighteen and youth under eighteen with up to three years' imprisonment or probation. The statute marked the first time that lesbian sex had been criminalized in Germany and it set the age of consent for opposite-sex sexual activities at fourteen, establishing a very different standard for heterosexual youth. In years to come, the Stasi, East Germany's secret police, continued to surveil and harass LGBT activists and government officials linked homosexuality to weakness, disloyalty, and abnormality.[20]

Nine months after the GDR abolished Paragraph 175, Canadian lawmakers considered Pierre Trudeau's Bill C-150. During debates on the bill in April and May 1969, both liberals and conservatives conceded that criminalization did not stop homosexual activities and thus rendered sodomy laws unenforceable. But liberals led by Justice Minister John Turner took the argument further, claiming that however immoral or repugnant individual legislators found homosexuality, the issue should not be a matter of law. They met strong opposition from a coalition of conservatives led

---

[19]Heather Worth, Jing Jing et al., "'Under the Same Quilt': The Paradoxes of Sex between Men in the Cultural Revolution," *Journal of Homosexuality* 64:1 (2017): 61–74.

[20]Jennifer V. Evans, "Decriminalization, Seduction, and 'Unnatural Desire' in East Germany," *Feminist Studies* 36:3 (Fall 2010): 553–77.

by members of the Ralliement Créditistes Party who tied homosexuality to subversion, child molestation, and pathology. Ultimately, the liberals prevailed and on May 14th, Bill C-150 passed third reading by a House of Commons vote of 149 to 55. The Senate also approved the legislation and on August 25, 1969, Canada legalized same-sex sexual activities between consenting adults over the age of twenty-one. Sex between more than two people or involving participants twenty years old or younger remained illegal, though the age of consent for heterosexual activities remained eighteen.[21]

In addition to these restrictions, the Canadian state kept in place other means of controlling gays and lesbians. George Klippert, the man whose life sentence triggered calls for reform of Canadian laws on same-sex sexual activities, was not released from prison until 1971. In June 1969, the House of Commons tabled a report of the Royal Commission on Security recommending lifting the ban on gays and lesbians in civil service jobs that did not require security clearances. Nor did Canadian lawmakers lift prohibitions on gays and lesbians serving in the Royal Canadian Mounted Police and the armed forces. Discourse defining homosexuality as a mental illness also remained deeply rooted in Canadian culture.[22]

Like their East German and Canadian counterparts, West German lawmakers decriminalized same-sex consensual relations between adult men. The political dynamics in West Germany changed after the Social Democratic Party won a parliamentary majority in 1969 and created a coalition with liberals. Advocates of decriminalizing sodomy since the 1890s, the Social Democrats immediately capitalized on the diminished role of the Christian Democrats and their emphasis on traditional families. No longer constrained by the economic and demographic anxieties of the immediate postwar era and rocked by massive student protests in 1968, many West Germans no longer believed that the government should impose its moral judgments on individual citizens whose behavior did not harm anyone. Many Protestant religious leaders also advocated legalizing consensual sex between adult men. Reformers also noted that communist East Germany had already abolished Paragraph 175, taking a step toward human rights that democratic West Germany had yet to make.

These arguments won broad support in the Bundestag. On May 9, 1969, liberals and conservatives joined forces and overwhelmingly voted to abolish key sections of Paragraph 175. As in East Germany and Canada, the decision stemmed from a belief in limiting government intervention in private lives, not acceptance of homosexuality. Most legal reformers still

---

[21]Stuart Chambers, "Pierre Elliott Trudeau and Bill C-150: A Rational Approach to Homosexual Acts, 1968–69," *Journal of Homosexuality* 57:2 (2010): 256–61.
[22]David Kimmel and Daniel Robinson, "Sex, Crime, Pathology: Homosexuality and Criminal Code Reform in Canada, 1949–1969," *Canadian Journal of Law and Society* 16:1 (2001): 163–4.

viewed gays and lesbians as psychologically unbalanced. Old fears that gay men preyed upon youth informed the lawmakers' decision to set the age of consent for same-sex relations at twenty-one, a provision that remained in effect until 1973 when it was lowered to eighteen. While West German citizens were adopting more tolerant attitudes toward premarital and extramarital sex and different types of family structures, their openness did not yet encompass homosexual activities and relationships. If such attitudes were to change, LGBT people would have to break down the legal, political, and societal obstacles keeping them in the shadows and limiting their civil rights.[23]

The homophile movement in the United States was poorly positioned to drive such radical change. By the late 1960s, ONE and Mattachine were no longer publishing their respective magazines. Daughters of Bilitis would soon disband its national board. In Philadelphia, Clark Polak struck a plea bargain in which he agreed to close *Drum*, Janus, and the Homosexual Law Reform Society in order to avoid a two-year jail sentence for obscenity charges.[24] In mid-1969, a time of fervent antiwar activism, black militancy, and an emerging women's liberation movement, the US homophile movement was losing its momentum.

But in June 1969, the Stonewall riots electrified LGBT people around the world and helped fuel a global gay liberation movement. In New York City, most gay bars were owned by mobsters who bribed police in order to avoid closures and raids. Patrons risked arrest, public exposure, and job loss. Conditions were often seedy. Popular for its dancing and go-go boys, the Stonewall drew a mixed crowd of middle- and working-class gays and lesbians, many of whom were Latino or African-American. Drag queens, homeless LGBT youth, sex workers, and gender nonconforming people also frequented the Christopher Street bar. Swept up in the social tumult of the era, patrons resisted when police raided the Stonewall shortly before midnight on June 27th. As police dragged patrons out of the bar and loaded a paddy wagon, a crowd on the street started throwing insults, bottles, beer cans, coins, and cobblestones. Hundreds joined street protests that rocked the East Village for several days. Four police officers were injured and thirteen demonstrators were arrested. Although Stonewall was far from the first time LGBT people resisted authorities and the gay liberation movement built on decades of homophile activism, the uprising marked a major shift in the tone and visibility of LGBT advocacy.[25]

The riots inspired immediate organizing. On July 1st, activists staged a "gay pride" rally on Christopher Street. The following day, protestors

---

[23]Robert G. Moeller, "Private Acts, Public Anxieties, and the Fight to Decriminalize Male Homosexuality in West Germany," *Feminist Studies* 36:1 (Fall 2010): 535–41.
[24]Marc Stein, *Rethinking the Gay and Lesbian Movement* (New York: Routledge, 2012), 78.
[25]Martin Duberman, *Stonewall* (New York: Dutton, 1993); David Carter, *Stonewall: The Riots That Sparked the Gay Revolution* (New York: St. Martin's, 2004).

picketed outside of the offices of *The Village Voice* in response to its negative depiction of the Stonewall uprising. On July 9th, Mattachine New York held a "homosexual liberation" meeting attended by over 100 people. A week later, a similar meeting drew twice as many participants, but forty attendees declared the homophile group too conservative and walked out. On July 24, several of these dissidents formed the Gay Liberation Front (GLF), fusing the radicalism of the student and antiwar movements with a more assertive LGBT activism. The name was quite intentional. "Gay" signaled the activists' rejection of the homophiles' accommodationist views and of medical discourses defining homosexuality as pathology. "Liberation" reflected their broad aims for personal freedom, political equality, and social justice. "Front" marked GLF's affinity with anti-imperialist organizations like the National Liberation Front in Vietnam. By the early 1970s, dozens of GLF chapters had been formed all over the United States and in several other nations.[26]

Throughout the early 1970s, gay liberation groups coexisted with established homophile organizations and newly formed gay rights coalitions. In early 1970, homophiles joined forces to protest a revision of a law being considered in Franco's Spain. The Ley de Peligrosidad Social (Law of Social Perils) defined known or suspected homosexuals (along with prostitutes, drug addicts, and drunkards) as morally dangerous. Simply identifying as gay or lesbian, regardless of sexual conduct, could be punished with imprisonment.[27] Writing from Paris, Arcadie's Marc Daniel wrote Antony Grey to warn of "infamy, blackmail, and despair" that would result from the law. Arcadie aimed to enlist "all of the homophile organizations in the world," psychiatrists, academics, and religious leaders in writing to the Spanish Embassy and the Spanish Ministry of Public Health to implore them not to pass a law that would have such grave consequences. Pointing to the brutality of the Franco regime, Daniel noted that such a law would be much more strictly and harshly enforced than the Labouchère Law ever had been in England. But these efforts failed to stop the Franco regime from implementing the law.[28]

The gay liberation movement quickly spread to other nations. In the fall of 1970, gay men and lesbians in London began holding GLF meetings that

---

[26]Stein, *Rethinking the Gay and Lesbian Movement*, 81–2.
[27]For important historic context and the law's ramifications, see Geoffroy Huard, "Spain from Franco's Repressive Regime to Same-Sex Marriage," *From Sodomy Laws to Same-Sex Marriage*, 95–107.
[28]Marc Daniel to Antony Grey, January 22, 1970, and Albany Trust to Spanish Ambassador, March 9, 1970, in HCA/Albany Trust, Series 7, folder 20/c, Records of the Albany Trust, Hall-Carpenter Collection, London School of Economics, London, England (hereafter HCA). See also Javier Fernández Galeano, "Is He a 'Social Danger:' The Franco Regime's Judicial Prosecution of Homosexuality in Málaga under the Ley de Vagos y Maleantes," *Journal of the History of Sexuality* 25 (2016): 1–31.

soon drew over 200 people per month. On November 27, GLF held its first public demonstration in protest of the arrest of an activist for importuning. Like its US counterpart, GLF London defined itself as "a people's movement" and rejected traditional organizational leadership structures. Calling for gays and lesbians to fight for their own freedom, GLF was bitterly critical of homophile organizations like the Albany Trust and the Committee for Homosexual Equality. Proud and unapologetic about their sexual identity, GLF groups around the world adopted slogans like "Avenge Oscar Wilde" and wore symbols like purple lambda signs and clenched fists. They reclaimed the pink triangle that the Nazis used to identify gay men in concentration camps as a symbol of resistance and resilience.[29] They organized "zaps" targeting establishments deemed hostile to gays and lesbians, engaged in public displays of same-sex affection, and held joyous dances welcoming gay and straight people alike. Throughout the early 1970s, gay liberationist groups also formed in the Netherlands, Belgium, Canada, New Zealand, and Australia.[30]

In 1971, West German filmmaker Rosa von Praunheim and sociologist Martin Dannecker released their film *Nicht der Homosexuelle ist pervers, sondern die Situation, in der er lebt (It is Not the Homosexual Who Is Perverse, But the Situation in Which He Lives)*. The protagonist Daniel moves to Berlin and has several dispiriting adventures in the gay subculture. He finally finds personal affirmation at a gay commune, where he and others reject lives of superficiality, hiding, and conformity and decide to fight state-sanctioned homophobia. The film was screened at cinemas and universities across West Germany and helped to inspire the creation of several new radical gay organizations. Applying insights and tactics derived from their work in the transnational student movement, the founders of groups like Homosexuelle Aktion Westberlin offered a leftist critique of capitalism, imperialism, and integrationist strategies advocated by homophiles.[31]

Similar groups arose in France and Italy. In March 1971, radical activists launched the Front Homosexuel d'Action Révolutionnaire (FHAR) in France. The group published two short-lived periodicals and staged several provocative demonstrations before dissolving in 1974.[32] Inspired by FHAR, bookseller Angelo Pezzano founded Fronte Unitario Omosessuale

---

[29]In October 1973, Homosexuelle Aktion Westberlin became the first organization in the world to adopt the pink triangle as a gay rights symbol. On the origins, evolution, and controversies of the pink triangle as a logo for transnational LGBT activism, see Newsome, "Homosexuals after the Holocaust," 120–40.

[30]Weeks, *Coming Out*, 185–92.

[31]Christopher Ewing, "The Color of Desire: Contradictions of Race, Sex, and Gay Rights in the Federal Republic of Germany" (PhD diss., City University of New York, 2018): 48, 54.

[32]Michael Sibalis, "Gay Liberation Comes to France: The Front Homosexuel d'Action Révolutionnaire (FHAR)," *French History and Civilization* (2005): 265–76.

IMAGE 4.2 London Gay Liberation Front demonstration, *c.* 1972.

Rivoluzionario Italiano in Turin later the same year. The group's acronym FUORI! was Italian for "out," a reference to the importance gay liberationists placed on coming out of the closet and readily identifying oneself as gay or lesbian. Inspired by Marxism, FUORI! initially placed gay liberation in a larger context of class conflict between the bourgeoise and the proletariat. FUORI! founded a magazine of the same name but struggled to make it financially viable. By 1973, the group repositioned itself and forged an alliance with the Radical Party. Within a year, FUORI! abandoned its revolutionary posture in favor of a reformist orientation, a move that alienated some of the organization's founding members.[33]

In Latin America, new gay liberation organizations formed in opposition to authoritarian regimes. In 1971, three years after Mexican security forces fired at thousands of students gathered in the Tlatelolco section of Mexico City to protest political repression, activists formed the Frente de Liberación Homosexual de México (FLH) to challenge a new democratic (but still repressive) government to end its harassment of gay men. Argentina's Nuestro Mondo (Our World) emerged in the late 1960s and morphed into a coalition of unionists, feminists, radical youth, intellectuals, and gays and lesbians called the Frente de Liberación Homosexual de Argentina (FLH). The disparate groups shared a leftist, anti-imperialist worldview and defined liberation as a collective struggle against capitalism. They viewed police harassment of gay men as a particularly extreme example of how the military regime suppressed all citizens, homosexual and heterosexual alike, at a time of increasing sexual openness and gender egalitarianism. In 1970, Argentinian poet Juan José Hernández visited the United States and learned about Stonewall. But he was profoundly inspired by Huey Newton's recently published "A Letter to the Revolutionary Brothers and Sisters about the Women's Liberation and Gay Liberation Movement." Co-founder of the Black Panthers, Newton called for those fighting racism to join forces with those fighting sexual oppression in a collective struggle against imperialism and capitalism. Newton's message greatly resonated with FLH activists and a Spanish translation of his letter became a widely circulated FLH document. In March 1973, after months of intense civilian resistance to the military regime, Argentina briefly transitioned to democracy and the new left-wing government stopped persecuting dissidents and homosexuals.

The changes proved fleeting and within a few months, the nation slid back into authoritarianism and police harassment of gay men resumed. FLH responded by publishing an underground magazine called *Somos* that was filled with news about gay liberation groups all over the world.[34] It also called attention to right-wing violence against gays in neighboring Chile. In June 1974, FLH released a statement accusing the Chilean government of attempting to impose a social order "modeled on the ideas of the Holy Inquisition" and repressing homosexuals as well as "workers, students, and patriots." Leaders of the ruling junta, FLH claimed, routinely "raped, tortured, castrated, and tormented" gay men and then left their bodies "for

---

[33]On the founding of FUORI! and the context in which it arose, see Dario Pasquini, "'This Will Be the Love of the Future': Italian LGBT People and Their Emotions from the Fuori! and Massimo Consoli Archives, 1970–1984," *Journal of the History of Sexuality* 29:1 (January 2020): 52–7.

[34]Pablo Ben and Santiago Joaquin Insausti, "Dictatorial Rule and Sexual Politics in Argentina: The Case of the Frente de Liberación Homosexual, 1967–1976," *Hispanic American Historical Review* 97:2 (May 2017): 297–325.

several days in the public streets in order to intimidate the population, to sow terror." FLH concluded with a call for the "Latin American and world homosexual communities to repudiate the Chilean regime and help its victims and opponents."[35] But FLH members soon faced similar dangers. After a military coup overthrew President Isabel Perón in March 1976, the group collapsed and several FLH members fled the country. Those who remained endured the most violent epoch in Argentinian political history.[36]

Brazil's LGBT citizens were also victims of dramatic shifts in state policies. The collapse of the authoritarian Estado Novo regime at the end of World War II marked the beginning of nearly two decades of economic growth, mass migration to cities, and consumerism. At the same time, vibrant gay subcultures in Rio de Janeiro and São Paulo gained more visibility through nightclubs, public beaches, carnival balls, and publications like *O Snob*.[37] But by the late 1960s, gays and lesbians became more guarded amid domestic political tumult. In 1968, four years after a military coup upended the nation's government, mass demonstrations in opposition to the ruling generals arose. In response, the junta issued decrees that closed Congress and restricted many civil liberties. In October 1969, the regime installed General Emílio Garrastazu Médici as president and escalated its brutal crackdown on dissidents and critics. Thousands were jailed and tortured.

The political repression inevitably affected Brazil's LGBT citizens. State police periodically raided nightclubs and arrested patrons. To avoid the government censorship, the editors of *O Snob* and other gay publications ceased production. Yet the regime remained focused on its direct political enemies and did not close gay establishments. Indeed, from 1972 on, new discos and saunas catering to gay men with disposable income opened, thanks to the nation's flourishing economy. Nonetheless, as gay liberation groups formed all over Europe and the United States in the early 1970s, the domestic political atmosphere was not conducive to similar organizing in Brazil.[38]

At the same time, gay pride marches and festivals commemorating the Stonewall riots occurred all over the world. On June 28, 1970, thousands of gay, lesbian, bisexual, and transgender New Yorkers participated in a Gay Pride march. By 1972, activists were participating in annual gay liberation events in London, Chicago, Los Angeles, Dallas, Boston, Milwaukee, West Berlin, Paris, Stockholm, San Francisco, Philadelphia, Atlanta, Miami, and Washington, DC. In contrast to the staid clothing and demeanor of homophiles who had demonstrated in front of the

[35]"Chile Junta Hits Gays with Reign of Terror," *The Advocate*, June 5, 1974, 20.

[36]Ben and Insausti, "Dictatorial Rule and Sexual Politics in Argentina." See also RFSL Sweden, A First Report on the Situation of Gays in Chile, IGA 2nd Annual Conference, Barcelona, Spain, April 4–7, 1980, HCA/Ephemera/217, HCA.

[37]On these developments, see Green, *Beyond Carnival*, 147–98.

[38]Green, *Beyond Carnival*, 242–66.

White House and Independence Hall in 1965, gay pride marches were a flamboyant, raucous celebration of the diversity of the LGBT community. Although a shared refusal to accept persecution and discrimination linked the militant homophiles and the gay rights marchers, the expression of these demands shifted dramatically.[39]

Despite differences in style and tactics among individual activists and grass roots organizations, the timing was right for more visible and assertive types of international LGBT advocacy. In September 1970, UN Secretary-General U Thant accepted a missive from the Homophile Youth Movement of the United States declaring that "the civil and legal rights of homosexuals should be insured under the legislation of every country and the world homophile movement should be assisted in its fight for pride, dignity, identity, and social and legal justice." Thant referred the letter to a subcommittee of the UN Commission on Human Rights.[40] Two years later, Swedish journalist Björn Vilson launched a one-man crusade to persuade the UN to investigate the status of gays around the world, to establish a public information campaign about the global persecution of sexual minorities, and to host an international conference on the legal and political challenges facing "millions existing in constant dread of having their homosexuality exposed." Vilson penned dozens of letters to UN officials and staged solo public demonstrations in Sweden.[41] Although neither of these actions inspired formal UN action, they portended a new phase of global LGBT advocacy, one in which activists once again demanded the protections accorded other minorities by international law and supranational bodies.

LGBT advocates also held international conferences and formed nongovernmental organizations to define policy positions and to ensure representation in global human rights deliberations and decision-making. In 1974, Ian C. Dunn, the founder of the Scottish Minorities Group (SMG), and Derek Ogg co-organized the first International Gay Rights Congress after realizing how many foreign activists were present at the first national meeting of the Campaign for Homosexual Equality, a British gay rights organization that had rejected the quiet assimilation of the Albany Trust.[42] Prior to the Congress, Ogg traveled to the United States to fundraise and to solidify ties with US activists. In New York, he met with Bruce Voeller, leader of the recently formed National Gay Task Force (NGTF).[43] In Washington, DC, Ogg visited Frank Kameny, who expressed great enthusiasm about

---

[39]Teal, *The Gay Militants*, 322–3.

[40]"U.N. Commission to Study Request to Aid Homosexuals," *The Advocate*, September 2–15, 1970, 13.

[41]"Swede Calls for U.N. Action for Homosexuals," *The Advocate*, May 23, 1973, 114.

[42]In 1969, Ian Dunn organized the first meeting of what became the Scottish Minorities Group (SMG), the northern counterpart to CHE. See "First International Gay Rights Conference Set," *The Advocate*, November 6, 1974, 19.

[43]"Heavyweight National Gay Group Formed," *The Advocate*, November 7, 1973, 1.

attending the forthcoming meeting. The Congress organizers paid for Kameny's airfare to ensure that he could.

In December 1974, 200 delegates from seventeen different countries convened in Edinburgh, Scotland. A small contingent of lesbians, overwhelmingly outnumbered by their male colleagues, repeatedly addressed the need for the gay and lesbian movement to endorse international feminism and tackle sexism within the gay and lesbian community. They castigated the conference organizers for failing to place women in any significant leadership roles at the Congress and covering only the travel expenses of male delegates.[44] Unable to attend the conference, an underground GLF group in Spain sent a report detailing the arrest and imprisonment of gays and lesbians by the Franco regime.[45] FLH activists in Buenos Aires provided the delegates an equally bleak account of antigay persecution in Argentina. A report from Australia offered more positive news about growing numbers of Australian gay organizations and gay activists lobbying Parliament to decriminalize consensual sex between male adults.[46] To highlight the fact that the Sexual Offenses Act had excluded Scotland and Northern Ireland, the organizers issued a press release stressing that the Congress was "being held in one of the few countries of the Western world where male homosexual activity is strictly illegal." Despite repeated difficulties in persuading grass roots activists of the importance of promoting and financially supporting international LGBT rights organizing, many of the attendees continued advocating the creation of a new organization devoted to advancing gay and lesbian equality worldwide as women's rights, environmental concerns, disability rights, and racial and ethnic equality were becoming part of global human rights discourse.[47]

---

[44]A Report on the First International Gay Rights Congress, Edinburgh, December 18–22, 1974, HCA/Ephemera/164, HCA.

[45]Under the terms of a 1970 law, the Franco regime included gays and lesbians among a list of "social perils" that the state sought to suppress. Formed in 1971, the Spanish Movement for Gay Liberation held meetings in private homes, but soon risked prosecution for violating a state law requiring a permit for gatherings of more than twenty people. The group enlisted the help of Arcadie, France's largest gay organization, in publishing a newsletter called *AGHOIS*. Activists in Barcelona sent the text to Paris. After printing each issue, Arcadie then sent individual copies back to Spain. But Spanish authorities discovered the scheme and contacted French authorities, who pressured Arcadie to stop printing *AGHOIS*. Subsequent efforts to get copies printed in Germany and Sweden and then smuggled back to Spain failed. See Mark Thompson, "Gay Liberation in Spain: Struggle and Secrecy—For a Better Future," *The Advocate*, November 19, 1977, 17, 22.

[46]Jim Foster, "International Congress Report," *The Advocate*, January 29, 1975, 5, 8–9; Ben and Insausti, "Dictatorial Rule and Sexual Politics in Argentina," 319; Minto, "Special Relationships," 379.

[47]On the communications, financial, and logistical challenges that arose after the Congress, see, for example, International Gay Rights Congress correspondence, April 27, 1975–September 11, 1975, HCA/Ephemera/166, HCA.

The following year, many of the intersections of these movements were evident at the World Conference on Women held in June and July 1975 in Mexico City. The first international conference organized by the UN to focus exclusively on women's issues, the meeting drew 1,200 delegates at a time when Cold War tensions were flaring. In a different part of Mexico City, approximately 6,000 representatives from nongovernmental organizations attended an unofficial, parallel meeting called the International Women's Year Tribune. The Tribune, a landmark event in transnational feminism and lesbianism, ignited contentious debates. While lesbians from several nations and cultures argued that sexual liberation was integrally linked to struggles against racism, apartheid, and imperialism, some representatives protested and dismissed sexual rights as a distraction from more pressing economic and political concerns. Similar debates would resurface at global forums in years to come.[48]

Established human rights organizations like Amnesty International (AI) were simultaneously grappling with how to reconcile LGBT rights with their missions and strategies. Established in 1961, AI is a nongovernmental organization working on behalf of "prisoners of conscience" whose governments imprisoned, tortured, or executed them because of their opinions or religious beliefs. In 1977, recognizing the impossibility of defending every individual defined as a "prisoner of conscience" (PoC) under these expansive terms, AI adopted the Mandate, a set of rules for interpreting and implementing its larger aims.[49] On many occasions since then, the Mandate Review Committee has recommended that several issues including abolition of the death penalty, prosecuting perpetrators of war crimes and genocide, and blocking the global arms trade be subsumed into AI's broader human rights agenda. But the decision to include individuals imprisoned on the basis of their sexual orientation proved a contentious seventeen-year process.

Amnesty's early years coincided with remarkable gains for lesbian, gay, bisexual, and transgender people. Following the June 1969 Stonewall Riots, police harassment of LGBT establishments in many US cities declined and half of the fifty states repealed their sodomy laws. In December 1973, the American Psychiatric Association removed homosexuality from its list of mental disorders, and the following year, the US Civil Service Commission lifted its ban on the employment of gay men and lesbians by the federal government. Several dozen US cities, including Detroit, Boston, Los Angeles, San Francisco, and Houston, incorporated sexual orientation

---

[48]Jocelyn Olcott, "Cold War Conflicts and Cheap Cabaret: Sexual Politics at the 1975 United Nations International Women's Year Conference," *Gender & History* 22:3 (November 2010): 733–54.
[49]Stephen Hopgood, *Keepers of the Flame: Understanding Amnesty International* (Ithaca, NY: Cornell University Press, 2006), 93.

into their municipal nondiscrimination protections in housing, public accommodations, and employment. Across the United States, openly gay candidates ran for public office and heterosexual candidates sought political support from the LGBT community. Such advances were echoed in many nations. In the early 1970s, Austria, Costa Rica, Finland, Norway, and Malta decriminalized homosexuality. The Netherlands made sixteen the age of consent for same-sex and opposite-sex sexual activities. In 1977, Quebec became the world's first jurisdiction larger than a municipality to outlaw discrimination based on sexual orientation.[50]

In August 1978, during a conference of the Campaign for Homosexual Equality held in Coventry, England, thirty men representing seventeen organizations from fourteen countries founded the International Gay Association (IGA), the world's first nongovernmental organization devoted to global LGBT equality. IGA's two major aims were to coordinate international political action for gay rights and to facilitate the exchange of information on the oppression of gay men and lesbian women throughout the world. The members agreed to meet again in Amsterdam the following year and set an ambitious list of priorities including asking the European Economic Community Commission to end employment discrimination on the basis of sexual orientation; surveying candidates for the European Parliament on their views on gay rights; and having IGA members lobby their respective national Amnesty International (AI) organizations to expand the definition of "prisoners of conscience" to include individuals imprisoned solely because of their sexual orientation or consensual same-sex behavior between adults.[51] On September 30, 1978, IGA held its first worldwide protest as member organizations across Europe, Canada, and Australia coordinated actions against proposed antigay laws introduced in Greece. The demonstrations, press releases, and letters to Greek officials helped persuade the Athens government to withdraw the draft legislation.[52]

IGA member groups and others repeatedly challenged the United States to repeal antigay provisions of its immigration laws. In June 1979, Carl Hill, a 32-year-old British gay man who worked as a photographer for London's *Gay News*, was arrested by immigration officials who noticed his "Gay Pride" button upon his arrival at San Francisco International Airport on a planned trip to cover the Gay Freedom Day Parade. After holding Hill for three hours and ordering him to undergo an examination performed by a Public Health Service psychiatrist when he refused to leave the

---

[50]For a chronology of these events, see Joanne Myers, *Historical Dictionary of the Lesbian and Gay Liberation Movements* (Latham, MD: Scarecrow Press, 2013), 24–53.
[51]Robert Mehl, "CHE Conference in Europe: International Gay Group Formed," *The Advocate*, November 29, 1978, 7, 11.
[52]IGA News, Vol. 1, No. 1 (November 1978): 3–4.

United States voluntarily, INS agents finally permitted Hill and his partner Michael Mason, the editor of *Gay News*, to go to their hotel. A week later, Don Knutson, an attorney from the public interest law firm Gay Rights Advocates, convinced US District Judge Stanley Weigel to issue a temporary restraining order against the Public Health Service on the grounds that homosexuality was not "a defect or disease" that the health officials were legally authorized to diagnose.[53] On August 3, the Hill case prompted US Surgeon General Julius Richmond to order the Public Health Service to stop conducting psychiatric evaluations of suspected homosexuals arriving at US ports of entry in order to issue medical certificates of excludability. The policy change, Richmond explained, reflected "current and generally accepted canons of the medical profession, which no longer considers homosexuality to be a mental disorder." But that same day, immigration officials at the San Francisco International Airport detained two Mexican nationals suspected of being gay. Shortly before the two were scheduled to be deported on a 1:30 a.m. flight, Eduardo Martinez and Javier Cruz were allowed to contact Don Knutson, who persuaded a judge to issue a restraining order. The judge scheduled a hearing to determine the legality of the Public Health Service's refusal to perform psychiatric investigations and whether the INS could exclude aliens on the basis of homosexuals without medical certifications. Ten days later, the INS issued a nationwide directive deferring enforcement of the antigay immigration ban until its legal status could be reassessed. The agency canceled the Martinez and Cruz trial scheduled for the next day and allowed them to be formally admitted into the United States.[54]

While LGBT activists hailed the decision as a major victory, thorny legal issues remained. INS claimed that the policy could not be permanently enacted without congressional action.[55] IGA noted the inconsistency with which the policy had been applied throughout the entire existence of the statute. Well-known gays like Elton John and Quentin Crisp entered the United States without incident while Kim Friele, the lesbian who served as secretary general for Norway's Forbundet av 1948, "has been fighting this for a few years now."[56] IGA objected vociferously to the fact that Secretary

---

[53]"Gay Britisher Barred from U.S., Then Let In," *The Advocate*, July 26, 1979, 7.

[54]"Immigration Finally Relents, Will No Longer Bar Gays," *The Advocate*, September 20, 1979, 13; Don Knutson, "Immigration Lifts Its Lamp to Gays—Reluctantly," *The Advocate*, October 4, 1979, 7, 14.

[55]"Congressmembers Ask INS to Change Policy," *The Advocate*, October 4, 1979, 9–10.

[56]IGA Memo 0003/79/IGA, August 10, 1979, HCA/Ephemera/163, HCA. Friele was a long-time gay rights activist who took the previously secret Forbundet av 1948 public while serving as the organization's president from 1966 to 1971. She was instrumental in Norway's decriminalization of homosexual acts in 1972 and declassification of homosexuality as a mental illness six years later. For a biographical overview, see https://nbl.snl.no/Kim_Friele.

of State Cyrus Vance directed US consulates abroad to deny visas to known and suspected gays and lesbians.[57]

In late 1979 and early 1980, IGA's efforts benefited from widespread media denunciation of a Justice Department opinion calling for the continued enforcement of the antigay provisions of US immigration law. A *Washington Post* editorial called the law "absurd" and several other major US newspapers also took stands against the ban.[58] Syndicated columnist Carl Rowan, noting that the law also precluded the entry of drunkards, adulterers, and gamblers, said that strict enforcement would create "nightmarish lines stretching outside our airports for miles." Opposition intensified in January 1980 after Gay Rights Advocates filed a $1 million lawsuit on behalf of Mexican fashion designer Jaime Chavez whom INS officers detained on December 29, 1979, after finding dresses in his suitcase and noticing him wearing "remnants of makeup" and "women's rings." Senator Alan Cranston, a Democrat from California, announced that he would introduce federal legislation eliminating the term "sexual deviation" from the US Immigration and Nationality Act.[59] Congressmen Henry Waxman, Anthony Beilenson, and Julian Dixon, Democrats from California, introduced a similar bill in the US House of Representatives.[60]

By March 1980, IGA had coordinated several high-profile actions against the law. Clint Hockenberry, IGA's American liaison, testified before the US Senate Committee on Immigration.[61] Edmund Lynch, the Dublin-based head of IGA's Information Secretariat, wrote to President Jimmy Carter, asking him to amend the legislation and underscoring the incongruity of current US immigration law and Carter's advocacy of global human rights.[62] At Amsterdam's Schiphol Airport, members of COC wore police uniforms and asked arriving American tourists whether they were gay or lesbian, explaining how foreign nationals perceived to be homosexual could be treated by US immigration officials. As many as 135 representatives in the Dutch Parliament signed a petition demanding repeal of the INS policy against foreign homosexuals. The Dutch also planned to file a formal protest at the Council of

---

[57]IGA Memo 0006/IGA/79, November 20, 1979, HCA/Ephemera/173, HCA.
[58]"Major Dailies Oppose INS Policy," *Washington Blade*, January 10, 1980, 6.
[59]Michael D. Green, "Senate to Get Bill Striking INS Ban," *Washington Blade*, January 10, 1980, 3.
[60]Lou Chibbaro, Jr., "Justice to Reconsider Immigration Policy," *Washington Blade*, February 7, 1980, 3; "House Bill Would End Antigay INS Policy," *The Advocate*, April 3, 1980, 7.
[61]Testimony of Clint C. Hockenberry before United States Select Commission on Immigration and Refugee Policy, January 21, 1980, HCA/Ephemera/215, HCA.
[62]Edmund Lynch to Jimmy Carter, January 29, 1980, HCA/Ephemera/215, HCA.

Europe (CoE) on the grounds that the US policy violated the provisions of the Helsinki Accords protecting the right to travel between countries.[63] Swedish and Dutch diplomats raised the same objections at the UN.[64] Nonetheless, the Carter administration equivocated.

While gay rights advocates confronted the complexities of US immigration law, they scored several victories. On March 26, 1977, Frank Kameny and a dozen leaders from the National Gay Task Force met with Midge Constanza, a public liaison for the Carter administration, in the first-ever official White House meeting dedicated to gay and lesbian rights. Later that year, Harvey Milk won election to the San Francisco Board of Supervisors, becoming the nation's seventh openly gay or lesbian candidate elected to public office. Prior to his assassination by a colleague in November 1978, Milk was instrumental to the city's passage of a gay rights ordinance and the defeat of a statewide ballot initiative that would have barred gays and lesbians and supporters of gay rights from working in public schools. The following year, after several Swedish activists skipped work after "calling in homosexual" and occupied offices at the National Board of Health and Welfare, Sweden became the world's first country to declassify homosexuality as a mental illness. As part of a wave of post-Franco reforms, Spain decriminalized homosexuality.[65]

At the same time, IGA grappled with how to expand its international reach. In response to concerns raised about sexism and underrepresentation of women in the organization, IGA created a women's caucus and adopted a more inclusive name, the International Association of Gay/Lesbian Women and Gay Men. In December 1980, seventy-six women from seventeen different countries traveled to Amsterdam to attend the first conference organized by the International Lesbian Information Secretariat, one of IGA's three secretariats. They participated in workshops and plenary sessions,

---

[63]The Helsinki Accords were a major diplomatic agreement signed by thirty-five nations on August 1, 1975. Aimed at easing Soviet-American tensions, the accords resolved European boundary disputes dating from World War II. The signatories, which included every European country except for Albania as well as the United States and Canada, also pledged to respect human rights and fundamental freedoms including the rights to emigrate and travel. Human rights activists instantly recognized the gravity of these provisions and began tracking and publicizing violations of the agreement. See Sarah Snyder, *Human Rights Activism and the End of the Cold War: A Transnational History of the Helsinki Network* (Cambridge, UK: Cambridge University Press, 2013).

[64]The Council of Europe is an intergovernmental organization that was founded in 1949. In 1953, it established the European Convention on Human Rights. The Convention is enforced by the European Commission and the European Court of Human Rights in Strasbourg, France. IGA Memo 0007/IGA/80, March 16, 1980, HCA/Ephemera/163, HCA; Michael D. Green, "Dutch Parliament Protests INS Exclusion of Gays," *Washington Blade*, January 24, 1980, 1, 4.

[65]Myers, *Historical Dictionary of the Lesbian and Gay Liberation Movements*, 24–53; Shaunacy Ferro, "The Time Swedes Called in Gay to Work," *Mental Floss*, April 28, 2015, https://www.mentalfloss.com/article/63529/time-swedes-called-gay-work.

exchanged organizing strategies, and discussed how lesbians might be better integrated into domestic and transnational gay rights activism.[66]

IGA also confronted its failure to represent developing nations and communist countries. During IGA's first annual conference, the delegates adopted a resolution committing members to gathering information on lesbians and gay men and making contact with local activists "in Third World countries," Eastern Europe, and the People's Republic of China. Several member groups were assigned countries on which to report at the next annual IGA conference.[67] In July 1980, IGA delegates shared news of burgeoning gay rights activism in Brazil, Nicaragua, Guatemala, and Chile.[68]

As transnational activists worked to increase their visibility and political power, religious conservatives mobilized in opposition to gay rights. In January 1977, after Dade County, Florida (which contains Miami) outlawed employment and housing discrimination on the basis of sexual orientation, Anita Bryant—best known as a beauty pageant queen, singer, and spokesperson for the Florida Citrus Commission—led a coalition called Save Our Children that successfully pushed for the repeal of the ordinance. The campaign drew on fundamentalist Christian doctrine that equated homosexuality with sin and claimed that homosexuals "recruited" and molested children. On June 7, 1977, Dade County voters overwhelmingly defeated the ordinance. Save Our Children also proved instrumental in persuading the Florida legislature to prohibit gays from adopting children, a ban that was not lifted until 2008. Following her victories in Florida, Bryant led successful efforts to repeal gay rights ordinances in Eugene, Oregon, and Wichita, Kansas. But her supporters failed to win passage of the Briggs Initiative (Proposition 6), a California ballot measure that would have barred LGBT teachers or anyone who supported LGBT equality, from working for the state's public schools.[69]

Terrified and enraged by the backlash, LGBT activists in the United States and elsewhere vociferously protested Bryant's antigay crusade. Immediately following the repeal vote in Miami, forty-five US groups formed the Coalition for Lesbian and Gay Rights. Activists in locales as diverse as Chicago, New Orleans, Denver, Norfolk, and Lime Rock, Arkansas publicly demonstrated against Bryant. In June 1977, over 250,000 people attended San Francisco's Gay Freedom Day parade, some carrying signs depicting Anita Bryant alongside notorious figures like Idi Amin, Joseph Stalin, and Adolf Hitler. In solidarity, activists in Sydney, Australia marched on the

[66]ILIS Conference 1980, Amsterdam, HCA/Ephemera/163, HCA.

[67]Proposals and Resolutions with Agreements as to Their Implementation, International Gay Association, 1st Annual Conference, April 14, 1979, HCA/Ephemera/163, HCA.

[68]*IGA Newsletter* 80–2 (July 1980), IGA News/*Newsletter*, box-ILGA Bulletin 1978–1989, IHLIA.

[69]Myers, *Historical Dictionary of the Lesbian and Gay Liberation Movements*, 24–53.

same day, but met violent resistance from police who beat and arrested demonstrators.

In the Netherlands, the Stichting Vrije Relatierechten (SVR—Foundation for Free Relationship Rights) persuaded dozens of leading Dutch politicians and clergy to sign a full-page appeal that appeared in the *Miami Herald* a week before the Dade County repeal vote. Called "A Message from the People of Holland," the text began "We, from the land of Anne Frank, know where prejudices and discrimination can lead to" and urged voters not to "repeal human rights."[70] After Save Our Children prevailed in the Dade County vote and began organizing in other US cities, SVR organized a fundraiser at the Amsterdam Orchestra Hall called "Miami Nightmare" that raised the money to purchase an advertisement in *Time* magazine. Published in January 1978, the appeal was titled "What's Going on in America?" and invoked the Declaration of Independence, the Universal Declaration of Human Rights, and the Helsinki Accords before asserting, "President Carter's human rights policy can gain credibility only if the rights of homosexuals in the United States of America are bound inseparably to human rights for all people." The ad's illustrious signatories included Simone de Beauvoir, Sir John Gielgud, Günther Grass, and politicians and clergy from Belgium, The Netherlands, Italy, and Spain.[71] Bryant's assault on gay rights in the United States inadvertently unified Dutch gay and lesbian activists who had been bitterly divided over questions of tactics and identity. On June 24, 1978, COC abandoned its long-standing integrationist strategy and joined forces with radical gay and lesbian liberation groups including Rooie Flikkers and Lesbian Nation in a demonstration of international solidarity that paved the way for an annual Dutch Gay Pride day.[72]

Anita Bryant's antigay crusade had a more direct and powerful impact on Canada's gays and lesbians. In June and July 1977, LGBT activists in Toronto and Ontario marched in protest of Save Our Children. Many worried that the Dade County defeat portended the ultimate failure of Canadian advocates' ongoing efforts to win civil rights protections through amendments of municipal, provincial, and federal codes. Such fears were amplified by the exclusion of sexual orientation in the recently passed Canadian Human Rights Act. Although the law only pertained to federal employees, it boded ill for the adoption of gay rights protections at the provincial and municipal levels.[73]

---

[70]Joost de Wals, "International Diffusion of Movement Mobilization: Dutch Actions against Anita Bryant and the Birth of Dutch Gay Pride" (MA Thesis, Katholieke Universiteit Nijmegen, 1996): 1–40. A reproduction of the *Miami Herald* ad is found on page 66.
[71]de Wals, "International Diffusion of Movement Mobilization," 47. A reproduction of the *Time* ad is found on page 67.
[72]de Wals, "International Diffusion of Movement Mobilization," 42–57.
[73]Julia Pyryeskina, "'A Remarkably Dense Historical and Political Juncture': Anita Bryant, the Body Politic, and the Canadian Gay and Lesbian Community in January 1978," *Canadian Journal of History* 53:1 (Spring/Summer 2018): 58–68.

IMAGE 4.3 Several noted Dutch figures attending a November 1980 repeat performance of "Miami Nightmare," a benefit concert staged three years earlier to raise funds for protests of Anita Bryant's anti-LGBT campaigns in the United States. From left to right: Singer without Name, Sylvia de Leur, Pia Beck, Manfred Langer, Henk Krol, and Robert Long.

LGBT Canadians therefore reacted quite negatively to the December 1977 announcement that Ken Campbell of Renaissance International had invited Anita Bryant to perform at Toronto's People's Church on January 15, 1978. A fundamentalist Christian, Campbell had protested the "satanic intrusion" of two gay liberation advocates speaking at his daughters' public school by withdrawing his children, enrolling them in a private Christian school, and temporarily refusing to pay the portion of his taxes earmarked for education. He and others registered Renaissance as a nonprofit charity and organized chapters across Canada. By late 1977, they had succeeded in persuading seven provinces to prohibit discussions of same-sex sexuality in public schools. Bryant's Toronto concert was only the first stop on a six-month national Christian Liberation Crusade.[74]

Gay rights advocates across Canada mobilized in protest. The demonstrations took on added urgency because of the Quebec National Assembly's December 16th vote to include sexual orientation in the provincial human rights charter and a police raid on the office of *The Body*

---

[74]Pyryeskina, "'A Remarkably Dense Historical and Political Juncture,'" 68–9.

Politic two weeks later.[75] A newspaper founded in 1971 by Toronto Gay Action and run by a collective, *The Body Politic* had recently published an article called "Men Loving Boys Loving Men." In response, Toronto police seized twelve boxes of *The Body Politic*'s financial records, subscriber lists, manuscripts, and correspondence. They then charged the newspaper's publisher, Pink Triangle Press, and three of the collective's officers with distributing obscene or immoral material through the mail. Determined to protect their hard-won legal gains and greatly alarmed by the intensification of police harassment, LGBT activists recoiled at the possibility of Bryant joining forces with Canadian fundamentalists.[76]

Although Save Our Children collapsed soon after Bryant concluded her Canadian tour, Canadian religious conservatives and LGBT advocates continued to clash. Throughout the early 1980s, police launched crackdowns on gay bathhouses and bars in Toronto, Edmonton, and Montreal. Renaissance International and other fundamentalist Christian organizations won key political victories over progay politicians even in progressive enclaves like Toronto. The publishers of *The Body Politic* endured a six-year legal ordeal and incurred $100,000 in attorneys' fees before prevailing after three different trials, six appeals, and two Supreme Court rulings. By the late 1980s, LGBT activists were winning major victories.[77]

Such progress was almost unfathomable to gays and lesbians living under autocratic regimes. In Iran, the situation was especially dire. Following the creation of the Islamic Republic of Iran in 1979, the regime instituted Sharia law and criminalized homosexuality, transsexuality, and transvestism. LGBT people were subjected to brutal punishments, including public lashings, stonings, and executions.[78] IGA affiliates in several nations protested the Khomeini regime's brutal treatment of its LGBT citizens. IGA member groups also highlighted antigay persecution in the Soviet Union. In Italy, FUORI! organized demonstrations protesting Article 121 of the Russian penal code, the 1960 law criminalizing same-sex sexual activities.[79]

---

[75]The police raid on *The Body Politic* was part of a larger wave of police repression aimed at gays and lesbians. For example, on October 22, 1977, 50 police officers in bulletproof vests and armed with machine guns stormed Truxx, a Montreal gay bar, and charged 146 men with a range of offenses including drug trafficking, gross indecency, and keeping a bawdy house. See Tom Warner, *Never Going Back: A History of Queer Activism in Canada* (Toronto: University of Toronto Press, 2002), 107–8.

[76]"Police Raid Body Politic" and "Quebec Gives Gay Rights," *The Advocate*, February 8, 1978, 10.

[77]Pyryeskina, "'A Remarkably Dense Historical and Political Juncture,'" 76–85. Gay rights activists throughout North America closely watched *The Body Politic* case. See, for example, "Body Politic Acquitted of 'Obscenity,'" *The Advocate*, March 22, 1979, 7.

[78]In early 1979, Enzo Francone, a member of IGA and Italy's Radical Party, was arrested while staging a one-man protest of these executions outside Tehran's central prison. IGA activists in Western Europe and the United States contacted Iranian embassies to protest and authorities released Francone less than two hours later. See News Brief, *The Advocate*, May 17, 1979, 8–9.

[79]FUORI! Working Paper, August 1978, HCA/Ephemera/649, HCA.

LGBT activists had a more complicated relationship with Cuba. Sharing fiercely anti-imperialist views, the radical left and the Gay Liberation Front felt a strong affinity for the Cuban Revolution. In 1969, as the New Left was splintering and opposition to the Vietnam War was soaring, former members of Students for a Democratic Society and officials from the Republic of Cuba created the Venceremos Brigades. As part of the coalition's goal of fostering solidarity and protesting the US government's embargo on Cuba, the Brigades sent American leftists to participate in the island's annual sugar harvest.

The experience proved challenging for gay and lesbian *brigadistas* whose political ideology collided with the homophobia common in the New Left and the Castro regime's hostility toward homosexuals. The Cuban government remained deeply committed to creating a socialist society exemplified by an *Hombre Nuevo* ("New Man") who rejected bourgeois values and who valued the collective good over individual success. The state therefore continued to persecute those whose flamboyant personal appearance, gender nonconformity, sexual behavior, or political dissent did not match these ideals. Cuban authorities used homosexuality as a pretext for purging universities, the arts, and the writers' unions. In April 1971, the Congress on Education and Culture issued an edict declaring "homosexual deviations" to be "socially pathological." "Antisocial" gays and lesbians were barred from having any influence on young people or from representing the Cuban Revolution internationally.[80] When feminist and gay and lesbian *brigadistas* criticized these actions, the National Committee of the Venceremos Brigade instituted a recruitment policy that barred openly gay and lesbian people from participating after January 1972. The exclusionary decision profoundly disillusioned gay and lesbian leftists who had previously viewed Cuba as a socialist utopia and who felt betrayed by their straight comrades.[81]

In the mid-1970s, the Cuban government instituted additional policies targeting public displays of homosexuality. In 1975, the Tribunal Suprema struck down the 1971 resolution calling for gays and lesbians to be fired from jobs in the arts. Some of those who had been purged received financial

---

[80]The celebrated novelist Reinaldo Arenas was the best known victim of Castro's policies on homosexuality and censorship. Arenas repeatedly clashed with state officials and was incarcerated from 1974 to 1976. After he emigrated to the United States in the 1980 Mariel boatlift, he vividly depicted the Cuban homosexual underground, his battles for artistic freedom, and the brutal treatment of gays by Castro's regime in his posthumously published 1993 autobiography, *Before Night Falls*. In 1984, exiled Cubans Néstor Almendros and Orlando Jiménez-Leal released *Improper Conduct*, a documentary featuring firsthand testimonies of gays and lesbian exiles victimized by the Cuban government. See Rafael Ocasio, "Gays and the Cuban Revolution: The Case of Reinaldo Arenas," *Latin American Perspectives* 29:2 (March 2002): 78–89.

[81]Ian Lekus, "Queer Harvests: Homosexuality, the U.S. New Left, and the Venceremos Brigades to Cuba," *Radical History Review* 89 (Spring 2004): 57–91.

compensation from the state. Rather than barring gays and lesbians from specific professions such as education and medicine, the government focused on restricting only those gays and lesbians who openly proclaimed or displayed their sexual orientation. In 1979, a new penal code decriminalized private consensual same-sex sexual activities between adults. However, "public ostentation" of a homosexual "condition" and engaging in homosexual acts witnessed by a third party remained illegal, as did engaging in homosexual sex with a male minor. "Public ostentation" of homosexuality was punishable with a fine or up to six months' incarceration. The new law mirrored the 1938 Social Defense Code used in prerevolutionary Cuba and contained prohibitions similar to those in place in Costa Rica, Mexico, Argentina, Brazil, the Dominican Republic, and Peru.[82] Cuban authorities continued to target effeminate gay men and masculine lesbian women for street sweeps, arrests, and detention.

In 1980, the Castro regime's campaign against "undesirables" escalated greatly during a mass exodus of Cubans fleeing to the United States. In the late 1970s, the Carter administration took several steps to improve US–Cuban relations, drawing the ire of conservatives angered by Cuba's support of Soviet military interventions in Africa and the Middle East. Cold War tensions intensified in early 1980 when opposition to Castro's policies and an economic downturn inspired dozens of desperate Cubans to seek asylum at the Venezuelan and Peruvian embassies in Havana, igniting violent altercations with Cuban police and creating food and water shortages at the diplomatic compounds. By early April, the number of asylum-seekers at the Peruvian embassy exceeded 10,000. To defuse the explosive and embarrassing situation, the Cuban government issued an announcement describing the asylum-seekers as "bums, antisocial elements, delinquents, and trash." On April 16, Cuba signed an agreement with Peru, the United States, and several other nations allowing an airlift of political refugees. Four days later, eager to facilitate the expulsion of "undesirables" like open homosexuals, the mentally ill, and criminals, Castro announced that anyone who wished to leave Cuba would be allowed to do so.[83] He suspended the airlift, opened the port of Mariel, and invited US émigrés to retrieve their relatives and others wishing to leave the island. Within a month, Cuban exiles had launched over 1,000 boat trips that retrieved over 13,000 Cuban refugees. By September 25, the day Castro closed Mariel, almost 125,000 Cubans (called Marielitos) had fled the island, an unknown

---

[82]Ian Lumsden, *Machos, Maricones, and Gays: Cuba and Homosexuality* (Philadelphia: Temple University Press, 1996), 71–82.
[83]For a brilliant analysis of the motives, implementation, and impact of this policy, see Susana Peña, "'Obvious Gays' and the State Gaze: Cuban Gay Visibility and U.S. Immigration Policy during the Mariel Boatlift," *Journal of the History of Sexuality* 16:3 (September 2007): 482–514.

number of whom were gays and lesbians. Castro repeatedly characterized the Marielitos as "scum," counterrevolutionaries, and criminals.[84]

The situation created a major dilemma for the Carter administration. A month before the Mariel boatlift began, Carter had signed the Refugee Act of 1980, a law designed to create uniform and systematic procedures for admitting and resettling refugees. Jettisoning a perceived previous bias toward accepting those fleeing communist governments, the Refugee Act defined a refugee as someone fleeing "persecution on account of race, religion, nationality, membership in a particular social group, or political opinion," a more geographically and ideologically expansive definition that aligned with that of the UN. But because sexual orientation was not among these categories and because US immigration authorities still barred "sexual deviants" from entering the United States, the Carter administration found itself forced to consider abandoning the antigay provisions of US immigration law already drawing heated criticism from LGBT advocates. US officials also faced pressure to revert to past refugee and asylum policies favoring those fleeing communism.[85]

With the world closely monitoring its self-professed commitment to human rights, the Carter administration weighed whether or not to let gay and lesbian Marielitos remain. Throughout the summer of 1980, US authorities vacillated, refusing to grant gay and lesbian Marielitos a waiver of INS policy. The Cranston bill lifting restrictions on gay and lesbian foreigners entering the United States received only lukewarm support from the Carter administration and died in the Senate.[86]

But after officials at the Department of State noted the incongruity of the US gay immigration ban and the Helsinki Accords, the Department of Justice modified INS rules. On September 9, 1980, US officials announced that immigration officials could enforce the antigay provisions of federal law only when foreign homosexuals offered "an unsolicited, unambiguous oral or written admission of homosexuality." These individuals could be brought before an immigration judge who would determine whether or not they must leave the country. Those who denied or refused to admit their homosexuality would be admitted to the United States. One's personal affect, wardrobe, or possession of gay paraphernalia or literature was no longer grounds for exclusion. Ironically, the same visibility and self-identification that put gay and lesbian Marielitos among the ranks of the "undesirables"

---

[84]Julio Capó, Jr. "Queering Mariel: Mediating Cold War Foreign Policy and U.S. Citizenship among Cuba's Homosexual Exile Community, 1978–1980," *Journal of American Ethnic History* 29:4 (Summer 2010): 78–81.

[85]Historically, refugees and asylees from communist nations like Hungary, Vietnam, Cambodia, and the Soviet Union were usually permitted admission to the United States whereas those fleeing authoritarian governments like the Duvalier regime in Haiti were often denied admission. Capó, Jr. "Queering Mariel," 82–92.

[86]Capó, Jr. "Queering Mariel," 92–5.

that Castro allowed to leave Cuba now imperiled their ability to remain in the United States. Yet there is no documented case of any gay or lesbian Marielito being deported. Ultimately, US officials' anticommunist ideology and determination to maintain the moral high ground on global human rights redounded to the gay and lesbian Marielitos' advantage.[87] Don Knutson of Gay Rights Advocates described the decision as "close to a total victory," but language requiring the exclusion of foreign homosexuals on the basis of "sexual deviance" remained enshrined in federal law.[88]

More litigation ensued. In November 1980, Carl Hill, the openly gay photographer for the London-based *Gay News*, returned to the United States to challenge INS policy and was again refused entry. When a federal immigration judge ruled on his behalf, the INS immediately appealed based on Hill's voluntary admission of his sexual orientation.[89] In May 1981, while Hill's case was still pending, a US District Court refused to dismiss a $1 million lawsuit filed by Jaime Chavez, the Mexican dress designer detained at San Francisco International Airport in December 1979. The same month, Hans Koops, an openly gay Dutch man, was issued a vacation visa after US immigration officials initially refused to do so on the basis of his sexual orientation. Two Dutch journalists wearing buttons reading "I'm Homosexual Too" accompanied Koops and were subjected to questioning by INS authorities before being "paroled" into the United States. The Lambda Legal Defense and Education Fund planned to file suit in both cases.[90]

The situation continued escalating. In May 1981, LGBT activists in several US and international cities demonstrated against the INS after the deportation of a gay man who was a dual British-Canadian citizen. In May, Phillip Fotheringham, twenty-three, was questioned by immigration authorities at New York's JFK airport, after they discovered a letter from his male lover in his luggage. After Fotheringham admitted he was gay, INS officials told him he would have to return to London on the next-available flight and placed him in the custody of TWA Airlines agents. Fotheringham claimed the INS authorities called him "sick," refused to return his passport, and denied him access to legal counsel. Upon returning to England, he immediately sued the INS and TWA for civil rights violations.[91] In June 1981, Congressmen Julian C. Dixon and Anthony C. Beilenson renewed efforts to repeal the antigay provisions of immigration law.[92]

---

[87]Donnel Nunes, "Rules on Immigration by Homosexuals Eased," *Washington Post*, September 10, 1980; Capó, Jr. "Queering Mariel," 95–8; Peña, "'Obvious Gays' and the State Gaze."
[88]"White House Waffles on Gay Immigration," *The Advocate*, July 10, 1980, 8; "Immigration Softens Its Antigay Policy," *The Advocate*, October 16, 1980, 9.
[89]"Foreign Gay Wins the First Round," *Washington Blade*, November 21, 1980, A–7.
[90]"Gay Side Wins One in Battle with INS," and "After the INS Delay, Dutch Man Allowed into U.S.," *The Advocate*, May 14, 1981, 8.
[91]"INS Deports Gay Man, Sparks Demonstrations," *The Advocate*, July 9, 1981, 10.
[92]"Bill to OK Gay Aliens Introduced in House," *The Advocate*, June 25, 1981, 9.

Propelled to victory in November 1980 by a coalition of social and fiscal conservatives, the Reagan administration had little sympathy for those challenging US immigration law. In August 1981, the INS Board of Appeals ruled against Carl Hill and upheld the agency's right to exclude foreign aliens "afflicted with psychopathic personality."[93] Gay Rights Advocates immediately brought Hill's case to the San Francisco US District Court. San Francisco's Gay/Lesbian Freedom Day Parade Committee also filed a challenge to the INS ban, arguing that denying American gays and lesbians the right to associate freely with foreigners was a violation of the First Amendment.[94] In September, LGBT activists on three continents simultaneously demonstrated against the INS. In Amsterdam, 100 people picketed the US consulate. In Berlin, Dublin, London, Oslo, Ottawa, Stockholm, Toronto, Wellington, and Sydney, advocates delivered letters of protest to US embassy officials. In Washington, DC, about 150 people gathered for a candlelight vigil outside the White House while similar demonstrations were held in Atlanta, Los Angeles, New York, San Diego, San Francisco, Philadelphia, and Tampa.[95] Shortly thereafter, a conservative group called Public Advocate issued a mass mailing warning that H.R. 3524, the bill seeking to repeal the antigay provisions of US immigration laws, would allow "alien homosexuals to flood America."[96]

While challenging US immigration laws, transnational LGBT activists were also seizing the power of supranational forums and international accords in confronting antigay repression.[97] Cognizant that eighteen of the Council of Europe's twenty states were legally bound by the terms of the European Convention on Human Rights adopted in 1953, advocates began closely monitoring claims of antigay discrimination filed with the European Commission of Human Rights (ECHR) and the European Court of Human Rights (ECtHR), the confidential and public forums set up to enforce the Convention. Should either body rule that "gay rights are human rights," activists recognized there would be tremendous implications across Europe.[98] In Great Britain, the Campaign for Homosexual Equality lobbied the government to support the addition of a gay rights clause to the 1975 Helsinki Accords and to advocate the decriminalization of homosexuality in Cyprus in proceedings of the European Parliament.[99]

---

[93]"INS Board Upholds Ban on Gay Aliens," *The Advocate*, August 20, 1981, 8.

[94]"The Immigration Mess," *The Advocate*, October 1, 1981, 17–18.

[95]"Immigration Protests Staged All over World," *The Advocate*, November 12, 1981, 8.

[96]"New Right Attack on Immigration Bill," *The Advocate*, December 24, 1981, 10.

[97]On the strategy of using supranational cooperation, see Campaign for Homosexual Equality, Proposals for Co-Ordinated Political Action Offered for Consideration by the International Committee Meeting, August 1978, HCA/Ephemera/649, HCA.

[98]"Gay Rights are Human Rights," July 9, 1978, HCA/Ephemera/649, HCA.

[99]Campaign for Homosexual Equality, Annual Report, 1980, HCA/CHE—Campaign for Homosexual Equality Collection, Series 1-Annual Reports, HCA.

In 1981, international LGBT activists scored a major victory when the European Court of Human Rights (ECtHR) ruled in favor of gay rights for the first time. In *Dudgeon v. the United Kingdom,* the court held that Section 11 of the Criminal Law Amendment Act (1885) that had criminalized male (but not female) homosexual acts in England, Wales, and Northern Ireland violated the European Convention on Human Rights. The plaintiff was Jeff Dudgeon, a shipping clerk in Belfast who also led the Northern Ireland Gay Rights Association (NIGRA). In 1976, after he and twenty other gay men were rounded up by police and questioned for hours about their private sexual activities, four of the men signed statements attesting to illegal homosexual acts. Dudgeon, however, refused and appealed his case to the European Commission of Human Rights in Strasbourg. When the commission ruled in his favor, Northern Ireland faced a choice between decriminalizing male homosexual activities or being expelled from the Council of Europe. *Dudgeon v. the United Kingdom* led to legislation decriminalizing male homosexual sex in Northern Ireland, thus aligning its legal code with the rest of the UK.[100] The case served as a precedent for similar ECtHR rulings in *Norris v. Ireland* (1988) and *Modinos v. Cyprus* (1993). US Supreme Court justice Anthony Kennedy also cited *Dudgeon* in his majority opinion in *Lawrence v. Texas* (2003), the landmark ruling that struck down sodomy laws in fourteen states and made same-sex sexual activities legal in all US states and territories.[101] In the wake of the *Dudgeon* ruling, LGBT advocates made litigation a critical element of their strategies for advancing gay rights worldwide.

LGBT advocates had cause for optimism. In 1981, Norway became the first country in the world to outlaw discrimination on the basis of sexual orientation and Colombia decriminalized homosexuality. The following year, France equalized the age of consent for heterosexual and homosexual sex, setting both at fifteen.[102] The Italian Department of Justice began allowing transsexuals to list their new gender on state documents, a step toward mitigating housing and employment discrimination based on perceived or actual gender identity.[103] Northern Ireland and New South Wales—following the precedents set by South Australia in 1975 and the Australian Capital Territory in 1976—legalized homosexuality. Quebec

---

[100]Scotland decriminalized consensual male homosexual sex in 1980. "A Gay Activist in Ireland," *The Advocate*, December 25, 1980, 16, 23.
[101]For an overview of key ECtHR rulings on LGBT issues, see European Court of Human Rights, Factsheet—Sexual Orientation Issues, https://www.echr.coe.int/Documents/FS_Sexual_orientation_ENG.pdf; Michael D. Goldhaber, *A People's History of the European Court of Human Rights* (New Brunswick, NJ: Rutgers University Press, 2009), 37–41. For an assessment of the legal ramifications of *Dudgeon v. United Kingdom*, see Angioletta Sperti, *Constitutional Courts, Gay Rights, and Sexual Orientation Equality* (London: Hart Publishing, 2017), 19–23.
[102]"French Activists Win Fight for Consent," *The Advocate*, September 30, 1982, 10.
[103]"Major Gain for Italian Transsexuals," *The Advocate*, May 13, 1982, 9.

granted same-sex couples domestic partnership rights. In Indonesia, three gay men founded Lambda International, the nation's first gay organization. They planned to engage in public education aimed at generating support for gay rights legislation. They hoped to forge coalitions with the *waria*, Indonesia's gender nonconforming community, who had been mobilizing since the late 1960s. In 1982, repealing sodomy laws imposed by the Salazar dictatorship, Portugal legalized consensual sexual activities between males aged sixteen or over.[104]

Throughout much of 1982, Carl Hill and the San Francisco Lesbian/Gay Freedom Day committee continued their three-year battle with the INS. On April 22, US District Court Judge Robert Aguilar handed Hill a major victory when he ruled that the INS could not bar gay foreign aliens without enforcing agency guidelines that mandated a psychological examination to verify the alien's homosexuality. The US Public Health Service had refused to conduct such exams since 1979. Unless the Department of Health and Human Services ordered the reinstatement of psychological evaluations of aliens suspected of homosexuality, INS could not legally enforce the exclusion of foreign gays.[105] On July 16th, Aguilar made permanent a temporary injunction that allowed foreign gays and lesbians to attend the San Francisco Gay Freedom Day Parade.[106] Gay rights advocates' euphoria about the decisions was cut short when the INS filed an appeal of the Hill ruling in the 9th Circuit.[107]

However disappointing these legal setbacks, LGBT activists in the United States still possessed far greater civil liberties than their counterparts in much of the developing world. In order to expand its global reach, IGA directed member groups to solicit information from activists in nations where organizing was not possible or not yet occurring and then report to IGA on their behalf. In 1982, Brazil's Grupo Somos presented a rather bleak assessment of LGBT life in Argentina. Although neither homosexual nor heterosexual consensual relations between adults over twenty-one were illegal, sex with individuals younger than twenty-one could be punished with three to eight years' imprisonment. Irrespective of the state of the law, homosexuality was widely condemned by Argentinian society and police routinely harassed and arrested gay men for offenses like crossdressing, vagrancy, and solicitation. These men had little legal recourse and were often forced to sign "confessions" kept in a public registry. Inclusion on

---

[104]Myers, *Historical Dictionary of the Lesbian and Gay Liberation, Movements,* 24–53; "Norway Gets Tough Progay Legislation," *The Advocate,* June 25, 1981, 9; "Gay Liberation Hits Indonesia," *The Advocate,* June 24, 1982, 8–9; "Gay Sex Legalized in Northern Ireland," *The Advocate,* December 23, 1982, 11; Linda Rapp, "Portugal," GLBTQ Archive, http://www.glbtqarchive.com/ssh/portugal_S.pdf.

[105]"Gays Win Major Victory in Immigration Battle," *The Advocate,* May 27, 1982, 9.

[106]"S.F. Judge Lifts Antigay Ban for All U.S. Borders," *The Advocate,* July 30, 1982, 9.

[107]"INS Appeals Progay Decision on Hill," *The Advocate,* August 5, 1982, 13.

the list often resulted in job loss. Gay men were also routinely blackmailed, physically assaulted, robbed, or murdered. "In this terrible climate there is no sign of improvement ..., " Grupo Somos concluded, "the primary goal of the police is to inspire terror ... every day more and more people ... choose exile."[108] The Austrian LGBT group HOSI described the perilous landscape for LGBT Colombians. Although noncoercive homosexual and heterosexual sexual relations between individuals aged fourteen or over were legal, authorities fined or dismissed teachers, civil servants, or judges who engaged in homosexual conduct.[109]

By the early 1970s, a new transnational LGBT rights movement was highlighting the persecution faced by many LGBT people around the world. Inspired by the counterculture and the protest movements of the era, this wave of international LGBT advocacy was more militant and more visible than its predecessors. While pushing for nondiscrimination protections at the local and national level, activists formed new global networks and organizations. They invoked human rights conventions and appealed to supranational bodies like the UN and the European Court of Human Rights. Advocates in democratic societies helped those living under autocratic regimes to publicize severe anti-LGBT repression. Already confronting an emerging coalition of religious conservatives who opposed homosexuality on moral grounds, transnational activists soon faced a terrifying new disease and the sudden end of the Cold War.

---

[108]*IGA Bulletin*, 82/4, December 12, 1982, 10.
[109]*IGA Bulletin*, 82/4, December 12, 1982, 11.

CHAPTER FIVE

Rage and Hope, 1981–2000

In the early 1980s, the onset of the Acquired Immune Deficiency Syndrome (AIDS) pandemic added terrifying urgency to the international LGBT rights movement. Enraged by state inaction and prejudice in the face of AIDS, activists pioneered confrontational tactics and rhetoric that expanded and reshaped transnational advocacy efforts. A decade later, the Cold War's sudden end brought new hopes and fears for the future of LGBT rights. Advocates seized opportunities for positive changes in formerly communist nations. Building upon victories in multinational forums in Europe, activists worked to elevate their status within the United Nations (UN) and to gain the support of NGOs working in the larger human rights movement. But LGBT people still faced brutal treatment by autocratic and fundamentalist governments and battled increasing resistance from political and religious conservatives in several democratic societies.

In the early 1980s, transnational LGBT advocates began mobilizing to draw attention to "a frightening epidemic of global proportions," AIDS. In mid-1983, Carlene Cheatam and Clint Hockenberry urged their international colleagues to support a national AIDS vigil being held in Washington, DC, on October 8:

> AIDS knows no national boundaries. As reported in Wien (Vienna), Sweden has 53 reported cases with three deaths; Germany has 35 cases with 5 deaths; France has 18 cases with 5 deaths; The Netherlands has 11 cases with 3 deaths; Brazil has 6 cases with 3 deaths; Austria has 14 cases with 2 deaths; and England has 21 cases with 5 deaths. In the United States alone, 2,090 have been diagnosed with AIDS with over 800 dead.

Recognizing that most foreign activists would not be able to travel to the United States, Cheatam and Hockenberry called for simultaneous candlelight marches in cities around the world.[1]

With the AIDS epidemic descending, International Gay Association (IGA) continued to combat global persecution and discrimination of gays and lesbians. In July 1984, over seventy delegates from eighteen countries gathered in Helsinki, Finland. They wrote letters condemning police raids and violence directed at the Mexican LGBT community. They protested the incarceration of the publisher of a Greek gay newspaper and the dismissal of a lesbian teacher in Australia. They reviewed ongoing campaigns to convince the UN and Amnesty International (AI) to defend gays and lesbians. They strategized about how to help LGBT activists in Latin America and Asia and welcomed their first member organizations from Africa and the Soviet Union. Because they defined the gay liberation movement as part of a larger struggle for human rights, IGA delegates officially opposed apartheid in South Africa.[2] The editorial team of the IGA *Pink Book* prepared to release an extensive report on LGBT rights worldwide.[3]

On September 30, 1984, more than 1,000 activists from North America, Latin America, and Europe converged on New York City to participate in the International March on the United Nations for Gay and Lesbian Freedom. The demonstration was endorsed by more than 100 LGBT international groups including the National Gay Task Force (United States), the Irish Gay Rights Movement (Republic of Ireland), Gay Freedom Movement of Jamaica (West Indies), and Grupo de Accion Gay (Argentina). Robert Pistor of the IGA Secretariat read letters from Soviet and Czech activists fighting for LGBT rights behind the Iron Curtain. On the eve of the opening ceremonies of the UN General Assembly, protestors marched from the Stonewall Inn to the UN Headquarters and demanded an end to medical, economic, political, and religious discrimination against gays and lesbians.[4]

On December 10, 1984, on United Nations International Human Rights Day, IGA members around the world held press conferences to mark the release of the organization's first *Pink Book*. Made possible by a grant from

---

[1]*IGA Bulletin*, 83/6, undated, 6–7. For an exhaustive, if flawed, contemporary account of the international dimensions of the early AIDS epidemic, see Randy Shilts, *And the Band Played On: Politics, People, and AIDS* (New York: St. Martin's Press, 1987). For a more recent, academic perspective, see Jacques Pepin, *The Origins of AIDS* (New York: Cambridge University Press, 2011).

[2]Press Release, 6th Annual Conference of the International Association of Lesbian/Gay Women and Gay Men, July 9–15, 1984, Helsinki, Finland, reprinted in *IGA Bulletin* 84/4, 1, Sub-File IGA 1984 Bulletin, Box—ILGA Bulletin 1978–1989, IHLIA.

[3]"Pink Book Editing Team Meets," *IGA Bulletin*, 84/4, 6, Sub-File IGA 1984 Bulletin, Box—ILGA Bulletin, 1978–1989, IHLIA.

[4]International March and Conference for Lesbian and Gay Freedom, *IGA Bulletin*, 84/4, 7–10, Sub-File IGA 1984 Bulletin, Box—ILGA Bulletin, 1978–1989, IHLIA; Gary Kinsman, "March on the United Nations," *Rites for Lesbian and Gay Liberation* (Toronto) 1:6 (November 1984).

the Dutch government and the volunteer labor of an IGA team, the *Pink Book* featured essays, maps, and a country-by-country survey detailing the status of LGBT people in individual nations all over the globe.[5]

But greater visibility of the international LGBT rights movement also illuminated many of its internal challenges. On June 30, 1985, over 500 IGA delegates and observers from eighteen nations convened in Toronto for the 7th annual IGA conference. A heated debate arose about whether IGA should broaden its focus to encompass other pressing human rights issues including racism and US interventions in Central America. Rather than commit to a wider core mission, the delegates issued a series of statements supporting "3rd world liberation movements which defend lesbian and gay rights" and condemning specific instances of antigay oppression, including "discriminatory immigration laws existing in many nations throughout the world" and "the video surveillance and entrapment of hundreds of men for consensual homosexual acts in Canadian washrooms." Continuing its efforts to widen its geographic reach, IGA voted to base its Action Secretariat in Montreal, the first IGA office not located in Europe. IGA encouraged established member groups to consider "twinning" with under-resourced groups in developing nations and then providing financial support, publications, and guidance on strategy. Delegations from Japan and Peru were in attendance for the first time and announced plans for new regional IGA conferences in Asia and Latin America. IGA strengthened its communications network by establishing information pools for Asia and for gays and lesbians serving in the military in addition to those for Latin America, Christian Churches, Leather and SM, and Eastern Europe.[6]

IGA simultaneously confronted the growing impact of the AIDS epidemic. It began devoting several pages of the quarterly *IGA Bulletin* to member groups' AIDS-related protests and news.[7] The 1985 annual conference formally denounced the Brazilian newspaper *A Tarde* for calling "the extermination of lesbians and gays as a remedy for AIDS" and condemned those who threatened to impose "compulsory registration or quarantine measures aimed at lesbians and gay men because of the AIDS-related virus."[8] "AIDS hysteria and increasing intolerance" were a major focus of IGA's 1986 annual conference.[9]

---

[5]*IGA Pink Book 1985: A Global View of Lesbian and Gay Oppression and Liberation* (Amsterdam: COC-Magazijn, 1985).

[6]Seventh World Lesbian and Gay Conference Ends in Canada, July 6, 1985, and IGA Conference Statement, *IGA Bulletin*, 4/85, 3–4, all in Sub-File IGA 1985 Bulletin, Box—ILGA Bulletin 1978–1989, IHLIA.

[7]See, for example, *IGA Bulletin* 1/85, 27–31, *IGA Bulletin*, 2/85, 28–30, and *IGA Bulletin*, 4/85, 22–6, all in Sub-File IGA 1985 Bulletin, Box—ILGA Bulletin 1978–1989, IHLIA.

[8]IGA Conference Statement, *IGA Bulletin*, 4/85, 4, Sub-File IGA 1985 Bulletin, Box—ILGA Bulletin 1978–1989, IHLIA.

[9]*IGA Bulletin*, 86/3, 1, Sub-File IGA 1986 IGA Bulletin, Box—ILGA Bulletin 1978–1989, IHLIA.

AIDS and the antigay vitriol it triggered intensified LGBT advocates' determination to push for equality. In 1984, following the collapse of a right-wing dictatorship that "disappeared" over 30,000 people during the "Dirty War," Argentinian gays and lesbian formed the Communidad Homosexual Argentina. The following year, French activists scored a major victory when the national government outlawed housing and employment discrimination based on sexual orientation. Belgium equalized the age of consent for heterosexual and homosexual sexual relations. In 1986, New Zealand passed the Homosexual Law Reform Act, legalizing consensual sex between men over age sixteen. Haiti decriminalized homosexuality. After years of lobbying by a coalition of socialists, radical leftists, and Landsforeningen for Bøsser og Lesbiske (the National Union of Gays and Lesbians, formerly Forbundet af 1948/F-48), the Danish Parliament voted 78–62 to grant same-sex couples the break on inheritance taxes extended to straight couples. But in the United States, the Supreme Court handed LGBT rights supporters a crushing defeat in *Bowers v. Hardwick* (1986), voting 5–4 to uphold the constitutionality of a Georgia law that criminalized oral and anal sex. Homosexuality was not decriminalized nationwide for another seventeen years.[10]

Concurrently, IGA addressed internal challenges while continuing to push the international community to engage LGBT issues. At its 1986 annual conference in Copenhagen, in an effort to acknowledge the critical importance of women in its ranks, IGA officially changed its name to the International Lesbian and Gay Association (ILGA) and reestablished a Women's Secretariat. ILGA also created a team charged with securing observer status for the organization at the UN and the Council of Europe (CoE). To protest the recent *Bowers v. Hardwick* decision, delegates picketed outside the US Embassy. Despite perpetual worries about the state of ILGA's finances, the organization committed to issuing a second edition of the *Pink Book*, this time relying on research assistance from the Gay Studies Department at the University of Utrecht. ILGA also launched a major effort to persuade the World Health Organization (WHO) to remove homosexuality from the *International Classification of Diseases* (ICD).[11]

While ILGA lobbied supranational organizations, other activists focused on national governments. In 1987, enraged by continued political indifference to those with HIV/AIDS, US protestors launched the AIDS Coalition to Unleash Power (ACT-UP), a direct action group that used provocative art, confrontational demonstrations, and scientific knowledge to generate awareness, improve medical treatment, and trigger policy

---

[10]Joanne Myers, *Historical Dictionary of the Lesbian and Gay Movements* (Latham, MD: Scarecrow Press, 2013), 24–53; Ernest Gill, "Danish Gay Couples Given Inheritance Tax Break," *The Advocate*, July 8, 1986, 15.

[11]Press Release, *IGA Bulletin* 86/4, 25, Sub-File IGA 1986 IGA Bulletin, Box—ILGA Bulletin 1978–1989, IHLIA.

change. ACT-UP chapters soon arose in many US and foreign cities.[12] In 1987, the Reagan administration's decision to add HIV and AIDS to the list of "dangerous and contagious diseases" that barred foreign citizens from entry to the United States infuriated HIV/AIDS activists. Four years later, organizers of the annual International AIDS Conference opted not to hold the meeting in Boston as a direct result of the policy. Despite condemnation by public health experts and scientists, the HIV exclusion remained in effect until 2010.[13]

While confronting the AIDS epidemic, activists in the UK also battled a Conservative government pursuing a harshly antigay agenda. The Tories were alarmed by the increasing visibility and impact of the British LGBT movement as evidenced in the 1985 election of openly lesbian Margaret Roff as mayor of Manchester and a successful alliance of the National Union of Mineworkers and Lesbians and Gays Support the Miners. Eager to capitalize on national survey showing that 75 percent of the population believed that homosexuality was "always or mostly wrong" on the eve of the 1987 general elections, Prime Minister Margaret Thatcher warned, "Children who need to be taught to respect traditional moral values are being taught that they have an inalienable right to be gay. All of these children are being cheated of sound start in life. Yes, cheated." Conservatives distributed pamphlets accusing the Labour Party of attempting to indoctrinate schoolchildren through progay books like *The Milkman's on His Way*. After the Tories won reelection, Conservative MP David Wilshire put forward Section 28, an amendment to the Local Government Act that prohibited local governments and schools in England and Wales from "promoting" homosexuality. The law's introduction and quick passage sparked vigorous protests. Renowned actor Ian McKellen came out as gay and joined 20,000 marchers protesting Section 28 in Manchester.

On April 30, 1988, 30,000 people, including delegations from Italy, Holland, Germany, Belgium, and Scandinavia, marched in London. Demonstrations against Section 28 were also held in Amsterdam, Rome, Sydney, Paris, Hamburg, Cologne, Milan, New York, San Francisco, Chicago, New Orleans, Washington, and Houston. On May 23, a group of lesbians stormed the set of the BBC's *Six O'Clock News*. But the protests failed to derail the law and Scotland soon passed nearly identical legislation. Under Section 28, many schools and councils closed LGBT youth support groups. In August 1988, the British government destroyed thousands of copies of its own health education booklet, *Teaching about HIV and AIDS*, and replaced them with a less explicit, more "moral" version that omitted any mention

---

[12]For a first-rate account of the inner workings and impact of ACT-UP, see David France, *How to Survive a Plague: The Inside Story of How Citizens and Science Tamed AIDS* (New York: Knopf, 2016).

[13]Stein, *Rethinking the Gay and Lesbian Movement*, 173.

of lesbian and gay organizations. Scotland did not repeal Section 28 until June 2000 and it remained law in England and Wales until November 2003. Six years later, Conservative leader David Cameron apologized for formerly supporting Section 28, calling it a "mistake" that was "offensive to gay people."[14]

Although ILGA's second *Pink Book* revealed that "only 5 percent of the planet's nations have legislation protecting lesbian and gay rights," the hostile political climate of the late 1980s did not preclude LGBT advocates from scoring significant victories in some nations.[15] In 1988, the Swedish government granted same-sex couples equal taxation and inheritance rights. Belize and Israel decriminalized homosexuality.[16] The same year, the European Court of Human Rights (ECtHR) ruled that Ireland's 1861 sodomy law and the Criminal Law Amendment Act of 1988 violated David Norris's rights to privacy and family life as articulated in Article 8 of the European Convention on Human Rights. A founder of Ireland's Campaign for Homosexual Law Reform, Norris and his attorney Mary Robinson took his case to the ECtHR after Norris lost an appeal before the Irish Supreme Court in 1983. In 1987, Norris became the first openly gay man elected to public office in Ireland and Robinson became the nation's first female president in 1990. In 1993, responding belatedly to the *Norris v. Ireland* ruling, Ireland decriminalized homosexuality.[17] In 1989, Denmark became the first country in the world to legalize civil unions for same-sex couples. The law granted pension, inheritance, property, and divorce rights but withheld the right to adopt children.[18] In 1990, after six years of lobbying by gay and lesbian activists and clever legislative maneuvering by openly gay Congressman Barney Frank, Congress repealed "psychopathic

---

[14]Peter Cummings, "Homophobic Legislation Threatens British Gays," *The Advocate*, January 19, 1988, 13, 17; Peter Cummings, "British Gays Step Up Protests of Antigay Bill," *The Advocate*, March 15, 1988, 14, 16–17; Peter Cummings, "A Lesbian Takeover at the BBC," *The Advocate*, July 5, 1988, 29; Peter Cummings, "U.K. Gays Take to the Streets," *The Advocate*, June 7, 1988, 33; Peter Cummings, "U.K. Destroys AIDS Leaflets," *The Advocate*, August 2, 1988, 30; "What Was Section 28? The History of the Homophobic Legislation 30 Years On," *Pink News*, May 24, 2018, https://www.pinknews.co.uk/2018/05/24/what-was-section-28-homophobic-legislation-30-years-thatcher/.

[15]10th Annual World Conference Statement, *IGA Bulletin* 88/4, 3–4, Sub-File IGA 1988 IGA Bulletin, Box—ILGA Bulletin 1978–1989, IHLIA. See also *The Second ILGA Pink Book: A Global View of Lesbian and Gay Liberation and Oppression* (Utrecht: Interfacultaire Werkgroup Homostudies Utrecht, 1988).

[16]Peter Cummings, "Israeli Knesset Reforms Sex Laws," *The Advocate*, June 7, 1988, 33; Myers, *Historical Dictionary of the Lesbian and Gay Liberation Movements*, 24–53.

[17]Peter Cummings, "Ireland's Sodomy Law Violates Rights, European Court Says," *The Advocate*, December 5, 1988, 23; Irish Legal Heritage: *Norris v. Ireland*, https://www.irishlegal.com/article/irish-legal-heritage-norris-v-ireland.

[18]Peter Freiberg, "Danish Measure Will Sanction Gay Weddings," *The Advocate*, July 4, 1989, 16.

personality" and "sexual deviancy" as grounds for barring foreign aliens from entering the United States.[19]

There were also signs of change behind the Iron Curtain. Under General Secretary Mikhail Gorbachev's *glasnost* policy, some restrictions on freedom of the press and freedom of expression were lifted in the Soviet Union. Although communist governments required all organizations to be registered with the state, Hungary authorized the creation of Homeros-Lambda, the country's first-ever gay group, and did not bar it from holding a national congress in May 1988.[20] In June 1988, audiences watching *Good Evening, Moscow* saw the first-ever televised appearance of Soviet gays, who reported that the national Communist Party was considering the legalization of consensual sex between men. Homosexuality was already legal in Albania, Bulgaria, Czechoslovakia, East Germany, Hungary, and Poland.[21] But ILGA's Eastern European Gay Information pool reported that the Nicolae Ceauşescu regime was arresting, torturing, and castrating gay men in Romania.[22]

The collapse of communism and the sudden end of the Cold War created new challenges for gays and lesbians in the Soviet Union and Eastern Europe. In February 1990, Eugenia Debryanskaya, Roman Kalinin, and eight others formed the Moscow Organization of Sexual Minorities, later renamed Moscow Gay and Lesbian Union. They began publishing a newspaper called *Tema*, Russian for "theme" and slang for homosexuality. Between 10,000 and 15,000 copies of each issue were printed and passed on from person to person. The volunteer staff answered about 250 readers' letters per week. Some readers described instances of vicious antigay police violence. The group's major aim was to secure the repeal of Article 121, the law under which men engaging in consensual homosexual activity could be imprisoned for up to five years, and to aid those incarcerated because of their sexual orientation. Although lesbianism was not criminalized, lesbians were routinely subjected to involuntary committal in psychiatric facilities. In addition to changing laws, the group aimed to change popular attitudes.[23]

These realities inspired Julie Dorf to found the International Gay and Lesbian Human Rights Commission (IGLHRC) in 1990. Born in Wisconsin and raised in a Republican-leaning Jewish family, Dorf majored in Soviet Studies at Wesleyan University and became involved in the Latin American

---

[19]Stein, *Rethinking the Gay and Lesbian Movement*, 173.
[20]In Brief, *The Advocate*, July 5, 1988, 29.
[21]Peter Cummings, "Soviets Consider Dropping Antigay Law," *The Advocate*, August 2, 1988, 30.
[22]In Brief, *The Advocate*, June 7, 1988, 33.
[23]Masha Gessen, "Moscow Activists Push for Gay Glasnost," *The Advocate*, December 18, 1990, 50–1.

solidarity and anti-apartheid movements of the 1980s. In 1984, she traveled to the Soviet Union and met several gay and lesbian people. As a bisexual and human rights activist, she was deeply troubled by stories of gay men incarcerated for violating Article 121. She returned to the United States with a richer understanding of the uses of antigay sentiment as a tool for quashing political dissent. After graduating from college and moving to San Francisco, Dorf was inspired by the radicalism of ACT-UP and began working to generate awareness of global gay and lesbian issues. With expenses of international advocacy mounting, Dorf registered IGLHRC as a 501(c) nonprofit organization in order to bolster fundraising. She opened a small office in the Castro District and hired a program director. IGLHRC set to work on lobbying AI to broaden its Mandate and forging ties with activists in Latin America and Eastern Europe.[24]

Advocates in nations newly emerging from communist rule were eager to make foreign connections. In July 1990, thirty Eastern European delegates attended the annual ILGA conference convened in Stockholm. Many had never before visited a Western country. Several expressed frustrations at resurgent ethnic tensions, economic struggles, and right-wing political rhetoric arising in many of their countries. Ryszard Kisiel, the editor of the Polish gay magazine *Filo*, reported that Lech Walesa, the leader of the Solidarity movement, publicly pledged that he would "eliminate homosexuals" if he won election as Poland's president. Kisiel called upon Western European and American attendees to lobby Walesa to moderate his views. East German attendees worried that the looming reunification of East and West Germany could result in the adoption of an increase in age of consent for same-sex sexual relations. Where the German Democratic Republic (GDR) had repealed Paragraph 175 and set the same age of consent for heterosexual and homosexual sex, the Federal Republic of Germany (FRG) set the age of consent for homosexual sex at eighteen, four years higher than for heterosexual sex. Nor had the FRG repealed Paragraph 175, though it was rarely enforced. Nonetheless, ILGA dissolved its Eastern European Information Pool, recognizing that Eastern European activists no longer needed outside assistance and could now work for change within their own nations.[25]

The 1990 annual ILGA meeting also revealed delegates' concerns about the large number of US activists in attendance. European groups, long the driving force behind ILGA, worried that the United States would attempt to control ILGA instead of cooperating. Striking a conciliatory tone, Paula Ettelbrick, of New York City-based Lambda Legal Defense and Education Fund, praised the Scandinavian advocates who shared

[24]Thoreson, *Transnational LGBT Activism*, 29–32.
[25]Chris Bull, "Antigay Fallout from Eastern European Revolutions Dominates ILGA Conference," *The Advocate*, August 14, 1990, 8–11.

expertise on domestic partnership laws.[26] Indeed, in years to come, Northern European countries would join forces with Latin American countries in pushing the international community to embrace gay and lesbian rights far earlier and far more consistently than the United States did.

Despite these differences, ILGA delegations continued joining forces on behalf of gays and lesbians facing serious repression. Throughout 1990, ILGA affiliates attempted to confirm and protested reports that the Iranian government had executed several gays and lesbians.[27] On May 17, 1990, following an ILGA lobbying campaign, the WHO endorsed the removal of homosexuality from the tenth edition of ICD, a coding system for a wide variety of signs, symptoms, and causes of diseases and injuries. In declaring that homosexuality should no longer be considered a mental illness, the WHO aligned itself with major professional organizations like the American Psychiatric Association and the US Public Health Service.[28] On August 10, groups around the world demonstrated at Argentinian embassies to spotlight the nation's antigay persecution. Although conditions had improved since the nation's military dictatorship ended in 1983, leaders from Communidad Homosexual Argentina (CHA) claimed police arrested and detained gays with no cause, sometimes forcing them to sign confessions for crimes like drug possession or prostitution prior to releasing them. Under the terms of an ordinance in Buenos Aires, gays were barred from voting or holding public office.[29] A year later, CHA scored its first major victory and got the law overturned. The group was also appealing to the Argentine Supreme Court for formal recognition as an organization under the national civil code. Without such authorization, CHA could not conduct business, accept donations, or hold property. CHA argued that the prohibitions violated its members' constitutional rights and freedom of expression.[30]

ILGA members also coordinated efforts at the UN. Determined to secure the ability to circulate position papers and to influence key decision-making entities, the ILGA applied for consultancy status at the United Nations Economic and Social Council (ECOSOC), the body which oversees the UN's human rights work. On January 31, 1991, ILGA members were bitterly disappointed when the ECOSOC tabled the organization's application, thus prohibiting its reconsideration until 1993. The vote followed an intense

---

[26]"Big U.S. Role Worries Some, Delights Others," *The Advocate*, August 14, 1990, 10.

[27]Chris Bull, "The Iranian Case," *The Advocate*, September 25, 1990, 13.

[28]Today in History: WHO Removed Homosexuality from Its List of Mental Illnesses, *Roodeport Record*, May 17, 2018, https://roodepoortrecord.co.za/2018/05/17/today-in-history-who-removed-homosexuality-from-its-list-of-mental-illnesses-web/.

[29]Chris Bull, "Embassy Protests Focus on Argentinian Claims of Repression," *The Advocate*, September 11, 1990, 10.

[30]Robert Julian, "Argentina's Gays and Lesbians Are Locked Out of the System," *The Advocate*, June 18, 1991, 44–7.

debate that reflected extremely polarized views of homosexuality among the nineteen nations represented on the ECOSOC. After Libya's representative declared gays and lesbians "contrary to the law of life," several delegates from Arab nations pushed for the outright rejection of ILGA's application. Although several ECOSOC supported ILGA's bid, UN rules required a unanimous vote and delegations from Oman, Libya, and the Philippines voted in opposition.[31]

Five months after the setback, ILGA delegates gathered in Acapulco, Mexico, for their 13th annual conference. *The Advocate*, the longest continuously running gay and lesbian publication in the United States, marked the occasion with a special issue devoted to "the new international activism." Although the characterization of transnational gay and lesbian advocacy as "new" was inaccurate, the magazine offered compelling profiles of activists in Mexico, Eastern Europe, Argentina, and the Soviet Union fighting employment discrimination, inadequate resources and hostility for people with AIDS, antigay violence, and police harassment. Five editors of gay and lesbian publications based in London, Melbourne, Oslo, Berlin, and San José, Costa Rica provided their perspectives on the state of the gay rights movement.[32] The leaders of Australia's Gay and Lesbian Immigration Task Force described their successful six-year campaign to persuade their government to grant immigration rights to same-sex couples in 1991.[33]

The location of the ILGA conference was significant for several reasons. It was the first time the annual meeting was held in Latin America, a symbol of the international gay and lesbian movement's expanding reach. But the conference was originally scheduled to take place in Guadalajara, traditionally one of Mexico's most conservative cities and a stronghold for Christian fundamentalists. The announcement of the ILGA conference triggered a popular furor and antigay graffiti appeared around the city. Already receiving death threats, ILGA organizers canceled the conference after the mayor threatened to impose fines on any hotel or restaurant that served attendees and also refused to offer police protection. News of the cancellation prompted protests in front of Mexican consulates in Washington, DC, San Francisco, and Amsterdam.[34] Mexican officials intervened to get the ILGA conference rescheduled in Acapulco.[35] Writing

---

[31]Chris Bull, "Religious Opposition Derails Gay Group's U.N. Consultancy Bid," *The Advocate*, March 12, 1991, 23.

[32]"Global Warning: The New International Activism," *The Advocate*, June 18, 1991, 29–43, 48–9.

[33]Bill Calder, "Australia Reforms Immigration Law to Embrace Gays and Lesbians," *The Advocate*, June 18, 1991, 43.

[34]ILGA chose Guadalajara at the suggestion of member group Grupo Orgullo Homosexual de Liberación (GOHL). David Lida, "Multinational Gay and Lesbian Conference Cancelled," *The Advocate*, July 16, 1991, 44–5.

[35]G. Luther Whitington, "ILGA Holds Historic Meeting," *The Advocate*, August 13, 1991, 36.

to Mexico's ambassador to the United States, a group of twenty-eight US congressional representatives condemned the mayor of Guadalajara's bigotry and role in creating a climate that imperiled the lives and human rights of gays and lesbians in the city. The letter was quite likely the first time that Congress officially criticized another government for mistreating its gay and lesbian citizens.[36] The episode was a potent illustration not only of the challenges many activists faced in their home countries, but also of the power of international activism in effecting local change.

At the same time, IGLHRC solidified ties with local gay and lesbian activists confronting the volatile Soviet political landscape. *Tema*, the new gay newspaper, was described by *Pravda* as the voice of "necrophiliacs, zoophiliacs, and pederasts." In January 1991, Gorbachev established the Commission on Public Morality and the group soon accused *Tema* of disseminating pornography. Undeterred, Tom Boellstorff, the American who served as IGLHRC's Moscow-based representative, worked with local advocates in organizing the Soviet Union's first-ever gay and lesbian conference in late July. Risking public exposure, hundreds of Soviets attended five days of discussions in Leningrad and Moscow. A Soviet-American contingent staged a kiss-in outside the Moscow city council building and gathered outside the Bolshoi Theater, a well-known gay hangout, to protest Soviet and US sodomy laws.

Just three weeks later, communist hardliners launched a coup d'état on August 20. In response, Russian President Boris Yeltsin issued a decree calling for popular resistance. Boellstorff, *Tema*'s editor Roman Kalinin, and four others gathered in Boellstorff's apartment and used a computer, laser printer, and copier donated by US activists to create and print thousands of brochures reproducing Yeltsin's decree and stamped with the word "Tema." Emboldened by sympathetic coverage of their recent conference on the Cable News Network and in the Soviet press, gay and lesbian activists posted 4,000 copies of the leaflets and joined the huge crowds at the barricades. When the coup quickly failed, they were cautiously optimistic that a new democratic government would be amenable to legalizing homosexuality.[37]

As the Cold War neared its sudden and relatively peaceful end, activists from many countries mobilized campaigns targeting AI's inaction in expanding its Mandate. The National Gay and Lesbian Task Force, IGLHRC, ILGA, and the recently formed Queer Planet organized a multi-language postcard campaign targeting AI section members all over the world, urging them to support changing the Mandate to include gay prisoners of conscience (PoCs) imprisoned solely on the basis of their sexual identity. "We're here,

---

[36]Rick Harding, "Members of Congress Protest Homophobia in Mexico," *The Advocate*, September 10, 1991, 58.
[37]International News in Brief, *The Advocate*, September 10, 1991, 29; Masha Gessen, "Soviet Queers Fight Coup," *The Advocate*, September 24, 1991, 50.

we're queer, and we're still waiting for Amnesty to get used to it," Queer Planet proclaimed, using rhetoric adopted by advocates reclaiming the former pejorative "queer" and emulating ACT-UP's confrontational style. Flyers referred to AI as "Amnesty Heterosexual" and powerfully conveyed the stark realities gays faced in many nations. Samples included: "Cuba re-educates its queers with hard work in labor camps. ... When will Amnesty International notice?" and "Last year, Iran celebrated the new year by executing some queers. Why won't Amnesty International take action against these atrocities? When will queers be counted as prisoners of conscience?" A list of talking points called "Why Should AI Care about Homosexual Prisoners" asserted "Homosexual prisoners all over the world—from human rights activists to outspoken cultural personalities—from Greece to South Africa, from India to Canada, receive psychological and physical abuse and are raped by guards and fellow prisoners."[38]

Throughout 1990, a special ILGA committee contacted AI sections to determine how much support existed for changing the Mandate. Responses varied dramatically. Many sections refused to respond prior to the submission of the Mandate Review Committee's report at the 1991 International Council Meeting (ICM). While the Mexican, Finnish, and British sections stated they would support adopting prisoners held on grounds of homosexuality, the Venezuelan section, citing members' threats to leave AI if the Mandate were changed, called for maintenance of the status quo. The Tanzanian section was emphatically opposed, declaring: "We are negative towards adopting prisoners jailed because of their homosexuality and plan no discussion on this. No one is to be contacted on this in the future." The ILGA committee also launched media and public education campaigns that featured copies of the BBC documentary "Amnesty and Homosexuals," an ad campaign profiling gay and lesbian prisoners, and a training booklet called *Convincing AI*.[39]

These protests and years of internal debate and study set the stage for Amnesty's September 1991 ICM. After yet another impassioned debate, the delegates voted to amend the Mandate to include gays imprisoned solely on the basis of their sexual orientation, for advocating for gay rights, and/or for engaging in consensual same-sex sexual relations in private under AI's definition of "prisoners of conscience." Demet Demir, a Turkish transgender woman and advocate for sexual minorities who was repeatedly arrested, incarcerated, and tortured by police, was the first person Amnesty adopted as a prisoner of conscience on the basis of sexual orientation.[40] Although

---

[38]Queer Planet/IGA AI campaign materials, file—HCA/Woods/2/2b, Christopher Woods collection, HCA.

[39]ILGA packet on Amnesty International project, file—HCA/Woods/2/2a, Christopher Woods collection, HCA.

[40]A Gender Variance Who's Who, Demet Demir, https://zagria.blogspot.com/2008/05/demet-demir-1961-turkish-activist.html#.XTHcyC2ZMnW.

it took another two years for Amnesty to develop and approve guidelines for implementing the Mandate change, AI began publicizing the cases of gay PoCs from many nations including Turkey, Russia, Argentina, Greece, and Saudi Arabia.[41] National sections created gay task forces and started collaborating with activists in the international LGBT rights movement.[42] Other human rights groups like Human Rights Watch and Human Rights First followed AI's lead and also encompassed anti-LGBT abuses under their purview.

At the same time, IGLHRC began to grow and focused its energies on Latin America and Eastern Europe. After Argentina's Supreme Court denied CHA's petition for legal status on the grounds that homosexuality "offends the nature and dignity of the human person" and did not therefore merit constitutional protections for the freedom of expression, IGLHRC helped CHA become a registered nonprofit in 1992.[43] Through its Emergency Response Network, IGLHRC urged members to demand investigations of antigay violence in Ecuador, Mexico, and Brazil and to lobby for repeal of sodomy laws in Chile and Nicaragua. In Eastern Europe, IGLHRC called on Romania to align itself with the European Community's Human Rights Commission by repealing laws criminalizing same-sex sexual acts for both men and women and releasing gay men and lesbians being held in mental hospitals.[44]

In Russia, IGLHRC worked with local activists lobbying for repeal of Article 121.1, the provision of Russian penal law penalizing consensual sex between adult men with up to five years' imprisonment. When the law was repealed in 1993, Masha Gessen, an IGLHRC volunteer, compiled documentation ensuring that all prisoners serving sentences under Article 121 were released. Vladislav Ortanov, editor of the Moscow gay magazine *Risk*, noted that the Russian law was now more liberal than many US states

---

[41]Implementation on the Yokohama Mandate Decisions, May 19, 1992, folder—International Council Meeting [Mandate Review Committee], Yokohama, Japan, August 30–September 7, 1991, RG I—Board of Directors' Files, 1965–2003, subseries I.3—International Councils and Committees, 1968–1995, box I.3.5, AUISA. See also Guidelines: Amnesty International's Work on Behalf of Imprisoned Homosexuals, December 31, 1992, RG I—Board of Directors' Files, 1965–2003, subseries I.1—Board Meetings, 1965–2003, box I.1.15, AUISA.

[42]AIUSA Homosexuality Task Force Report, January 11, 1992, folder—BOD Meetings, January 31–February 2, 1992, RG—Board of Directors' Files, 1965–2003, subseries I.1—Board Meetings, 1965–2003, box I.1.14, AUISA.

[43]International News in Brief: Argentina, *The Advocate*, December 31, 1991, 25; Thoreson, *Transnational LGBT Activism*, 32.

[44]Chile was one of only two South American nations that still criminalized consensual homosexual acts between adults. In 1992, President Violetta Chamorro signed legislation recriminalizing homosexuality in Nicaragua—a law that remained in effect until March 2008. IGLHRC Emergency Response Network, Action Alert—March 1992, Folder—Emergency Response Network, Box—Newsletters-International Gay-Intersex, GLBT Historical Society, San Francisco, California (Hereafter GLBTHS).

IMAGE 5.1 After voting in 1991 to include individuals imprisoned on the basis of their sexual orientation as part of the organization's definition of "prisoners of conscience," Amnesty International (AI) made LGBT rights an integral part of its work for international human rights. Here, a member of AI's contingent at the 2011 London Pride Parade.

that still had sodomy laws in place. But he and other Russian advocates conceded legal reforms were only one part of changing hostile societal attitudes.[45]

In April 1993, ECtHR struck another major blow against sodomy laws in *Modinos v. Cyprus*. Following its precedents in *Dungeon v. United Kingdom* (1981) and *Norris v. Ireland* (1988), the ECtHR voted 8–1 on behalf of Alecos Modinos, a gay rights activist who had founded Apeleftherotiko Kinima Omofilofilon Kiprou, or "Cypriot Gay Liberation Movement," in 1987. After meeting years of fierce resistance while lobbying the government of Cyprus to decriminalize homosexuality, Modinos filed an individual petition with the ECtHR, claiming that the sodomy law in Cyprus violated his privacy rights as articulated in Article 8 of the European Convention on Human Rights. After the ECtHR sided with Modinos, Cyprus finally decriminalized homosexuality in May 1998.[46]

But the international LGBT rights movement suffered a major defeat when ILGA reapplied for consultative status at the ECOSOC. On March 29, 1993, the Committee on Non-Governmental Organizations, recognizing that differing views on the morality of homosexuality made it impossible to reach consensus, opted to deviate from standard practice of requiring unanimity for its decisions. The committee then voted 9–4 to make ILGA the world's first lesbian and gay NGO granted official status at the UN. ILGA had long been active at the UN through informal participation in the Department of Public Information, the WHO, preparatory committees serving the World Conference on Human Rights, the Women's Economic and Development Organization, and World AIDS Day, but now it could formally propose agenda items, submit recommendations, and send observers to meetings.[47]

ILGA's victory proved fleeting. In September 1993, the right-wing *Lambda Report*, a newsletter devoted to "monitoring the homosexual agenda in American politics and culture," disclosed that the North American Man/Boy Love Association (NAMBLA) and Vereniging Martijn, a Dutch pedophile group, were among ILGA's 400 member organizations in fifty nations. The story was picked up by mainstream media outlets including *The Washington Times*, the *Houston Chronicle*, Cable News Network's *Larry King Live*. The connection between ILGA and NAMBLA quickly drew the attention of US envoys at the UN who had backed ILGA's bid for consultative status. On October 19, 1993, John Blaney, a US special advisor at the UN,

---

[45]Thoreson, *Transnational LGBT Activism*, 32; Masha Gessen, "The Gay Gulag," *The Advocate*, February 23, 1993, 44–6; "Ballet Russe: Russia Drops Its Sodomy Law, but Additional Change May Be Elusive," *The Advocate*, July 13, 1993, 31.

[46]European Court of Human Rights, Case of *Modinos v. Cyprus*, Application No. 15070/89, 22 April 1993, https://hudoc.echr.coe.int/eng#{"itemid":["001–57834"]}.

[47]"UN Gives ILGA Official Status Despite Strong Opposition," *ILGA Bulletin* 3/93, June/August 1993, 5–6, Sub-File—1993 ILGA Bulletin, Box—ILGA Bulletin, 1990–2004, IHLIA.

asked ILGA to clarify its relationship with "reprehensible" NAMBLA and publicly warned that the United States could rescind its support for ILGA's NGO status. The Canadian and Australian UN delegations voiced similar views. On November 5, ILGA officers met with NAMBLA representatives in New York City and issued a statement saying that ILGA had refunded NAMBLA's 1993 dues and asked for its resignation. Should NAMBLA not withdraw, ILGA officers would recommend its expulsion at the June 1994 annual conference. The statement also emphasized that ILGA had never promoted pedophilia and that it consistently condemned child sexual abuse and exploitation. Sending the statement to the United States mission at the UN and the State Department, ILGA hoped it had defused the explosive situation.[48]

But the controversy only escalated. On January 26, 1994, the US Senate voted 99–0 to support a measure introduced by notoriously antigay Senator Jesse Helms (R-NC) that slashed $118 million in US contributions to the UN unless President Bill Clinton verified that there were no groups affiliated with the UN that condoned pedophilia. The vote exacerbated ILGA's already challenging problems. Insisting its opposition to age of consent laws was in keeping with homosexual tradition, NAMBLA was refusing to withdraw from ILGA as were fellow ILGA members Vereniging Martijn and Bundesverband Homosexualität, a German group with a pedophile caucus.[49] Fearing the loss of its hard-won UN consultative status, the ILGA voted to expel all three groups at its June 1994 annual conference.

The decision did not end the firestorm. On September 16, ECOSOC called an emergency meeting at the request of the US delegation, which alleged that ILGA was still affiliated with Verein für Sexuelle Gleichberechtigung (VSG), a German group that advocated the abolition of age of consent laws. After a two-hour discussion, the fifty-four national delegations of ECOSOC voted unanimously to strip ILGA of its consultative status. Blindsided by the emergency meeting and unable to verify that there were no other groups in its large, loosely organized membership that held views similar to VSG's, ILGA did not immediately pursue reinstatement. When the 49th United Nations General Assembly opened ten days later, there was no gay and lesbian group among the 1,500 NGOs with consultative status in attendance.[50] It would remain that way for nearly two decades.

Throughout the 1990s, those advocating LGBT equality around the world experienced landmark victories and crushing setbacks. In 1991, Hong Kong, the Bahamas, and Ukraine decriminalized homosexuality. In 1992 and 1993, Canada, Australia, Israel, and New Zealand abolished their bans

---

[48]Duncan Osborne, "The Trouble with NAMBLA," *The Advocate*, December 14, 1993, 40–1; ILGA Report on NAMBLA Debate, 1994, Folder on ILGA and Pedophilia, IHLIA.
[49]Duncan Osborne, "Ill Will toward ILGA," *The Advocate*, March 8, 1994, 27.
[50]Jorge Morales, "Undone at the U.N.?" *The Advocate*, November 1, 1994, 29–30.

on openly gay and lesbian people serving in the armed forces. But when President Bill Clinton advocated a similar policy for the US military, he bitterly disappointed his LGBT right supporters by accepting a "Don't Ask, Don't Tell" compromise that permitted gay and lesbian soldiers to serve only if they concealed their sexual identity—a policy that remained in effect until 2010. In 1993, the Intersex Society of North America became the world's first intersex rights organization. The same year, New Zealand passed the Human Rights Amendment, outlawing discrimination on the basis of sexual orientation or HIV status. In 1994, four years after the FRG and the GDR reunified, Germany repealed Paragraph 175, the sodomy law that Magnus Hirschfeld began protesting in 1897.

Between 1993 and 1996, Norway, Sweden, and Iceland legalized civil unions for same-sex couples. But in the United States, Congress overwhelmingly passed the Defense of Marriage Act, legislation barring federal recognition of any same-sex marriage or similar union conducted by a state. By contrast, in May 1996, South Africa became the first country in the world to adopt a constitution guaranteeing equal rights and protections on the basis of sexual orientation. Three months later, Buenos Aires became the first city in Spanish-speaking Latin America to prohibit discrimination on the basis of sexual orientation and repealed the infamous police edicts that allowed police to harass and detain young people, prostitutes, and gays and lesbians without any judicial oversight. Between 1996 and 1998, Canada, Fiji, and Ecuador banned discrimination on the basis of sexual orientation. On September 23, 1999, three Americans organized the first Celebrate Bisexuality Day during the ILGA annual conference held in Johannesburg. It evolved into a yearly global event calling for bisexual rights, visibility, and pride. On November 20, 1999, Gwendolyn Ann Smith founded the Transgender Day of Remembrance to commemorate the murder of Rita Hester, an African-American transgender woman who was killed in Allston, Massachusetts, in November 1998. It too became an annual international day of action. By 2000, Albania, Moldova, Ecuador, Venezuela, China, South Africa, Bosnia and Herzegovina, Kazakhstan, Tajikistan, and Chile had decriminalized homosexuality. The Netherlands and France established civil unions for same-sex couples.[51]

While lobbying many of the individual nations that made these changes, international LGBT advocacy groups also collaborated on landmark legal cases that had global ramifications. In 1985, after losing the extended parole he had been granted upon his arrival in the United States during the Mariel boatlift five years earlier, Fidel Armando Toboso-Alfonso applied for

---

[51]"Double Victory in Buenos Aires," Emergency Response Network, IGLHRC Action Alert, November 1996, Folder—Emergency Response Network, Box—Newsletters-International Gay-Intersex, GLBTHS; Myers, *Historical Dictionary of the Lesbian and Gay Liberation Movements*, 24–53.

asylum before an immigration judge in Texas. The judge ruled that Toboso-Alfonso qualified for asylum under the provisions of the Refugee Act of 1980 that protected persecuted members of a "particular social group." The Immigration and Naturalization Service (INS) appealed the ruling. When the case was heard by the US Board of Immigration Appeals (BIA) in 1990, Toboso-Alfonso had to prove that he would suffer persecution because of his sexual orientation if he returned to Cuba. Through news clippings and testimonials from other gay Marielitos, Toboso-Alfonso persuaded the BIA to grant him asylum on the basis of his sexual identity, thus rejecting the INS's argument that his "socially deviant" and illegal sexual conduct invalidated his asylum claim. In 1994, US Attorney General Janet Reno directed immigration officers and courts to treat *Matter of Toboso-Alfonso* as precedent. The case was pivotal in establishing that a well-founded fear of persecution on the basis of sexual orientation is a valid basis for making a claim for asylum in the United States.[52] In 1994, Suzanne Goldberg, Noemi Masliah, and Lavi Soloway founded the New York-based Lesbian and Gay Immigration Rights Task Force (later renamed Immigration Equality) to advocate pro-LGBT immigration policies and to provide free legal assistance to LGBT and HIV+ individuals seeking to emigrate to or be granted asylum by the United States.[53]

IGLHRC also played a major role in aiding LGBT people fleeing persecution. In 1992, IGLHRC helped a gay man from Argentina who became the first person granted asylum in Canada on the basis of sexual orientation. In 1993, IGLHRC attorney Tania Alvarez won a major victory when a San Francisco immigration judge granted asylum to Marcelo Tenorio, a gay man from Brazil who fled his country after being stabbed and beaten outside a gay nightclub in 1989. The case, along with *Matter of Toboso-Alfonso*, helped to establish fear of persecution on the basis of sexual orientation as grounds for political asylum under the Refugee Act of 1980. IGLHRC soon launched a highly effective Asylum Program, run by Sydney Levy.[54]

At the same time, AI drew global attention to antigay violence. In February 1994, AI issued *Breaking the Silence: Human Rights Violations Based on Sexual Orientation*, a 53-page report on human rights abuses of LGBT people in twenty-four countries including Colombian death squads killing gay men and transvestites, public executions of gay men in Iran, and the assassination of Renaldo Jose dos Santos, a Brazilian councilor who

[52]Capó, "Queering Mariel," 99–100. The 1990 BIA decision is found at https://www.justice. gov/sites/default/files/eoir/legacy/2012/08/14/3222.pdf.

[53]On the mission and history of Immigration Equality, see https://www.immigrationequality. org/about-us/#.XTJasy2ZOt8.

[54]Thoreson, *Transnational LGBT Activism*, 32–3; "Judge Grants Asylum Because of Gay Bashing in Brazil," *Florida Today*, August 5, 1993, 7A. The Matter of Marcel Tenorio decision is found at https://www.refworld.org/cases,USA_CA_9,3ae6b6c320.html.

had announced his bisexuality and whose decapitated corpse was found in a garbage dump. Following the report's release, Amnesty launched a six-month awareness campaign involving national advertisements and a US speaking tour by Dr. Luis Mott, founder and president of Brazil's Grupo Gay de Bahia. Mott discussed his research on more than 1,200 murders of gay men and lesbians in Brazil since 1980.[55]

Tasmanian gay rights and AIDS activist Nick Toonen made history when he prevailed in a complaint brought to the United Nations Humans Rights Committee (UNHRC). Between 1975 and 1990, the Campaign Against Moral Persecution (CAMP), an Australian gay and lesbian coalition founded in 1970, had successfully lobbied for the repeal of most of the state sodomy laws initially imposed when Australia was a British colony. In 1991, only the state Tasmania still criminalized private consensual male same-sex sexual activities, which were punishable with up to twenty-one years in jail. Toonen challenged the two relevant provisions of the Tasmanian Criminal Code, arguing these laws fueled harassment, discrimination, and violence against gay and lesbian Tasmanians. As a well-known advocate in a relationship with another man, Toonen claimed that laws criminalizing homosexual conduct imperiled his employment, personal safety, and rights to privacy and freedom of expression. He also argued that antigay statements made by Tasmanian politicians, religious authorities, and the general public created a climate of "official and unofficial hatred" that made it impossible for the Tasmanian Gay Law Reform Group to lobby effectively for the decriminalization of homosexuality. Accordingly, Toonen alleged that Sections 122 (a), (c), and 123 of the Tasmanian Criminal Code violated Articles 2(1), 17, and 26 of the International Covenant on Civil and Political Rights (ICCPR), a multilateral treaty adopted by the UN in 1976 and signed by Australia.

In November 1992, the UNHRC declared Toonen's claims admissible. Its ruling triggered a legal battle between the Australian federal government and Tasmania. Federal authorities ultimately rejected Tasmania's claims that Toonen's privacy rights had not been violated since there had been no state prosecutions for sodomy since 1984 and that Tasmania's sodomy laws were justified by the spread of HIV/AIDS and traditional morality. Noting that homosexuality had been decriminalized in all other Australian states and that three of Australia's six states and two self-governing territories had outlawed discrimination on the basis of sexual orientation, the Australian government asked the UNHRC to provide guidance on whether sexual orientation was a protected category under the ICCHR and whether

---

[55]John Gallagher, "No Amnesty for Bigotry," *The Advocate* March 22, 1994, 28–9; Dennis McMillan, "Amnesty International and Gay Rights," *San Francisco Sentinel*, June 8, 1994; Amnesty International advertisement, "In Many Countries, Coming Out of the Closet Means Facing More than Just Your Parents," *The Advocate*, August 23, 1994.

the Tasmanian sodomy laws, even though not recently enforced, violated Toonen's privacy rights or were a proportionate response to public health threats.

In 1994, the UNHRC issued its landmark decision in *Toonen v. Australia*. Concluding the privacy provisions of the ICCHR encompassed the right to private consensual sexual activity, the UNHRC ruled that the Tasmanian sodomy laws violated Toonen's privacy rights, despite their lack of recent enforcement. The Committee rejected the idea that sodomy laws were a reasonable measure to prevent the spread of HIV/AIDS, adding that such laws often increased the risk of exposure by deterring people in need of public health information. In interpreting Article 26 of the ICCHR, the UNHRC concluded that the reference to "sex" included sexual orientation. Accordingly, the UNHRC found Australia was breaching its obligations under the ICCHR and ordered its government to rectify the situation within ninety days. When Tasmania still refused to repeal its sodomy laws, the Australian government passed the Human Rights (Sexual Conduct) Act of 1994, thereby legalizing private consensual sexual activity between adults throughout Australia and prohibiting the making of laws that arbitrarily interfered with the sexual conduct of adults in private. Tasmanian LGBT advocates immediately challenged the legality of the Tasmanian sodomy laws and prevailed in their case before the Australian High Court, *Croome v. Tasmania* (1997). In response, the Tasmanian lawmakers finally decriminalized same-sex relations on May 1, 1997.[56]

Quite remarkably, Tasmania quickly embraced gay rights legislation, adopting the nation's most comprehensive nondiscrimination and relationship recognition law in 2003, and becoming the first state in Australia to legalize same-sex marriage in 2012.[57] But the ramifications of *Toonen v. Australia* were global. In recognizing the equal rights of lesbian, gay, bisexual, and transgender people for the first time, the UNHRC set a precedent that fundamentally altered the course of LGBT rights worldwide.

LGBT advocates made additional progress in other international forums. On February 8, 1994, the European Parliament (EP), an advisory body for the European Union (EU), voted 159–96 to adopt a resolution calling for member nations to grant their gay and lesbian citizens equal rights in

---

[56]"Major Gay Law Reform in Tasmania, Australia," Emergency Response Network, IGLHRC Action Alert, Vol. VI, No. 3, 1997, Folder—Emergency Response Network, Box—Newsletters-International Gay-Intersex, GLBTHS.

[57]Dan Harrison, "How a Tasmanian Gay Rights Battle Influenced the World," *Sydney Morning Herald*, April 10, 2014, https://www.smh.com.au/politics/federal/how-a-tasmanian-gay-rights-battle-influenced-the-world-20140412-zqt2p.html; Rodney Croome, "20 Years since Toonen Changed the World," *New Matilda*, April 11, 2014, https://newmatilda.com/2014/04/11/20-years-toonen-changed-world/; *Toonen v. Australia*, Communication No. 488/1992, U.N. Doc CCPR/C/50/D/488/1992 (1994), University of Minnesota Human Rights Library, http://hrlibrary.umn.edu/undocs/html/vws488.htm.

relationship recognition, adoption, social security, housing, and inheritance and to adopt a common age of consent for heterosexual and homosexual sexual activities. Although the resolution did not have the force of law, it drew strong opposition from Pope John Paul II in his weekly address on February 22. The Pontiff called upon Europeans to ignore any affirmation of "deviant behavior." The same day, the Vatican issued a letter condemning same-sex unions as "a serious threat to the future of the family and society."[58]

Undeterred by the possibility of additional resistance from the Vatican along with authorities in predominately Muslim countries, gay and lesbian rights activists collaborated with women's rights advocates at the UN's Fourth World Conference on Women, held in Beijing in September 1995. In preparing for the summit, IGLHRC staffer Rachel Rosenbloom compiled *Unspoken Rules: Sexual Orientation and Women's Rights*, a compendium of reports from thirty different countries. In Beijing, activists gathered 6,000 signatures on a petition demanding that sexuality be added to the conference agenda and ran a Lesbian Tent at the NGO Forum. When a contingent of lesbian activists unfurled a banner reading "Lesbian Rights are Human Rights" during the plenary session, they were detained by security officials until US Representative Bella Abzug negotiated their release. In an impassioned, protracted discussion, delegates debated whether or not to include a call to end discrimination based on sexual orientation in the non-binding Platform for Action, but dropped the provision from the final draft.[59]

In 1996, LGBT activists used the fiftieth anniversary of the UN to call attention to endemic and widespread violence against LGBT people around the world. On October 17, as heads of states attended ceremonies at the headquarters of the UN, the first-ever International Tribunal on Human Rights Violations against Sexual Minorities also convened in New York. Individuals from El Salvador, the United States, India, Argentina, Zimbabwe, and Romania described the anti-LGBT abuses and discrimination they had suffered to a panel of distinguished human rights experts. After hearing the testimonials, the panel issued recommendations calling for the UN and human rights groups to defend the rights of LGBT people worldwide.[60]

The European Commission on Human Rights (ECHR) soon ruled that those rights included the right not to be stigmatized by laws that set different

---

[58]"European Parliament Passes Gay Rights Resolution—Pope Responds," Emergency Response Network, IGLHRC Action Alert, March/April 1994, Folder—Emergency Response Network, Box—Newsletters-International Gay-Intersex, GLBTHS.

[59]Thoreson, *Transnational Activism*, 34; Rone Tempest and Maggie Farley, "Beijing Meeting Affirms Sexual Rights of Women," *Los Angeles Times*, September 16, 1995, https://www.latimes.com/archives/la-xpm-1995-09-16-mn-46385-story.html.

[60]"Lesbians and Gays Demand Action from UN on Human Rights Violations," *ILGA Bulletin*, January–March 1996, 23, Sub-File—1996 ILGA Bulletin, Box—ILGA Bulletin, 1990–2004, IHLIA.

ages of consent for heterosexuals and homosexuals. In July 1997, ECHR's *Sutherland v. United Kingdom* sided with Euan Sutherland, an activist from Stonewall, a British LGBT rights group founded in 1989. Sutherland filed a complaint that fixing the age for legal same-sex relations at eighteen, two years higher than for opposite-sex relations, violated his privacy rights as articulated under Article 8 of the European Convention for the Protection of Human Rights and Fundamental Freedoms. Although Sutherland had not been prosecuted for violating the British age of consent law, he argued that he had a legitimate fear of arrest based on the state's 169 convictions for such violations in 1991. After hearing a range of opinions from legal and medical authorities, the ECHR found different ages of consent discriminatory and unjustified. In response, the UK government agreed to equalize its age of consent laws. In 2000, after two previous bills lowering the UK's age of consent for homosexual acts to sixteen failed, the legislation was reintroduced and adopted by Parliament.[61]

In addition to challenging unjust laws, transnational advocates continued monitoring and confronting antigay repression. After publishing its third *Pink Book* in 1993, ILGA began publishing annual Gay Rights Human Rights reports. In 1996, at the request of Gays and Lesbians of Zimbabwe (GALZ), IGLHRC organized a multinational campaign denouncing Zimbabwe President Robert Mugabe and legislators from the ruling Zimbabwe African National Union (ZANU PF) party for calling for the "eradication of homosexualism" and the arrest of gays and lesbians.[62] In Namibia, President Sam Nujoma declared that "homosexuals must be condemned and rejected in our society," after the Rainbow Project, a coalition of gays and lesbians, announced that Prime Minister Hage Geingob had assured them that sexual orientation was protected under the terms of Article 10.2 of the Namibian Constitution adopted in 1990.[63] LGBT activists targeted the Romanian government with several actions, including a boycott of Romanian wines, after it repeatedly refused to

---

[61]European Court of Human Rights, *Case of Sutherland v. the United Kingdom*, Application No. 25186/94, https://hudoc.echr.coe.int/eng#{"itemid":["001-59354"]}.

[62]"Anti-Gay Rhetoric Escalates in Zimbabwe," Emergency Response Network, IGLHRC Action Alert, January 1996, Folder—Emergency Response Network, Box—Newsletters-International Gay-Intersex, GLBTHS.

[63]"Namibia's Nujoma Attacks Homosexuals," Emergency Response Network, IGLHRC Action Alert, January 1997, Folder—Emergency Response Network, Box—Newsletters-International Gay-Intersex, GLBTHS. In June 1999, Namibian gay rights groups won a major victory when Namibia's high court ruled that gay and lesbian couples had exactly the same rights as straight couples. The decision was a strong rebuke to President Nujoma, Home Minister Jerry Ekandjo, and other conservative members of the ruling SWAPO (now known as the South West Africa People's Organisation) party who claimed that homosexuality was un-African. See "Favorable Ruling on Gay and Lesbian Couples in Namibia," *ILGA Bulletin*, Issue 2/99, 6, Sub-File—1999 ILGA Bulletin, Box—ILGA Bulletin, 1990–2004, IHLIA.

decriminalize private consensual same-sex activities between adults, as a condition for its admission to the CoE in 1993 and compliance with the European Convention on Human Rights.[64]

ILGA increased its ability to advance LGBT rights in Europe when it gained consultative status at the CoE in January 1998, nine years after it initially applied. Obtaining official NGO status affirmed ILGA's many years of lobbying the CoE for the decriminalization of same-sex relations and the equalization of age of consent laws for heterosexuals and homosexuals. ILGA had been instrumental in the CoE's decision to require former communist states in Eastern Europe to repeal their sodomy laws as part of gaining admission—a policy that triggered legal reforms in Lithuania, Albania, Moldova, Macedonia, Armenia, and Azerbaijan.[65] European LGBT groups were also instrumental to the inclusion of sexual orientation in the nondiscrimination provisions in Article 13 of the Treaty of Amsterdam (1999), an agreement that reformed and expanded the powers of the EU originally articulated in the Treaty of Maastricht seven years earlier.[66]

ILGA was also gaining power at the UN. On October 8, 1998, in an historic first, the United Nations High Commissioner for Human Rights Mary Robinson met with Jennifer Wilson and Jordi Petit, ILGA's joint Secretaries General, and Kurt Krickler, co-Chair of ILGA Europe, to discuss making LGBT rights an integral element of the UN's work to promote and defend human rights. Robinson had been David Norris's attorney in the landmark *Norris v. Ireland* case. Robinson appointed a liaison to ILGA and requested that ILGA provide materials to help increase awareness of LGBT issues at the UN. Robinson also encouraged ILGA to produce annual

---

[64]Upon Nicolae Ceauşescu's rise to power in 1968, the Romanian penal code was revised to make same-sex relations between men or between women illegal, both in private and in public. Although Romania amended the first paragraph of Article 200 that criminalized same-sex relations in private when it applied for membership to the EU in 1995, it retained other portions of Article 200 that outlawed homosexual acts "which cause public scandal," "inciting or encouraging" people to engage in same-sex relations, and "propaganda" about homosexuality. Penalties ranged from one to five years' imprisonment. "Romanian Penal Code Reform Rejected," Emergency Response Network, IGLHRC Action Alert, January 1996 and "Romanian Parliament Retains Notorious Anti-Homosexual Law: Police Persecution of Gays & Lesbians Expected to Escalate," Emergency Response Network, IGLHRC Action Alert, November 1996, Folder— Emergency Response Network, Box—Newsletters-International Gay-Intersex, GLBTHS; "ILGA Leads Global Boycott to Protest Romanian Penal Code," *ILGA Bulletin*, April-June 1997, 5, Sub-File—1997 ILGA Bulletin, Box—ILGA Bulletin, 1990–2004, IHLIA.

[65]In early 1998, the CoE compromised forty member states, every one of Europe's forty-five countries except for Belarus, Bosnia and Herzegovina, Monaco, the Vatican, and Yugoslavia (Serbia/Montenegro). "ILGA Receives NGO Consultative Status with CoE," *ILGA Bulletin*, 1/98, January–March, 1, 31, Sub-File—1998 ILGA Bulletin and "Council of Europe Pressure Brings Progress for Lesbian, Gay and Bisexual Rights in Europe," *ILGA Bulletin*, 3/00, 7, sub-file—2000 ILGA Bulletin, Box—ILGA Bulletin, 1990–2004, IHLIA.

[66]European Parliament, Fact Sheets on the EU—The Maastricht and Amsterdam Treaties, http://www.europarl.europa.eu/factsheets/en/sheet/3/the-maastricht-and-amsterdam-treaties.

reports detailing human rights abuses of gays and lesbians around the world, information that Robinson believed could facilitate the appointment of a special UN rapporteur on LGBT rights. While neither Robinson nor the ILGA representatives could have predicted how long it would take to achieve all of these aims, the meeting was an important milestone.[67]

By the late 1990s, bisexuals were assuming a more visible and assertive role in the international LGBT movement. In 1995, ILGA established a Bisexuality Information Pool. Administered by Wayne Roberts of the Australian Bisexual Network, the pool became a valuable source of information and recruited bisexual groups from around the world to join ILGA.[68] In April 1998, more than 900 people attended the 5th International Conference on Bisexuality held at Harvard University. Organized primarily by Boston's Bisexual Resource Center, it was the largest-ever gathering of bisexual advocates from around the globe. Conference planners announced future meetings in Rotterdam and Sydney and the launch of a new website listing all known bisexual groups and resources worldwide.[69]

The rapid integration of the internet as a tool for global visibility, organizing, and protest was only one of the ways that the international LGBT rights movement broadened its scope at the turn of the twenty-first century. In 2000, ILGA secured funding from the European Commission that enabled it to launch an LGBT human rights project in Latin America. Orchestrated by Guatemala's OASIS and other member groups from ILGA's Latin America caucus, the project included Spanish and Portuguese language versions of *ILGA Bulletin* and publication and distribution of a guide for LGBT activists edited by MUMS—United Sexual Minorities Movement of Chile. ILGA affiliates presented the handbook at ten seminars in cities across Latin America and the Caribbean. They also coordinated regional conferences and introduced a new regional version of *ILGA Bulletin*.[70]

Simultaneously, ILGA affiliates in Africa documented human rights abuses. The June 2000 edition of *The Flash*, ILGA Africa's newsletter, included an extensive report on the status of gays and lesbians in several African nations. It described the criminalization of homosexuality in Botswana, Zambia, and Cameroon. Although consensual same-sex relations between partners eighteen and older were legal in Egypt, societal attitudes remained hostile and rising Islamic fundamentalism posed additional

---

[67]"UN High Commissioner for Human Rights with International Lesbian & Gay Group in Historic First," Vol. 16, Issue 21, Ambush, http://archive.ambushmag.com/is2198/news4.htm.
[68]"ILGA Bisexuality Information Pool," January–March, 4, Sub-File—1998 ILGA Bulletin, Box—ILGA Bulletin, 1990–2004, IHLIA.
[69]"Largest Ever International Conference on Bisexuality Held in Boston," *ILGA Bulletin*, 2/98, April–June 1998, 23, Sub-File—1998 ILGA Bulletin, Box—ILGA Bulletin, 1990–2004, IHLIA.
[70]"ILGA Announces GLBT Human Rights Project for Latin America," *ILGA Bulletin*, Issue 2/00, 3, Sub-File—1998 ILGA Bulletin, Box—ILGA Bulletin, 1990–2004, IHLIA.

threats to LGBT Egyptians. Uganda was an especially harsh environment. Homosexuality was not only illegal, but also taboo. Known or suspected gay men were disowned by their families, expelled from schools, made homeless, arrested, and imprisoned. Despite equally daunting obstacles in Zimbabwe, GALZ was celebrating its tenth anniversary and a marked increase in LGBT visibility. But its statistics also revealed the extraordinary courage entailed in being an activist confronting the dictatorship led by Robert Mugabe. GALZ noted a doubling of its membership—from three or four people in 1990 to about ten in 1998. Where only one gay man in the entire nation was willing to speak to the media when the organization was founded, now five gay men and two lesbians regularly did interviews.[71]

At the same time, Romanian gay and lesbian advocates escalated their efforts.[72] In June 2000, as Romania's application to join the EU entered the negotiations phase, the Romanian Chamber of Deputies voted to repeal Article 200, the nation's sodomy law. But with 432 gays and lesbians in jail for Article 200 offenses, leaders of ACCEPT, Romania's only LGBT rights organization, remained skeptical. The support of the Senate was required for decriminalization and the powerful Orthodox Church was fiercely opposed to legal reforms. Furthermore, Article 201 of the Romanian Penal Code remained in place and contained vague provisions outlawing "acts of sexual perversion, committed in public or if producing public scandal."[73]

In October 2000, these injustices drew intense media attention when ILGA-Europe convened its annual meeting in Bucharest. Facing threats of counterdemonstrations, conference organizers arranged for the largest security presence in ILGA history. Guards kept the few protestors who showed up at a safe distance from the attendees. Joined by the US ambassador to Romania and Dutch and German elected officials, 100 ILGA delegates from twenty-seven countries drafted an open letter to the president of Romania's Senate, reminding him of the nation's repeated failure to honor its commitment to repeal Article 200.[74]

In December 2001, the Romanian Parliament finally repealed the notorious Article 200. The lawmakers also outlawed discrimination on the basis of sexual orientation. The moves followed ten years of lobbying by

---

[71]ILGA Africa, *ILGA Bulletin*, Issue 3/00, 4–7, Sub-File—2000 ILGA Bulletin, Box—ILGA Bulletin, 1990–2004, IHLIA.

[72]For historic context and comparisons to other post-communist nations in Eastern Europe, see Conor O'Dwyer, *Coming Out of Communism: The Emergence of LGBT Activism in Eastern Europe* (New York: New York University Press, 2018).

[73]"Council of Europe Pressure Brings Progress for Lesbian, Gay and Bisexual Rights in Europe," *ILGA Bulletin*, 3/00, 7, Sub-File—2000 ILGA Bulletin, Box—ILGA Bulletin, 1990–2004, IHLIA; Karin Popescu, "Gays Tell Romania to Stop Treating Them as Criminals," *Reuters*, October 4, 2000, http://www.glapn.org/sodomylaws/world/romania/ronews18.htm.

[74]"ILGA-Europe Calls on Romanian Senate to Repeal Laws Criminalizing Same-Sex Relations," *ILGA Bulletin*, 3/00, 9, Sub-File—2000 ILGA Bulletin, Box—ILGA Bulletin, 1990–2004, IHLIA.

ACCEPT and ILGA, the longest and largest campaign in the organization's history. Pressure by the EU and the EP was also essential in Romania's decision to embrace LGBT rights. But while the enlargement of the EU had created great opportunities for it to compel membership-seeking nations like Bulgaria, Cyprus, and Hungary to enact pro-LGBT reforms, ILGA leaders also pointed to the hypocrisy inherent in the failure of long-time EU members such as Austria, Ireland, Portugal, and the UK to ensure full LGBT equality for their own citizens.[75]

The onset of the HIV/AIDS pandemic and the abrupt end of the Cold War created extraordinary challenges and opportunities for global advocates of LGBT equality. Enraged by apathy and inaction in response to HIV/AIDS, more radical transnational groups arose and successfully pushed the mainstream international LGBT rights movement and governments to respond more vigorously to the global health crisis. The HIV/AIDS emergency added urgency to activists' campaigns for the legalization of same-sex sexual activities and the institution of nondiscrimination protections and relationship recognition for LGBT people. Simultaneously, transnational networks of LGBT advocates reached more geographically expansive foreign audiences and grappled with racial, gender, and economic inequities embedded within the movement. Despite these daunting obstacles, activists pushed the UN and other supranational governance organizations to embrace LGBT equality. As the twentieth century ended, the international LGBT rights movement was prepared to defend its fragile gains and to demand full citizenship in individual nations and the global community.

---

[75]"Romania Repeals Anti-Gay Law," *ILGA-Europe* Newsletter, Winter 2002, 9, IHLIA.

CHAPTER SIX

Global Equality, Global Backlash, 2001–20

Over the last two decades, the international LGBT rights movement has broadened its geographic scope, won critical legal victories, and gained support from key supranational institutions. But this increased visibility and success often met intense resistance. While many nations instituted sweeping protections for LGBT individuals and couples, others remained intractably opposed to amending their legal codes to decriminalize same-sex relations. At times, politicians joined forces with conservative religious leaders in making LGBT people proxies for larger debates over national identity and globalization. Tensions also arose among LGBT people. Advocates in the Middle East denounced the use of LGBT rights to justify imperialism and xenophobia while LGBT individuals in the West invoked xenophobia and racism as tools for protecting LGBT equality. Although LGBT rights became an integral part of the larger human rights agenda, there were constant reminders that national gains could be reversed and that global progress is not a foregone conclusion.

At the turn of the twentieth century, although international LGBT rights advocates were making impressive gains in Europe, they were less successful in effecting change in predominately Muslim nations. The Cairo 52 case was a particularly notable example. On May 11, 2001, Egyptian State Security officers and members of the vice squad raided a floating gay nightclub called the Queen Boat and arrested thirty-three men. The next day, they arrested an additional nineteen men at other random locations. Because Egyptian law did not specifically mention homosexuality, police broadly interpreted a 1961 law designed to combat prostitution and charged fifty of the men with "habitual debauchery" (*fujur*) and "obscene behavior." Two men were charged with "contempt of religion" under Article 98f of the Penal Code. All fifty-two men pleaded innocence. During their incarceration, some of the men were subjected to torture and humiliation. Throughout nearly six months of detention, all were held incommunicado and spent twenty-two hours a day in two extremely crowded cells that had no beds. Many had no legal representation. At least five were forced to pull down their pants and show their underwear to authorities. Police presumed that wearing colored underwear was a sign of homosexuality. Although each man was wearing white underwear, all were still assumed to be gay. Several of the men were forced to undergo "forensic" genital and anal examinations to "prove their homosexuality," presumably to determine whether or not they had ever engaged in anal intercourse. Human Rights Watch and IGLHRC condemned the procedures, describing them as "profoundly degrading and humiliating." They invoked the 1994 declarations by the United Nations Human Rights Committee that unequal treatment on the basis of sexual orientation and the criminalization of consensual same-sex acts were violations of international law. While Egyptian advocates at the Hisham Mubarak Law Center defended the accused, other Egyptian human rights organizations sided with the government.[1]

The Egyptian media widely covered the case and greatly prejudiced public perceptions of the men. Journalists not only printed their names, addresses, and photographs, but also depicted them as tools of Europe or Israel. Echoing the government, the Egyptian press claimed that the arrests were necessary to protect traditional values and that foreign criticism of the case stemmed from the desire to impose Western culture and notions of human rights on Egyptian society. When their trials began in June, the men were brought before the Egyptian State Security Court, a court whose verdicts could not be appealed and could be overturned only by the president. On August 15, protests of the government's handling of the Cairo 52 were held in cities all over the world. Members of the US Congress and Germany's Bundestag wrote Egyptian President Hosni Mubarak to condemn the trials.[2]

On November 14, 2001, despite revelations of inadequate legal counsel, false arrests, falsified evidence, and violations of police procedure, twenty-one of the men were convicted of the "habitual practice of debauchery." Another man was found guilty of "contempt for religion" and a third, alleged to be the "ringleader" of a homosexual "cult," was convicted of both charges and given the maximum sentence of five years' hard labor. A teenager charged with the same offenses was tried by the juvenile court and sentenced to three years of imprisonment, followed by three years' probation.[3]

---

[1]OutRight (formerly IGLHRC), "Egypt: Egyptian Justice on Trial—The Case of the Cairo 52," Fact Sheet October 15, 2001, https://www.outrightinternational.org/content/egypt-egyptian-justice-trial-case-cairo-52.

[2]OutRight "(formerly IGLHRC), "Egypt: Egyptian Justice on Trial."

[3]Sarah Kershaw, "Cairo, Once 'the Scene', Cracks Down on Gays," *New York Times*, April 3, 2003, https://www.nytimes.com/2003/04/03/world/cairo-once-the-scene-cracks-down-on-gays.html.

In response to the verdicts, ILGA-Europe urged allies in the European Union (EU) and the European Parliament (EP) to pressure Egypt to comply with the human rights provisions of the recently signed Euro-Mediterranean Association Agreement between member states of the European Community and the Arab Republic of Egypt. Although a motion to delay debate and voting on the Association Agreement failed in the EP, both the EU and EP pledged to monitor Egypt's treatment of gays and lesbians and demanded that it stop its human rights abuses. The French artist Jean-Michel Jarre launched an appeal to President Mubarak, calling for immediate release of the twenty-three men serving two to five-year prison terms. On the whole, 127 EP members joined over 6,000 people, including notable figures like actors Catherine Deneuve, Juliette Binoche, and Anthony Delon, in signing the appeal. In February 2002, Egyptian Ambassador Soliman Awaad visited Het Roze Huis, the gay and lesbian center in Antwerp, and claimed that Egypt would consider the appeals of all twenty-three men—a statement that ran counter to the fact that no decisions of the State Emergency Court were subject to appeal. Awaad stressed that Egyptian law did not mention homosexuality. The men had been convicted not because of their alleged orientation, he insisted, but "because of lewdness and contempt of religion." Enraged by Awaad's claims and Egyptian police's recent arrest of eight men charged with "the practice of debauchery" in Damanhour, international condemnation of Egypt's record on gay rights escalated.[4]

In response to the global outcry, President Mubarak ordered a retrial and moved the cases to civil court. But on March 15, 2003, after months of litigation, all twenty-one defendants convicted in the first trial were convicted again and, in some instances, sentenced to three years instead of the originally imposed one to two years. Twenty-nine men were acquitted. Two others had their convictions upheld. In years to come, the Egyptian government launched other mass arrests of gay men and subjected them to the same public humiliation and mistreatment experienced by the Cairo 52 as part of larger efforts to assert authority and quash dissent.[5]

Not coincidentally, Egypt played a major role in the April 2002 defeat of ILGA's application for consultative status at the UN Economic and Social Council. By a 29–17 vote, ECOSOC handed ILGA a major defeat. While the opposition included several nations well known to be antigay

---

[4]"Continuing Pressure on Egypt," *ILGA-Europe Newsletter*, Winter 2002, 12–13, IHLIA.
[5]Scott Long, "The Trials of Culture: Sex and Security in Egypt," *Middle East Report* 230 (2004): 12–20; Nicola Pratt, "The Queen Boat Case in Egypt: Sexuality, National Security, and State Sovereignty," *Review of International Studies* 33:1 (2007): 129–44; Christiana Lilly, "The Cairo 52: 13 Years Later—Its Impact and Legacy," *South Florida Gay News*, June 19, 2015, https://southfloridagaynews.com/World/the-cairo-52-13-years-later-it-s-impact-and-legacy.html.

like Egypt, Sudan, Zimbabwe, and Uganda, ILGA members were shocked when Spain also blocked ILGA's application. Spain was the only nation among EU member countries and accession states that did not support ILGA. The fact that Spain currently held the presidency of the EU made the vote all the more stunning given the guarantee of freedom from discrimination based upon sexual orientation enshrined in the EU's Charter of Fundamental Rights. When asked to justify their opposition, delegates falsely accused ILGA of calling for the abolition of age of consent laws and supporting pedophilia. In reality, ILGA supported age of consent laws, but called for their equal application for both opposite-sex and same-sex relations. ILGA had also repeatedly demonstrated its support for the United Nations Convention on the Rights of the Child, especially its provisions against the sexual abuse of children. When opponents protested ILGA's refusal to provide ECOSOC its membership list, ILGA emphasized the need to protect advocates working in many of the nations who opposed ILGA's application. Unable to reapply for consultative status until 2005, ILGA called on Spanish members to protest their government's no vote and for the EU to repudiate Spain's position.[6]

At the same time, LGBT advocates in the Middle East were articulating a stinging critique of the Israeli government and colonialist models of LGBT advocacy. In 2002, the Israeli Foreign Ministry asked LGBT groups to participate in a film promoting Israel as a progressive, gay friendly country and tourist destination. The move outraged supporters of Palestine who viewed it as "pinkwashing"—a way of diverting attention from Israel's colonial occupation and repression of Palestine and portraying the Palestinians as backward and homophobic. In response, alQaws (Arabic for "rainbow") severed its ties with the Israeli LGBT group Jerusalem Open House in 2007 and changed its name to alQaws for Sexual and Gender Diversity in Palestinian Society. It launched a "pinkwatching" campaign that monitored Israel's record of imperialist and anti-Muslim actions and called for a global boycott of LGBT events and travel in Israel. To alQaws, queer solidarity is inextricably linked with rejection of colonialism, apartheid, racism, classism, and sexism.[7] Critics argue that allegations of pinkwashing devalue the LGBT Israelis' achievements and ongoing challenges. They claim that it is possible to celebrate gay pride in Israel and simultaneously

---

[6]"Homophobia Defeats ILGA's Bid for Consultative Status," *ILGA-Europe Newsletter*, Spring 2002, 12–13, IHLIA.

[7]Walaa Alqaisiya, "Decolonial Queering: The Politics of Being Queer in Palestine," *Journal of Palestine Studies* 47:3 (Spring 2018): 29–44; Walaa Alqaisiya, Ghaith Hilal, and Haneen Maikey, "Dismantling the Image of the Palestinian Homosexual: Exploring the Role of alQaws," in *Decolonizing Sexualities: Transnational Perspectives, Critical Interventions*, Sandeep Bakshi, Suhraiya Jivraj, and Silvia Posoco, eds. (London: Counterpress, 2016), 126–40.

condemn the Israeli government's occupation of Gaza and the West Bank, along with anti-LGBT persecution attitudes and discrimination among Palestinians.[8]

Pinkwashing arises in contexts other than the Israeli-Palestinian conflict and is closely associated with the concept of homonationalism. Originally coined by queer studies scholar Jasbir K. Puar, homonationalism is the use of a nation's positive record on LGBT issues as a means of promoting racist, xenophobic, and/or imperialistic policies.[9] The story of the late Dutch politician Pim Fortuyn is illustrative. In 2002, Fortuyn, an openly gay man campaigning in national elections, described Islam as "a backward culture" that rejected modernity. He called for the Netherlands to close its borders to Muslim immigrants in order to protect its liberal society and tradition of LGBT acceptance from imported Muslim intolerance, sexism, and homophobia. On May 6, 2002, shortly after completing a radio interview, Fortuyn was assassinated by Volkert Van der Graaf, a left-wing environmental and animal rights activist.[10] At his 2003 trial, Van der Graaf explained that he murdered Fortuyn in order to stop him from using Muslims as "scapegoats" and exploiting "the weak members of society" in his quest for political power. Van der Graaf was convicted and sentenced to eighteen years of incarceration. He was released on parole in 2014.[11]

Homonationalism infuriates activists who inextricably link LGBT equality to a larger struggle for human rights. They embrace intersectionality—the view that all forms of racial, gender, sexual, political, social, and economic oppression are interconnected and must therefore be simultaneously combatted.[12] But, as evidenced by white gay men who supported the xenophobic and anti-Muslim views of far-right French politician Marine Le Pen despite her call for a ban on same-sex marriage in 2017, complexities and contradictions that complicate the quest for international LGBT equality persist.[13]

---

[8]See, for example, Miriam Elman, "Reverse Pinkwashing: Exploiting Isolated Israeli Anti-Gay Violence to Excuse Widespread Palestinian LGBT Persecution," *Legal Insurrection*, August 6, 2015, https://legalinsurrection.com/2015/08/reverse-pinkwashing-exploiting-isolated-israeli-anti-gay-violence-to-excuse-widespread-palestinian-lgbt-persecution/.

[9]Jasbir K. Puar, *Terrorist Assemblages: Homonationalism in Queer Times* (Durham, NC: Duke University Press, 2007).

[10]Marlise Simons, "Rightist Candidate in the Netherlands Is Slain, and the Nation Is Stunned," *New York Times*, May 7, 2002, https://www.nytimes.com/2002/05/07/world/rightist-candidate-in-netherlands-is-slain-and-the-nation-is-stunned.html.

[11]Andrew Osborn, "I Shot Fortuyn for Dutch Muslims," *The Guardian*, March 27, 2003, https://www.theguardian.com/world/2003/mar/28/thefarright.politics; "Dutch Free Killer of Anti-Islam Politican Pim Fortuyn," *BBC*, May 2, 2014, https://www.bbc.com/news/world-europe-27261291.

[12]For an example of this view, see the statement on intersectionality by the Equality Network, a Scottish LGBT rights group, https://www.equality-network.org/our-work/intersectional/.

[13]Will Chalk, "Why Gay French Men Are Voting Far Right," *BBC*, April 19, 2017, http://www.bbc.co.uk/newsbeat/article/39641822/why-gay-french-men-are-voting-far-right.

Despite the tensions reflected by the emergence of pinkwashing and homonationalism, LGBT advocates in Europe scored some significant victories in the early 2000s. On July 24, 2003, the European Court of Human Rights (ECtHR) ruled on behalf of an Austrian man challenging a provision of the Austrian Rent Act that denied same-sex partners successive tenancy rights in the event of the death of a domestic partner of the same sex—a right guaranteed to partners of the opposite sex. The Court held that Austria's law violated Article 8, the "respect for home" provision of the European Convention for Protection of Human Rights and Fundamental Freedoms. It was the first time the Court recognized any rights of same-sex partners.[14]

In October 2003, the fifteen governments of the member states of the EU agreed to a sweeping nondiscrimination directive issued after nearly two years of negotiations on how to implement Article 13 of the Treaty of Amsterdam. The directive prohibited employment discrimination on the basis of religion, disability, age, and sexual orientation. Thirteen additional nations seeking to join the EU would be required to enact these protections as a requirement of membership.[15]

While the EU advanced LGBT rights, ILGA continued to expand its global reach. In November 2003, ILGA held its annual conference in Manila, the first time the meeting was held in Asia. Approximately 150 delegates from dozens of countries gathered to celebrate ILGA's twenty-fifth anniversary and to strategize for the future. Claudia Roth, the German Commissioner for Human Rights, addressed the delegates and applauded Brazil's recent introduction of a resolution on "Human Rights and Sexual Orientation" at the UN Commission on Human Rights (UNCHR), the first-ever draft resolution to include sexual orientation. Although Germany and the EU had supported the proposal, it drew vociferous opposition from the Vatican, Pakistan, and Egypt. With debate at a standstill, Brazil tabled the resolution and the UNCHR adjourned, postponing a vote until March 2004. Roth struck a hopeful note when she declared that the measure would pass and that progress toward global LGBT equality would continue.[16]

But when the UNCHR reconvened in March 2004, Brazil declined to resubmit the resolution. Facing domestic opposition led by the Catholic Church and international pressure from Arab states threatening to boycott a forthcoming trade summit to be held in the country, Brazil backed away from the nondiscrimination resolution, startled that a measure it

---

[14]European Court of Human Rights, *Karner v Austria*, July 24, 2003, https://hudoc.echr.coe. int/eng#{"itemid":["001-61263"]}.

[15]"ILGA-Europe Welcomes EU Anti-Discrimination Directive," *ILGA-Europe Newsletter*, Winter 2003, 8, IHLIA.

[16]"The First ILGA World Conference in Asia," *ILGA-Europe Newsletter*, Winter 2003, 7, IHLIA.

assumed would be uncontroversial generated such an uproar. The draft resolution lapsed the following year.[17]

At the beginning of the twenty-first century, many nations were making significant strides toward LGBT equality. In 2000, Azerbaijan, Georgia, and Gabon decriminalized homosexuality. Great Britain lifted its ban on openly gay and lesbian people serving in the armed forces and set sixteen as an equal age of consent for heterosexual and homosexual relations. Germany's Bundestag issued an official apology for Nazi persecution of gays and lesbians and for the "harm done to homosexual citizens up to 1969." Tokyo passed an LGBT-inclusive nondiscrimination law and held its first pride parade. In the United States, Vermont became the first state to legalize civil unions. During a pride parade in Phoenix, Arizona, the light pink and blue transgender rights flag was flown for the first time.

In 2001, the Netherlands became the first country in the world to legalize same-sex marriage. Albania, Liechtenstein, and Estonia equalized the age of consent. Domestic partnership laws for same-sex couples took effect in the Czech Republic, South Africa, Finland, and Germany. For the first time, Panama legally recognized an LGBT organization, the Asociación Hombres y Mujeres Nuevos de Panama (New Men's and Women's Association of Panama). South Korea outlawed discrimination based upon sexual orientation. In 2002, Buenos Aires became the first Latin American city to legalize civil unions and Ontario became the first Canadian province to do so. Austria and Croatia took similar steps shortly thereafter. In 2003, in a monumental victory for LGBT rights in the United States, the Supreme Court struck down remaining state sodomy laws in its *Lawrence v. Texas* ruling. That same year, Belgium became the second country in the world to legalize same-sex marriage and Iraq decriminalized homosexuality.

In 2004, following South Africa, Sweden, and New Zealand, Portugal became the fourth nation in the world to include a provision outlawing discrimination based upon sexual orientation in its constitution. New Zealand adopted the Civil Unions Act. Defying a wave of state measures that barred same-sex marriage, Massachusetts became the first US state to grant same-sex couples full marriage rights. A year later, Spain became the third country in the world to legalize same-sex marriage. Canada soon followed and also legalized adoption by same-sex couples. After a Supreme Court ruling in favor of same-sex marriage that went into effect on December 1, 2006, South Africa became the first African nation and the fifth country worldwide to legalize same-sex marriage.[18]

---

[17]Françoise Girard, "United Nations: Negotiating Sexual Rights and Sexual Orientation," in Richard Parker, Rosalind Petchesky, and Robert Sember, eds., *SexPolitics: Reports from the Front Lines*, 311–58, Sexuality Policy Watch, 2004, https://www.sxpolitics.org/frontlines/book/pdf/sexpolitics.pdf.

[18]Myers, *Historical Dictionary of the Lesbian and Gay Liberation Movements*, 24–53.

These victories coexisted with a concerted effort to generate increased awareness of anti-LGBT violence and discrimination around the world. On June 1, 2003, a Canadian organization named Fondation Émergence launched a National Day Against Homophobia. The event inspired Louis-Georges Tin, a French academic and advocate for black gay men, to begin planning an annual international demonstration against homophobia. More than 24,000 individuals and several organizations including ILGA, IGLHRC, the World Congress of LGBT Jews, and the Coalition of African Lesbians singed a statement in support of the initiative. Organizers chose May 17, the anniversary of the 1990 decision by the World Health Organization to remove homosexuality from its list of mental disorders. The date (formatted 17.5) also coincided with an unofficial German event commemorating historic resistance to Paragraph 175. On May 17, 2005, International Day Against Homophobia (IDAHO) demonstrations were held all over the globe. Activities included the first-ever public LGBT rallies held in China, Congo, and Bulgaria. The event's name expanded to include Transphobia in 2009 and Biphobia in 2015. Annual May 17 demonstrations and cultural events are now celebrated and officially recognized all over the world.[19]

But increased visibility of global homophobia did not inspire the ECOSOC to give LGBT organizations consultancy status. On January 26, 2006, the United States joined the staunchly anti-LGBT governments of Cameroon, China, Cuba, Pakistan, the Russian Federation, Senegal, Sudan, and Zimbabwe in supporting an Iranian resolution blocking ILGA-Europe's effort to win UN consultative status based on ILGA's previous association with NAMBLA more than a decade earlier.[20] On May 17, as activities marking the IDAHO were occurring all over the world, the ECOSOC again rejected ILGA-Europe's application for consultative status. In explaining her call for the immediate rejection of the application, Iran's delegate said that ILGA-Europe was part of ILGA, whose application for readmission had been repeatedly denied. She also questioned ILGA-Europe's explanations of how its work advanced human rights. ILGA-Europe was not permitted to respond to her objections. The following day, despite the objections of several delegates about due process violations, the ECOSOC voted 9–7 to reject the consultancy application filed by Lesben und Schwulenverband in Deutschland (Lesbian and Gay Federation in Germany).[21]

---

[19]"17 May 2005: The First International Day against Homophobia," *Sur in English*, May 17, 2019, http://www.surinenglish.com/lifestyle/201905/17/2005the-first-international-against-20190517102414-v.html; Louis-Georges Tin biography, http://frenchculture.org/sites/default/files/2012-pres-tin2.pdf; International Day against Homophobia, Transphobia, & Biphobia, https://may17.org.

[20]Warren Hoge, "Rights Groups Fault U.S. Vote in U.N. on Gays," *New York Times*, January 27, 2006, A6.

[21]"UN Denies Consultative Status to ILGA-Europe," ILGA-Europe, May 18, 2006, https://www.ilga-europe.org/resources/news/latest-news/un-denies-consultative-status-ilga-europe.

LGBT activists, dozens of nongovernmental organizations (NGOs), and the EU kept pressuring the ECOSOC. On December 11, 2006, the ECOSOC finally approved the applications for consultancy status filed by ILGA-Europe, Landsforeningen for Bøsser og Lesbiske (Danish National Association for Gays and Lesbians), and the Lesbian and Gay Federation in Germany. For the first time, ECOSOC recognized the critical importance of allowing LGBT NGOs to participate in UN proceedings.[22] Its vote came just days after fifty-four UN member states supported a joint statement sponsored by Norway decrying human rights violations based upon sexual orientation and gender identity. The statement's inclusion of gender identity marked a significant advance in international recognition of transgender rights.[23]

Concurrently, activists recognized the need for a legal framework for stopping human rights abuses of LGBT people around the world. In November 2006, human rights experts gathered at a meeting of the International Commission of Jurists held at Gadjah Mada University in Yogyakarta, Indonesia. Sonia Onufer Corrêa, Research Associate at the Brazilian Interdisciplinary AIDS Association, and Vitit Muntarbhorn, a law professor and UN Special Rapporteur on human rights for the Democratic People's Republic of Korea, co-chaired the sessions. Over the course of three days, they unanimously agreed on a set of twenty-nine principles on sexual orientation and gender identity and named them after the city in which they convened. The Yogyakarta Principles identified pervasive patterns of discrimination and violence against LGBT people and made specific recommendations for actions that the UN, states, NGOs, the media, and human rights groups could take to ensure full equality for LGBT people everywhere. On March 26, 2007, the finalized version of the Yogyakarta Principles was released at the United Nations Human Rights Council (UNHRC) in Geneva.[24] In December 2008, inspired by the Yogyakarta Principles, sixty-six mostly European and Latin American countries supported a UN declaration co-sponsored by France and the Netherlands calling for the universal decriminalization of homosexuality, but the United States joined China, Russia, the Roman Catholic Church, and the Organization of the Islamic Conference in opposing the non-binding measure. Ambassador Jorge Argüello of Argentina read the declaration

---

[22] "ILGA-Europe Gets Consultative Status with United Nations!" ILGA-Europe, https://www. ilga-europe.org/resources/news/ilga-europe-gets-consultative-status-united-nations.

[23] 2006 Joint Statement, 3rd Session of the Human Rights Council, ARC International, December 1, 2006, http://arc-international.net/global-advocacy/sogi-statements/2006-joint-statement/.

[24] The Yogyakarta Principles are published in their entirety in all six United Nations languages at http://www.yogyakartaprinciples.org. See also Human Rights Watch, "Yogyakarta Principles," A Milestone for Lesbian, Gay, Bisexual, and Transgender Rights, March 26, 2007, https:// www.hrw.org/news/2007/03/26/yogyakarta-principles-milestone-lesbian-gay-bisexual-and-transgender-rights.

into the record, the first time a declaration on gay rights was recorded in the official proceedings of the UN General Assembly.[25]

Determined to rectify the disjuncture between US obstruction on international LGBT rights and American leadership on other human rights issues, Secretary of State Hillary Clinton began championing LGBT equality. In November 2009, on the eve of World AIDS Day, Clinton announced that the United States would not tolerate the criminalization of homosexuality in nations receiving US aid aimed at combatting HIV/AIDS. Her statement signaled an unprecedented level of commitment by a US administration to international LGBT issues. It coincided with weeks of private US diplomatic efforts to persuade Ugandan officials to drop pending legislation imposing the death penalty for those who repeatedly engaged in gay sex or exposed others to HIV.[26]

At a June 2010 State Department celebration of LGBT Pride Month, Clinton emphasized that the US Department of State's Bureau for Democracy, Human Rights, and Labor tracked the treatment of LGBT people in its country-specific human rights reports and that it had begun offering emergency aid to human rights activists in Africa, South Asia, and the Middle East at risk because of their LGBT status or pro-LGBT advocacy. "Just as I was very proud to say the obvious more than 15 years ago in Beijing that human rights are women's rights and women's rights are human rights," Clinton declared, "well, let me say today that human rights are gay rights and gay rights are human rights."[27]

Translating rhetoric into action, the United States also played a major role in helping the International Gay and Lesbian Human Rights Commission (IGLHRC) gain consultancy status at the United Nations Economic and Social Council. On July 19, 2010, after three years of obstruction and delays, the ECOSOC voted 23–13 in favor of IGLHRC's application. More than 200 NGOs from fifty-nine countries supported ILGHRC's accreditation, including Sexual Minorities Uganda (SMUG) and Brazil's Associação Brasileira de Lésbicas, Gays, Bissexuais, Travestis e Transexuais, which had become the tenth LGBT NGO to win ECOSOC consultancy status a few months earlier.[28] On June 30, 2011, prevailing over the entrenched

---

[25]Neil MacFarquhar, "In a First, Gay Rights Are Pressed at the U.N.," *New York Times*, December 19, 2008, A22. In June 2011, the Organization of the Islamic Conference formally changed its name to the Organization of Islamic Cooperation.

[26]Kerry Eleveld, "Clinton Condemns International Homophobia," *The Advocate*, November 30, 2009, http://www.advocate.com/news/daily-news/2009/11/30/clinton-condemns-international-homophobia.

[27]Hillary Rodham Clinton, Remarks at an Event Celebrating Lesbian, Gay, Bisexual, and Transgender (LGBT) Month, June 22, 2010, https://2009-2017.state.gov/secretary/20092013clinton/rm/2010/06/143517.htm.

[28]"A Victory against Homophobic Silencing of Civil Society," ILGHRC Press Release, July 19, 2010, https://outrightinternational.org/content/united-nations-grants-official-status-us-based-international-lgbt-rights-group.

opposition of a majority of African and Islamic nations, ECOSOC voted 29–14 to restore ILGA's consultancy status after suspending it seventeen years earlier.[29]

The same month, in contrast to the Bush administration's opposition to a similar resolution that failed in 2008, the Obama administration's UN envoys joined eighty-five nations in passing a South African-sponsored resolution condemning anti-LGBT violence and discrimination, a first for the UNHRC.[30] President Barack Obama spoke before the United Nations General Assembly three months later and asserted: "No country should deny people their rights to freedom of speech and freedom of religion, but also no country should deny people their rights because of who they love, which is why we must stand up for the rights of gays and lesbians everywhere."[31] No sitting US president had ever before offered such unequivocal support for global LGBT equality.

The shifts in US policies coincided with significant advances in several nations. In 2006, the Czech Republic and Slovenia legalized domestic partnerships and Germany outlawed discrimination on the basis of sexual orientation. That same year, Fiji decriminalized consensual homosexual acts between adults. Serbia and the Isle of Man adopted legislation equalizing the age of consent for same-sex and opposite-sex acts. In 2007, Nepal decriminalized homosexuality. The following year, a newly independent Kosovo adopted a constitution including sexual orientation as a protected category. Uruguay became the first South American nation to recognize civil unions. In 2009, Norway and Sweden legalized same-sex marriage and Hungary instituted a domestic partner registry. Icelandic voters elected Jóhanna Sigurðardóttir the world's first openly gay or lesbian head of state. Issuing a decision that proved short-lived, India's High Court struck down much of Section 377, thus legalizing most same-sex sexual acts. Burundi, however, criminalized same-sex relations. In 2010, same-sex marriage became legal in Argentina and Iceland and Denmark legalized the adoption of children by same-sex couples.[32]

These events helped sustain pro-LGBT advocacy at the UN. In November 2011, the UN Commissioner of Human Rights issued a report documenting pervasive discrimination and violence against LGBT people around the world. In response to this "pattern of human rights violations," High Commissioner Navi Pillay called on UN member states to investigate

[29]"ILGA Granted UN Consultative Status," *Freedom House Press Release*, June 30, 2011, https://freedomhouse.org/article/ilga-granted-un-consultative-status.

[30]"U.N. Council: Gay Rights Are Human Rights," *The Advocate*, June 17, 2011, http://www.advocate.com/news/daily-news/2011/06/17/un-gay-rights-are-human-rights.

[31]"Obama Addresses Global Gay Rights in UN Speech," *The Advocate*, September 21, 2011, http://www.advocate.com/news/daily-news/2011/09/21/obama-addresses-global-gay-rights-un-speech.

[32]Myers, *Historical Dictionary of the Lesbian and Gay Liberation Movements*, 24–53.

and prosecute hate crimes motivated by anti-LGBT animus; adopt LGBT-inclusive policies on asylum; decriminalize consensual same-sex relations and equalize age of consent laws governing heterosexual and homosexual conduct; adopt nondiscrimination laws including sexual orientation and gender identity; ensure LGBT citizens the freedoms of movement, assembly, and expression; institute LGBT-inclusive sensitivity and bias training for law enforcement officials; and accord transgender people the ability to change their gender and name on official documents.[33]

In keeping with the UNHRC's recommendations, Obama and Clinton formalized steps elevating international LGBT rights as a priority in US foreign policy. On December 5, 2011, Obama issued a presidential memorandum "directing all agencies engaged abroad to ensure that U.S. diplomacy and foreign assistance promote and protect the human rights of LGBT persons." Obama ordered intensified efforts to combat the criminalization of homosexual identity or conduct, to fight anti-LGBT discrimination, to protect LGBT refugees and asylum seekers, and to ensure "swift and meaningful U.S. responses to human rights abuses of LGBT persons abroad." On the same day, Clinton addressed the UNHRC in Geneva and announced the creation of a new $3 million Global Equality Fund to support the work of NGOs working on international LGBT issues. While neither Obama nor Clinton vowed to tie US foreign aid to a nation's record on LGBT equality, the symbolism of their statements was powerful.[34]

John Kerry, Clinton's successor as Secretary of State, expanded America's global LGBT equality initiatives. In April 2013, USAID launched the LGBT Global Development Partnership, a $16 million public-private initiative that promoted LGBT rights around the world over four years.[35] In February 2015, Kerry appointed Randy Berry, an

---

[33]"Discriminatory Laws and Practices and Acts of Violence against Individuals Based on Their Sexual Orientation and Gender Identity," Report of the United Nations High Commissioner for Human Rights, November 17, 2011, https://www2.ohchr.org/english/bodies/hrcouncil/docs/19session/a.hrc.19.41_english.pdf.

[34]Dan Robinson, "Obama Elevates Gay Rights as a Foreign Policy Priority," *Voice of America*, December 5, 2011, http://www.voanews.com/content/obama-elevates-gay-rights-as-a-foreign-policy-priority-135136743/174955.html; Steven Lee Myers and Helene Cooper, "U.S. to Aid Gay Rights Abroad, Obama and Clinton Say," *New York Times*, December 6, 2011, http://www.nytimes.com/2011/12/07/world/united-states-to-use-aid-to-promote-gay-rights-abroad.html?pagewanted=all&_r=0; Hillary Rodham Clinton, Remarks in Recognition of International Human Rights Day, Palais des Nations, Geneva, Switzerland, December 6, 2011, https://photos.state.gov/libraries/belize/231771/PDFs/Remarks%20in%20Recognition%20of%20International%20Human%20Rights%20Day.pdf; and The White House; Office of the Press Secretary, "Presidential Memorandum—International Initiatives to Advance the Human Rights of Lesbian, Gay, Bisexual, and Transgender Persons," December 6, 2011, https://obamawhitehouse.archives.gov/the-press-office/2011/12/06/presidential-memorandum-international-initiatives-advance-human-rights-l.

[35]Michael K. Lavers, "Advocates Welcome U.S. Efforts to Promote Global LGBT Rights," *Washington Blade*, December 7, 2014.

openly gay long-time foreign service officer, to be the first U.S. special envoy to promote global gay rights.[36] Over the next year, he traveled to forty-two countries.[37]

The United States and several other nations continued pushing the UN to integrate LGBT rights into global human rights conventions and treaties. In August 2015, the UN Security Council received its first-ever briefing on LGBT issues at a meeting co-hosted by the United States and Chile. It followed the June 2015 release of a report by the UN Commissioner for Human Rights that found that thousands of people had been horrifically injured or killed worldwide because of their sexual orientation or gender identity. The briefers included UN Deputy Secretary General Jan Eliasson, Jessica Stern of IGLHRC, a gay Iraqi refugee using the pseudonym "Adnan," and Subhi Nahas, a Syrian LGBT activist. Both "Adnan" and Nahas fled their nations after receiving death threats from Islamist extremists opposed to homosexuality. The key goal of the briefing was to highlight the Islamic State's brutality against gays as a means of winning support from member nations who might be ambivalent or even hostile to gay rights, but who strongly opposed Islamist extremist terrorism.[38]

In June 2016, following a joint campaign led by 628 NGOs from 151 countries (about 70 percent from the Global South), the UNHRC voted 23–18 to create an independent expert charged with monitoring anti-LGBT violence and discrimination around the world. It was the UN's strongest demonstration to date of a commitment to integrating sexual orientation and gender identity into international human rights law.[39] In September 2016, Vitit Muntarbhorn of Thailand, the retired law professor and long-time UN official who had co-chaired the 2006 meeting at which

---

[36]Michael K. Lavers, "State Department Names Randy Berry as LGBT Envoy," *Washington Blade*, February 23, 2015.

[37]Michael K. Lavers, "Randy Berry Makes First Year as LGBT Envoy," *Washington Blade*, April 25, 2016. Under the Trump administration, the State Department abolished Berry's position, along with those of several other special envoys. See Ernesto Londoño, "Pride Flags and Foreign Policy: U.S. Diplomats See Shift on Gay Rights," *New York Times*, June 9, 2019, https://www.nytimes.com/2019/06/09/world/americas/pride-flags-us-embassies.html?nl=todaysheadlines&emc=edit_th_190610?campaign_id=2&instance_id=10067&segment_id=14141&user_id=009e3a5e9e977a807281a8e42634915a&regi_id=582352630610.

[38]Samantha Power, "Making History: The First UN Security Council Meeting on LGBT Rights," *Medium*, August 24, 2015, https://medium.com/@AmbassadorPower/making-history-the-first-un-security-council-meeting-on-lgbt-rights-f0ec18d216b; Frank Bruni, "Gay and Marked for Death," *New York Times*, August 21, 2015, https://www.nytimes.com/2015/08/23/opinion/sunday/frank-bruni-gay-and-marked-for-death.html?_r=0.

[39]J. Lester Feder, "The U.N. Votes to Create Its First LGBT Rights Watchdog," *Washington Blade*, June 30, 2016; Human Rights Watch, "UN Makes History on Sexual Orientation, Gender Identity," June 30, 2016.

the Yogyakarta Principles were drafted, was appointed to the post.[40] After Muntarbhorn resigned a year later due to health problems, the UNHRC appointed Victor Madrigal-Borloz, a Costa Rican attorney and anti-torture activist, to succeed him.[41]

But overall, the movement for international LGBT equality had mixed success and inspiring victories continued to coexist with crushing defeats. In December 2011, the United States ended its ban on openly gay and lesbian people serving in the armed services and opened the ranks to transgender individuals five years later. In 2011, Colombia outlawed discrimination on the basis of sexual orientation. Two years later, Cuba passed similar legislation. Between 2012 and 2018, Denmark, Brazil, Uruguay, New Zealand, France, UK, Scotland, Finland, the United States, Ireland, several states in Mexico, Colombia, Greenland, Germany, Bermuda, and Malta legalized same-sex marriage.[42] In 2012, Argentina adopted a landmark law that allows people to change their gender marker on official documents without first requiring proof of medical or psychological treatment.[43] In May 2014, the African Commission on Human and Peoples' Rights, a body created by the African Charter on Human and Peoples' Rights in 1987, adopted a resolution denouncing violence and other human rights violations based on sexual orientation or gender identity—the first time a pan-African organization had ever adopted such a stance.[44]

Since early 2018, there have been major advances in Latin America and Asia with global ramifications. In January 2018, the Inter-American Court of Human Rights issued a sweeping decision that could result in the legalization of same-sex marriage and the expansion of transgender protections in up to twenty Central and South American countries. Issued in response to an inquiry from Costa Rica, the decision sets a precedent for the

---

[40]Human Rights Campaign, UN Appoints First-Ever Independent Expert on Sexual Orientation and Gender Identity, September 30, 2016. An effort to block the creation of the independent expert led by African and Islamic states failed decisively in December 2016, see "New Attempt to Block United Nations Mandate on Sexual Orientation and Gender Identity Proves Unsuccessful," *ILGA Bulletin* 69, December 19, 2016 (December 15–22, 2016).

[41]Michael K. Lavers, "Costa Rican Lawyer Named New UN LGBTI Rights Watchdog," *Washington Blade*, December 6, 2017, https://www.washingtonblade.com/2017/12/06/costa-rican-lawyer-named-new-un-lgbti-rights-watchdog/.

[42]Myers, *Historical Dictionary of the Lesbian and Gay Liberation Movements*, 24–53.

[43]Emily Schmall, "Transgender Advocates Hail Law Easing Rules in Argentina," *New York Times*, May 24, 2012, https://www.nytimes.com/2012/05/25/world/americas/transgender-advocates-hail-argentina-law.html.

[44]International Service for Human Rights, "African Commission Adopts Landmark Resolution on LGBT Rights," May 22, 2014, https://www.ishr.ch/news/african-commission-adopts-landmark-resolution-lgbt-rights.

twenty-three signatories to the American Convention on Human Rights.[45] In response, Costa Rica became the first Central American nation with legal same-sex marriage in 2020.[46]

In September 2018, India's Supreme Court unanimously struck down Section 377 and decriminalized consensual same-sex relations. The decision reversed a 2013 decision upholding the colonial-era sodomy law and came three years after an effort to repeal the law failed. The ruling had tremendous implications for other former British colonies throughout the world whose

IMAGE 6.1 Activists in Kolkata, India, celebrate a landmark May 2019 Supreme Court ruling striking down Section 377, an 1861 British law that criminalized same-sex relations. The decision is inspiring challenges to similar laws still enshrined in the statutes of former British colonies all over the world.

---

[45]Although each individual country will have to apply the ruling to its own laws, it had immediate implications for nineteen nations then lacking marriage equality including Barbados, Bolivia, Chile, Costa Rica, Dominica, Dominican Republic, Ecuador, El Salvador, Guatemala, Grenada, Haiti, Honduras, Jamaica, Mexico, Nicaragua, Panama, Paraguay, Peru, and Suriname. See Zack Ford, "This Court Just Issued a Sweeping LGBTQ Victory for the Western Hemisphere," *Think Progress*, January 10, 2018, https://thinkprogress.org/inter-american-marriage-equality-transgender-rights-096258591a40/.

[46]Juan Carlos Ulate, "'Love Will Prevail:' Costa Rica's Same-Sex Couples Can Marry in 2020," *Reuters*, November 16, 2018, https://www.reuters.com/article/us-costa-rica-lgbt/love-will-prevail-costa-ricas-same-sex-couples-can-marry-in-2020-idUSKCN1NL06T.

legal codes retained sodomy laws originally imposed by Great Britain.[47] Although a May 2019 ruling by Kenya's high court left the sodomy law in place, Botswana's high court struck down two colonial-era laws a month later, becoming the first African country to decriminalize same-sex relations through a judicial ruling.[48]

In May 2019, Taiwan became the first Asian nation to legalize same-sex marriage. After the country's high court ruled in May 2017 that denying same-sex couples marriage rights was unconstitutional, LGBT advocates lobbied the national legislature for months in the face of conservative opposition. They persisted even after voters approved a November 2018 public referendum limiting civil marriage to heterosexual couples. When the legislature passed legislation legalizing same-sex marriage seven months later, thousands of LGBT Taiwanese and their allies took to the streets to celebrate. Jennifer Lu, leader of Marriage Equality Coalition Taiwan, declared "traditional culture is not against LGBT culture. That's the message we want to send to the world."[49]

Yet it is far from certain that LGBT rights will become a global norm. While many nations have recently made striking recent advances toward LGBT equality, others have greatly intensified anti-LGBT persecution. In 2011, Malawi expanded its sodomy law to criminalize same-sex sexual activities between women. Four years later, the nation outlawed same-sex marriage and defined one's sex or gender as the one assigned at birth. While the law also contained provisions outlawing child marriage and bestowing property rights for widows, the legislation's protections for children and women coexisted with an emphatic rejection of LGBT and intersex rights.[50]

In January 2014, Nigerian President Goodluck Jonathan signed a law that criminalized same-sex relations, same-sex marriage, and participation in "gay clubs, societies, or organizations." A month later, Uganda President Yoweri Museveni signed similar legislation, thwarting four years of international

---

[47]Michael K. Lavers, "India Supreme Court Ruling Decriminalizes Homosexuality," *Washington Blade*, September 6, 2018, https://www.washingtonblade.com/2018/09/06/india-supreme-court-ruling-decriminalizes-homosexuality/.

[48]Stephanie Busari, Farai Sevenzo, and Lillian Leposo, "Kenyan Court Upholds Law Making Gay Sex Illegal," *CNN*, May 24, 2019, https://www.cnn.com/2019/05/24/health/kenya-lgbtqi-ruling-intl/index.html; Max Bearak, "Botswana Legalizes Gay Sex, Striking Down Colonial-Era Laws," *Washington Post*, June 11, 2019, https://www.washingtonpost.com/world/africa/botswana-legalizes-homosexuality-striking-down-colonial-era-laws/2019/06/11/7b3f9376-8c0f-11e9-b08e-cfd89bd36d4e_story.html.

[49]Nick Aspinwall, "Taiwan Becomes First in Asia to Legalize Same-Sex Marriage," *Washington Post*, May 17, 2019, https://www.washingtonpost.com/world/asia_pacific/taiwan-becomes-first-country-in-asia-to-legalize-same-sex-marriage/2019/05/17/d60e511e-7893-11e9-bd25-c989555e7766_story.html.

[50]Aaron Morrison, "Malawi Gay Rights: New Marriage Law Further Criminalizes LGBT Relationships and Identities, Group Says," *International Business Times*, April 17, 2015, https://www.ibtimes.com/malawi-gay-rights-new-marriage-law-further-criminalizes-lgbt-relationships-identities-1886670.

efforts to stop passage of the Anti-Homosexuality Act, often referred to as the "Kill the Gays" bill. After the United States, Sweden, Denmark, and Norway responded by cutting or diverting aid to Uganda, some Africans questioned why anti-LGBT activities seemed to be given primacy in a region rife with a host of human rights abuses. Other Africans supported American evangelicals like Lou Engle, Scott Lively, and Larry Jacobs in their efforts to export especially vitriolic anti-LGBT attitudes.[51]

In February 2017, police in the Russian republic of Chechnya arrested a gay man for substance abuse and then arrested several of the contacts discovered on the man's cell phone. Although neither drug use nor homosexuality is illegal in Russia, police jailed and tortured others in order to compel them to reveal more names. Even though many of the men arrested did not self-identify as gay, the illegal prosecutions escalated. Those lucky enough to survive weeks of mistreatment were released to their families, but faced serious repercussions resulting from police revealing their sexual identity in the predominately Muslim society.

In April 2017, the Moscow-based journalist Elena Milashina reported the existence of detention camps for gay men in Chechnya. Further investigation confirmed that more than 100 men convicted of homosexual offenses were being held in two camps near Grozny, the republic's capital. Claiming there were no homosexuals in Chechnya, the authorities responsible for the incarcerations refuted the journalists' allegations. Through the intervention of the Russian LGBT Network, several dozen detainees and other LGBT Chechens were evacuated to St. Petersburg and Moscow. With the help of the Russian Ministry of Foreign Affairs, about thirty obtained international passports and were subsequently granted refugee status in Canada or Europe.[52]

---

[51]See, for example, Melani McAlister, *The Kingdom of God Has No Borders: A Global History of American Evangelicals* (New York: Oxford University Press, 2018), 247–67; Amar Wahab, "'Homosexuality/Homophobia Is Un-African?' Un-Mapping Transnational Discourses in the Context of Uganda's Anti-Homosexuality Bill/Act," *Journal of Homosexuality* 63:5 (2016): 685–718; "We Need to Talk about Colonialism before We Criticize International Anti-LGBTQ Legislation," *Autostraddle*, January 22, 2014, http://www.autostraddle.com/we-need-to-talk-about-colonialism-before-we-criticize-international-anti-lgbtq-legislation-218306/; Norimimitsu Onishi, "U.S. Support of Gay Rights in Africa May Have Done More Harm Than Good," *New York Times*, December 20, 2015; NPR Goats and Soda, "When the U.S. Back Gay and Lesbian Rights in Africa, Is There a Backlash?" August 30, 2016, https://www.npr.org/sections/goatsandsoda/2016/08/30/491818892/when-the-u-s-backs-gay-and-lesbian-rights-in-africa-is-there-a-backlash.

[52]Kyle Knight, "Gay Men in Chechnya Are Being Tortured and Killed," *The Guardian*, April 17, 2017, https://www.theguardian.com/commentisfree/2017/apr/13/gay-men-targeted-chechnya-russia; Masha Gessen, "The Gay Men Who Fled Chechnya's Purge," *New Yorker*, July 3, 2017, https://www.newyorker.com/magazine/2017/07/03/the-gay-men-who-fled-chechnyas-purge; Tracy E. Gilchrist, "Rainbow Railroad Helps 31 Persecuted Chechen Gay and Bisexual Men to Safety," *The Advocate*, September 3, 2017, https://www.advocate.com/world/2017/9/03/rainbow-railroad-helps-31-persecuted-chechen-gay-bisexual-men-safety.

With such divergent global attitudes toward LGBT rights, pride events around the world often become a flashpoint. During the 1970s, pride parades spread from the United States to Western Europe to Australia. In the 1990s, several Latin American countries began holding annual pride celebrations, as did South Africa, the Philippines, Japan, Israel, India, and Thailand. With the end of the Cold War and the expansion of the EU, pride festivals arose in Hungary, Poland, Serbia, Croatia, and Bosnia and Herzegovina. More recently, pride events have been organized in China, Cuba, and Jamaica.

While most pride festivals are peaceful and joyous celebrations of the diversity of the LGBT community, they have drawn criticism and fierce hostility in many places. Some activists condemn pride festivals for their commercialization and amplification of Western elite white male interpretations of gay culture. Israeli pride festivals have drawn the ire of pro-Palestinian advocates who characterize the events as pinkwashing, the attempt to use a nation's tolerance of LGBT rights as a means of diverting attention from anti-democratic practices and repression of other groups.[53] Much smaller than its Tel Aviv counterpart, Jerusalem Pride is also criticized by ultra-Orthodox Jews who view it as blasphemous. In 2005, Yishai Schlissel was convicted of attempted murder after stabbing three attendees. In July 2015, a month after being released from prison, Schlissel returned to the event and stabbed six marchers, one of whom—sixteen-year-old Shira Banki—died. Unrepentant in his repeatedly expressed antigay views, Schlissel was sentenced to life imprisonment.[54]

In Eastern Europe and Russia, pride events have become particularly divisive. In Serbia in October 2010, right-wing hooligans and ultranationalists broke windows, set cars ablaze, and threw stones, firecrackers, and bombs at police officers guarding marchers at Belgrade Pride. Fifty-seven people were injured and officials suspended the event due to security concerns.[55] But four years later, under heavy pressure from the EU (which Serbia was seeking to join), the government allowed Belgrade Pride to resume. With thousands of police providing security, 1,000 participants peacefully marched, following a small protest by Orthodox and right-wing demonstrators.[56] In 2018, Prime

---

[53]Francesca Romana Ammaturo, "Pride Parades and Marches," in Global Encyclopedia of Lesbian, Gay, Bisexual, Transgender, and Queer History, Howard Chiang, ed. (Chicago: Gale, 2019), Vol. 3, 1281–7.

[54]Isabel Kershner, "Ultra-Orthodox Israeli Stabs 6 at a Gay Pride Parade for the Second Time, Police Say," New York Times, July 30, 2015, https://www.nytimes.com/2015/07/31/world/middleeast/man-attacks-gay-pride-marchers-in-jerusalem-for-second-time-police-say.html; "Jerusalem Gay Pride Stabbing: Ultra-Orthodox Yishai Schlissel Jailed for Life," BBC News, June 26, 2016, https://www.bbc.com/news/world-middle-east-36634148.

[55]"Serbia Gay Pride March Attacked with Bombs, Stones," CNN, October 10, 2010, https://www.cnn.com/2010/WORLD/europe/10/10/serbia.gay.violence/index.html.

[56]Zak Cheney-Rice, "Here's What Happened at Serbia's First LGBT Pride March in Four Years," Mic, September 30, 2014, https://www.mic.com/articles/100082/here-s-what-happened-at-serbia-s-first-lgbt-pride-march-in-four-years.

Minister Ana Brnabic, the first openly lesbian and first Serbian woman to hold the nation's highest office, and Belgrade Mayor Zoran Radojcic, joined a parade of several hundred people.[57]

On May 17, 2013, during a rally in Tbilisi, Georgia marking the International Day Against Homophobia and Transphobia, approximately 20,000 people, led by Georgian Orthodox priests, broke through security lines and attacked about fifty LGBT activists and their allies. Seventeen people were hurt in the melee. Two days before the event—the first-ever public demonstration against homophobia held in Georgia—Ilia II, the head of the Georgian Orthodox Church, called for its cancellation and described homosexuality as "an anomaly and a disease." Amnesty International (AI), several foreign embassies, and many Georgian NGOs condemned the violence. Georgian officials promised to investigate the episode and prosecute the assailants.[58] Although Georgia passed LGBT-inclusive nondiscrimination protections as part of its integration into the EU, homophobic attitudes remained deeply entrenched. When LGBT advocates announced plans to launch Georgia's first pride week in June 2019, they met opposition not only from the Orthodox Church and Levan Vasadze, a Georgian millionaire with ties to Russian business interests who had become the most visible leader of Georgia's anti-LGBT movement, but also from LGBT Georgians who worried that public demonstrations would jeopardize the freedom they were now enjoying underground.[59]

Similar religious and political tensions have arisen in Turkey. Pride celebrations were first launched in Istanbul in 2003. By 2014, the annual event drew over 100,000 people, by far the largest pride celebration in a majority Muslim nation. But in 2015, after organizers proceeded despite being denied a permit because the parade occurred during the Muslim holy month of Ramadan, Turkish police used a water cannon and rubber bullets to disperse marchers.[60] In 2016, the government, citing security concerns and the need to maintain public order in the wake of a failed coup attempt, banned pride events in Istanbul and instituted the same prohibition in

[57]"Serbian Prime Minister, Belgrade Mayor Join Gay Pride Parade," *Radio Free Europe/Radio Liberty*, September 16, 2018, https://www.rferl.org/a/gay-rights-activists-to-march-in-central-belgrade/29492367.html.

[58]Amnesty International, "Georgia: Homophobic Violence Mars Tbilisi Pride Event," May 17, 2013, https://www.amnesty.org/en/latest/news/2013/05/georgia-homophobic-violence-mars-tbilisi-pride-event/; Andrew Roth, "Crowd Led by Priests Attacks Gay Rights Marchers in Georgia," *New York Times*, May 17, 2013, https://www.nytimes.com/2013/05/18/world/europe/gay-rights-rally-is-attacked-in-georgia.html?hpw.

[59]Umberto Bacchi, "Georgia's First Pride Event Kicks Off amid Tensions, Threats," *Reuters*, June 18, 2019, https://www.reuters.com/article/us-georgia-lgbt-pride/georgias-first-pride-event-kicks-off-amid-tensions-threats-idUSKCN1TK003.

[60]Mehmet, Caliskan, and Yesmin Dikmen, "Turkish Police Use Water Cannon to Disperse Gay Pride Parade," *Reuters*, June 28, 2015, https://in.reuters.com/article/turkey-rights-gay-pride/turkish-police-use-water-cannon-to-disperse-gay-pride-parade-idINKCN0P80O420150628.

Ankara the next year.[61] Although homosexuality has been legal in Turkey since 1923, homophobic attitudes persist and the LGBT community became a target in a period of increased political repression under President Recep Tayyip Erdogan and his Justice and Development Party (AKP), which is rooted in conservative Islam. When approximately 1,000 protestors defied the pride ban and marched in Istanbul in June 2018, police attacked them with tear gas and rubber bullets and arrested eleven people.[62] In April 2019, the Turkish LGBT rights group Kaos GL prevailed in a legal appeal that resulted in an administrative court striking down the pride ban in Ankara.[63] Nonetheless, Istanbul authorities ignored pleas by AI to lift the "arbitrary ban" and forbade pride for the fifth year in a row. When hundreds of people marched in defiance in June, police once again forcibly dispersed the crowd.[64]

The Russian government has taken especially harsh measures to suppress pride events and LGBT organizations.[65] In 2005, to mark the thirteenth anniversary of the decriminalization of homosexuality in Russia, Nikolay Alexeyev, leader of the new group GayRussia, announced that he would apply for a permit to hold Moscow's first pride festival the following year. The city government led by Mayor Yuri Luzhkov banned all planned pride activities and rejected the application to hold a march on Tverskaya Street. The head of the Russian Orthodox Church, Chief Rabbi Berl Lazar, and the Muslim Grand Mufti Talgat Tadzhuddin all publicly opposed the march.[66] On May 27, 2006, when several dozen Russian LGBT advocates flanked by European allies marched in defiance, about 300 nationalist and neo-Nazi protestors attacked them while police did little to intervene. Oscar Wilde's grandson Merlin Holland and Volker Beck, an openly gay member of the German Bundestag, were among those who suffered vicious beatings.[67] Undeterred, the organizers continued to hold pride marches each year. In 2007, 2008, and 2012, they again faced brutal violence and arrests. In other years, they escaped such mistreatment only by keeping the location of demonstrations secret. In October 2010, the ECtHR lambasted Moscow

[61]"Turkish Capital Ankara Bans All Gay Rights Functions," *BBC*, November 19, 2017, https://www.bbc.com/news/world-europe-42043910.

[62]Sheena McKenzie, "Hundreds of LGBTI+ Campaigners March in Banned Istanbul Pride Parade," *CNN*, July 2, 2018, https://www.cnn.com/2018/07/02/europe/istanbul-pride-parade-intl/index.html.

[63]Alex MacDonald, "Court Lifts Ban on Pride Events in Ankara," Middle East Eye, April 19, 2019, https://www.middleeasteye.net/news/court-lifts-ban-lgbt-pride-events-ankara.

[64]Olivia Tobin, "Istanbul Pride 2019: Thousands March despite Being Banned by Authorities," *The Evening Standard*, June 30, 2019, https://www.standard.co.uk/news/world/hundreds-celebrate-istanbul-pride-despite-march-being-banned-by-authorities-a4178996.html.

[65]Francesca Stella, "Queer Space, Pride, and Shame in Moscow," *Slavic Review* 72:3 (2013): 458–80.

[66]Peter Tatchell, "Marching in Moscow," *The Guardian*, May 24, 2006, https://www.theguardian.com/commentisfree/2006/may/24/moscowbansgayprideparade.

[67]Doug Ireland, "Police, Fascists Crush Moscow Pride," *Gay City News*, May 7, 2006, https://www.gaycitynews.nyc/stories/2006/9/police-fascists-crush-moscow-2006-05-07.html.

authorities for discriminating against the pride organizers on the basis of sexual orientation and denying them freedom of assembly.[68]

Russian officials remained unrepentant and ignored the ECtHR ruling. In 2012, after St. Petersburg banned LGBT organizations and public events, the feminist punk band Pussy Riot held a concert in Moscow's Cathedral of Christ the Savior to protest Vladimir Putin and the Russian Orthodox Church. They were arrested for "hooliganism motived by religious hatred" and sentenced to two-year jail terms.[69] The same day Pussy Riot was sentenced, a Moscow court upheld the city's new 100-year ban on Moscow Pride.[70]

The battle between Russia's free speech and LGBT rights advocates and those defending "traditional" values from what they characterized as Western assaults on nature and religion had been escalating for years. After the collapse of the Soviet Union in 1991, state censorship ended and expressions of sexuality flooded Russian media and culture. But the transition from communism to global capitalism created profound economic inequality and disillusionment among the majority of Russians. By the early 2000s, President Vladimir Putin and a new oligarchic class joined forces with nationalists and conservative religious leaders in demonizing LGBT people as a root cause of moral decay, a declining birth rate, and poverty. Homophobic public discourse and anti-LGBT hate crimes soared. In June 2013, after several failed attempts to do so earlier, the Duma (Russia's parliament) unanimously adopted a new national law criminalizing the promotion of LGBT rights and spreading "propaganda of nontraditional sexual relations" among minors. Individuals found guilty of violating the statute face fines of up to 100,000 rubles ($1,750). Convicted organizations faced substantially higher fines and closure for up to ninety days. Foreign offenders faced fines and deportation. The propaganda law went into effect immediately and state authorities quickly used it to charge hundreds of LGBT youth advocates, mental health professionals, journalists, and teachers. The Putin regime encouraged religious conservatives and right-wing nationalists in Europe, the Middle East, and Africa to reject the promotion of LGBT rights by the EU and the UN.[71]

---

[68]Human Rights Watch, "Russia: European Court Rules Gay Pride Ban Unlawful," October 21, 2010, https://www.hrw.org/news/2010/10/21/russia-european-court-rules-gay-pride-ban-unlawful.

[69]Mark Memmott, "Two-Year Prison Terms for Russia's Pussy Riot Rockers," *NPR*, August 17, 2012, https://www.npr.org/blogs/thetwo-way/2012/08/17/158976733/coming-up-women-in-russian-punk-band-to-be-sentenced.

[70]Eyder Peralta, "Moscow Court Upholds 100-Year Ban on Gay Pride Events," *NPR*, August 17, 2002, https://www.npr.org/sections/thetwo-way/2012/08/17/159025451/moscow-court-upholds-100-year-ban-on-gay-pride-events.

[71]Miriam Elder, "Russia Passes Law Banning Gay 'Propaganda,'" *The Guardian*, June 11, 2013, https://www.theguardian.com/world/2013/jun/11/russia-law-banning-gay-propaganda; Dan Healey, *Russian Homophobia from Stalin to Sochi* (London: Bloomsbury Academic, 2017).

The political potency of such efforts is evident in Poland. In the spring of 2019, after Warsaw Mayor Rafal Trzaskowski issued a declaration calling for the integration of sex education and LGBT issues into high school curricula in accordance with World Health Organization guidelines, Jarosław Kaczyński, leader of the ruling right-wing Law and Justice party (PiS), denounced "LGBT ideology" as a "threat to families and children" and a "threat to Polish identity, to our nation, to its existence and thus to the Polish state." In response, thirty city and regional councils declared themselves "LGBT-free zones." In July 2019, when Bialystok, a northeastern city of 298,000 that is a stronghold for the PiS, celebrated its first-ever pride march, 1,000 marchers were ringed by police protecting them from about 4,000 counter-protestors throwing objects and shouting "God, honor, and motherland" and "Bialystok free of perverts!" Although Bialystok Pride was one of twenty-four pride celebrations held across Poland and polls show increasing support for LGBT rights among urban Poles, Catholic and state leaders have successfully encouraged popular animus toward secularization and rechanneled xenophobia used to animate voters at the height of the European migration crisis in 2015. Tapping into entrenched anti-LGBT attitudes is not difficult in a nation where same-sex marriage and adoptions

IMAGE 6.2 Religious conservatives and right-wing nationalists in several Eastern European countries and Russia have joined forces in opposing LGBT rights. In this photograph taken at the Equality March in Krakow, Poland, on May 19, 2018, anti-LGBT demonstrators hold a banner suggesting that LGBT equality threatens families.

are illegal. More ominously, the political climate has contributed to a rise in anti-LGBT hate crimes.[72]

These trends leave the ultimate outcome of the international LGBT rights movement uncertain. Supranational institutions like the ECtHR and the United Nations Human Rights Commission have helped to advance global LGBT equality, but such multilateral institutions are under duress in an age of resurgent populism. While there has been monumental progress for LGBT equality in individual nations, in dozens of countries same-sex relations remain illegal and cultural attitudes are still intensely hostile. The intervention of foreign activists into localized LGBT rights battles often inflames deep-seated anti-imperialism and sometimes results in intensified persecution of grassroots activists. But the courage and conviction of those fighting for the right to love and desire whomever they wish have never been extinguished by even the most repressive government and the struggle for worldwide LGBT equality will continue.

---

[72]Tara John and Muhammad Darwish, "Polish City Holds First LGBTQ Pride Parade despite Far-Right Violence," CNN, July 21, 2019, https://www.cnn.com/2019/07/21/europe/bialystok-polish-lgbtq-pride-intl/index.html; Rick Noack, "Polish Towns Advocate 'LGBT-Free' Zones while the Ruling Party Cheers Them On," Washington Post, July 21, 2019, https://www.washingtonpost.com/world/europe/polands-right-wing-ruling-party-has-found-a-new-targetlgbt-ideology/2019/07/19/775f25c6-a4ad-11e9-a767-d7ab84aef3e9_story.html?wpisrc=nl_headlines&wpmm=1.

Conclusion

This short volume could not possibly encompass the entirety of the history of the international LGBT rights movement, but it does point to many valuable avenues for future inquiry. Why have Northern Europe and Latin American countries embraced LGBT equality earlier than many leading Western democracies? How has religion both advanced and obstructed LGBT rights around the world? What does the rise of right-wing authoritarianism in democratic societies portend for the future of LGBT rights globally? How do more radical conceptions of queer identity and non-binary notions of gender complicate efforts to expand LGBT rights at the national and international levels? Will the somewhat inchoate international anti-LGBT rights movement cohere into a force that ultimately rolls back LGBT gains made in supranational institutions like the European Union and the United Nations (UN)? These are only a few of the questions scholars who wish to build on this narrative should explore.

Universalized notions of rights based upon sexual orientation and gender identity will remain hotly contested for the foreseeable future. Weak UN enforcement mechanisms and a strong reluctance to violate norms of national sovereignty compound the challenges of consistently applying human rights principles globally. If major international powers move beyond condemnatory rhetoric and informal diplomacy and begin using more forceful tactics like recalling ambassadors from nations that pass anti-LGBT laws, withdrawing foreign aid, or suspending visa privileges for officials responsible for such legislation, such moves risk further jeopardizing local activists already facing intense scrutiny, police harassment, and violence in these nations. Pressure from international LGBT advocacy groups also sparks anti-imperialist and nationalist resistance in many places. While the steps taken to forge a global consensus on LGBT equality are quite remarkable, it is clear there is much more to be done to ensure the safety and protection of LGBT people worldwide. One might hope that the story of global LGBT equality is a progress narrative that ends with acceptance of non-heteronormative and non-binary people everywhere, but the future is riddled with uncertainty.

The rapidity with which gains can be reversed has been potently demonstrated by the United States. While campaigning in the Republican presidential primaries in April 2016, Donald Trump opposed same-sex marriage but nonetheless presented himself as an advocate for LGBT rights, publicly criticizing a recently passed North Carolina law prohibiting the use of bathrooms that did not correspond with one's gender as defined at birth.[1] On June 12, Omar Mateen, a 29-year-old security guard, killed forty-nine people and wounded fifty-three others in a mass shooting at Pulse, a gay dance club in Orlando, Florida. Mateen, a Muslim born in the United States to Afghan immigrant parents, had vowed his allegiance to the Islamic State of the Levant and Iraq (ISIS) in a 911 call made during the shooting.[2] Two days later, Trump—by then the Republican nominee—condemned ISIS for throwing men assumed to be gay off buildings. He claimed that his proposed ban on the emigration of Muslims would protect the "freedoms and beliefs" of LGBT Americans more robustly than any policy espoused by Democratic nominee Hillary Clinton. Trump aligned himself with anti-Muslim activists like Dutch politician Geert Wilders and blogger Pamela Geller who pointed to persecution and violence against LGBT people by Islamic extremists as justification for immigration restrictions. Trump's use of the Pulse massacre, one of the deadliest mass shootings in US history, to promote homonationalism and nativism outraged many LGBT activists who noted that most of the Pulse victims were Hispanic. "He has no shame," said Jay Brown, spokesman for the Human Rights Campaign, the largest US LGBT advocacy organization. "Many gay people are also Muslims, Latinos and women," he added, "we are the very people around whom he has built an entire campaign belittling and maligning at every turn."[3]

Skepticism about Trump's professed commitment to LGBT rights proved justified. After Trump won the presidency, his administration embarked on a systematic reversal of pro-LGBT executive orders and federal policy changes made by the Obama administration. In addition to reinstituting a ban on transgender people serving in the armed forces, the Trump administration

---

[1]Maggie Haberman, "Donald Trump's More Accepting Views on Gay Issues Set Him Apart in G.O.P.," *New York Times*, April 22, 2016, https://www.nytimes.com/2016/04/23/us/politics/donald-trump-gay-rights.html.

[2]Ralph Ellis, Ashley Fantz, Faith Karimi, and Eliott C. McLaughlin, "Orlando Shooting: 49 Killed, Shooter Pledged ISIS Allegiance," *CNN*, June 13, 2016, https://www.cnn.com/2016/06/12/us/orlando-nightclub-shooting/index.html.

[3]Beth Reinhard and Reid J. Epstein, "Donald Trump Casts Himself as Gay-Rights Champion after Orlando Shooting," *Wall Street Journal*, June 15, 2016, https://www.wsj.com/articles/donald-trump-casts-himself-as-gay-rights-champion-after-orlando-shooting-1465988402.

rolled back expanded protections in adoption, health care, education, housing, and federal contracting. In October 2019, lawyers from the US Department of Justice appeared before the Supreme Court and argued that the provisions of the Civil Rights Act of 1964 that outlaw sex discrimination do not encompass sexual orientation or gender identity. The case has enormous implications for the future of LGBT rights in the United States.[4]

At the same time, the Trump administration is attempting to present itself as a champion of international LGBT rights. In a June 2019 tweet marking LGBT Pride Month, Trump claimed that his administration had launched a global campaign to decriminalize homosexuality in seventy countries—an announcement initially made by Richard Grenell, Trump's openly gay ambassador to Germany. But at the same time, the Trump administration was rejecting requests from US embassies asking to fly the rainbow flag on the official flagpoles outside their buildings—an annual LGBT Pride Month gesture that had become routine since Hillary Clinton declared "gay rights are human rights" in 2011. Some US diplomats and international LGBT rights advocates interpreted the move as a signal that the United States was abandoning its recent leadership role in advancing global LGBT equality.[5] They remained skeptical even after Trump addressed the UN in September 2019 and declared: "We stand in solidarity with LGBTQ people who live in countries that punish, jail, or execute individuals based on sexual orientation." Pointing to Trump's assaults on domestic LGBT rights and the US refusal to grant visas to gay and bisexual men fleeing human rights abuses in Chechnya, many LGBT activists accused Trump of dishonesty and hypocrisy.[6]

Trump's polarizing presidency and its contradictory rhetoric and actions are part of a larger wave of right-wing populism that has imperiled LGBT rights in several nations.[7] The case of Brazil is illustrative. In recent years,

---

[4]Sam Levin, "'A Critical Point in History': How Trump's Attack on LGBT Rights Is Escalating," *The Guardian*, September 3, 2019, https://www.theguardian.com/world/2019/sep/03/trump-attack-lgbt-rights-supreme-court; Kristen Berg and Moiz Syed, "Under Trump, LGBTQ Progress Is Being Reversed in Plain Sight," *ProPublica*, November 22, 2019, https://projects.propublica.org/graphics/lgbtq-rights-rollback.

[5]Josh Lederman, "Trump Admin Tells U.S. Embassies They Can't Fly Pride Flag on Flagpoles," *NBC News*, June 7, 2019, https://www.nbcnews.com/politics/national-security/trump-admin-tells-u-s-embassies-they-can-t-fly-n1015236.

[6]Rachel Savage, "Rights Advocates Call Trump's Pledge to Decriminalize Gay Sex 'a Lie,'" *Reuters*, September 25, 2019, https://www.reuters.com/article/united-nations-lgbt-usa/rights-advocates-call-trumps-pledge-to-decriminalize-gay-sex-a-lie-idUSL5N26G5ZK.

[7]John Ibbitson, "Rising Populism Threatens LGBTQ in West and around the World," *The Globe and Mail*, December 28, 2018, https://www.theglobeandmail.com/politics/article-rising-populism-threatens-lgbtq-in-west-and-around-the-world/?fbclid=IwAR2PrAa6DPoXnYHb1Z4gq6u95QE4cxkKhz50AmwjAEd1MZ_JkH8tq_vWYTk; Ian Lekus, "The Movement for LGBTQ Rights Is on the March around the World," *The Nation*, June 28, 2019, https://www.thenation.com/article/international-lgbtq-rights-legacy-imperialism/.

Brazil has instituted several LGBT protections, including the legalization of same-sex marriage in 2013 and a March 2018 law that allows people to change their legal gender identity without requiring surgery, hormonal treatments, or a medical diagnosis. Many LGBT Brazilians were therefore justifiably alarmed when Jair Bolsonaro campaigned for the presidency in 2018. Bolsonaro, a right-wing retired military officer, made no secret of his anti-LGBT views. "Yes, I'm homophobic," he once asserted, "and very proud of it." In 2011, he claimed that he would prefer to have "a dead son rather than a gay son." He also encouraged parents who suspected their children of being gay or lesbian to beat them back to "normal." Upon assuming office on January 1, 2019, Bolsonaro immediately prohibited the nation's human rights ministry from considering LGBT issues. The move sent a chilling message in a country with one of the world's highest rates of anti-LGBT violence.[8] But just six months later, Brazil's Supreme Court ruled that sexual orientation and gender identity should be protected under the nation's nondiscrimination law.[9]

Although resurgent right-wing populism has contributed to increases in violence against racial, religious, and sexual minorities in several countries, there is also cause for cautious optimism. Social media provides LGBT people living under repressive governments or in unfriendly societies the means to connect. In China, Blued, one of the world's most popular dating apps, is consciously apolitical, but is nonetheless helping to raise LGBT visibility and increase popular support for LGBT rights while avoiding censorship by the communist regime.[10] Muslim immigrants in Western Europe are using Grindr, an app best known for facilitating gay sex hookups, to find friendship and support in a place that is alien and sometimes hostile.[11] There are signs that the populist wave may prove short-lived. Recent mass protests against authoritarian regimes in Iran and Hong Kong and Global Climate Strike and Black Lives Matter rallies all over the world attest to

---

[8]Shannon Power, "Brazil's New President Strips LGBTI Rights on His First Day in Office," *Gay Star News*, January 3, 2019, https://www.gaystarnews.com/article/brazils-new-president-strips-lgbti-rights-on-his-first-day-in-office/.

[9]Joshua Bote, "Brazil's Supreme Court Criminalizes Homophobia and Transphobia," *USA Today*, June 14, 2019, https://www.usatoday.com/story/news/world/2019/06/14/brazil-supreme-court-bans-homophobia-transphobia-despite-bolsonaro/1454855001/.

[10]Yi-Ling Liu, "How a Dating App Helped a Generation of Chinese Come Out of the Closet," *New York Times Magazine*, March 5, 2020, https://www.nytimes.com/2020/03/05/magazine/blued-china-gay-dating-app.html?nl=todaysheadlines&emc=edit_th_200308&campaign_id=2&instance_id=16585&segment_id=21991&user_id=009e3a5e9e977a807281a8e42634915a&regi_id=582352630308.

[11]Andrew D. J. Shield, *Immigrants on Grindr: Race, Sexuality, and Belonging Online* (Cham, Switzerland: Palgrave Macmillan, 2019).

people's enduring willingness to combat injustice and demand reform.[12] In May 2019, despite the transnational anti-LGBT movement's attacks on "gender ideology" (a rhetorical device used to encapsulate hostility toward gender equity, transgenderism, and reproductive justice), the World Health Organization removed "gender identity disorder" from its list of mental illnesses—a major landmark in the global quest for transgender rights.[13]

According to a 2019 Gallup poll of more than 130,000 people in 167 nations, tolerance for LGBT individuals is rising markedly in almost every country in the world. Not surprisingly, the nations with the highest levels of support are Iceland, the Netherlands, Norway, Canada, and Denmark—all countries with a long history of protecting LGBT rights. Equally unsurprising is the persistence of homophobia and transphobia in several former Soviet states and across sub-Saharan Africa. Despite having respectively decriminalized consensual same-sex relations between men in 1988 and 2000, Tajikistan and Azerbaijan ranked among the five least tolerant nations. Male homosexuality remains illegal in the other three—Somalia, Senegal, and Mauritania.[14]

Although the ultimate outcome of the global quest for LGBT equality remains uncertain, courageous LGBT activists will undoubtedly continue fighting for love, dignity, safety, and living one's truth. That path has looked very different in different times and places and such differences will persist. But the road to justice never ends and there will always be pathbreakers willing to take the journey.

---

[12]Allana Akhtar and Juliana Kaplan, "A World on Fire: Here Are All the Major Protests Happening around the Globe Right Now," *Business Insider*, October 22, 2019, https://www.businessinsider.com/all-the-protests-around-the-world-right-now; Jen Kirby, "'Black Lives Matter' Has Become A Global Rallying Cry against Racism and Police Brutality," *Vox*, June 12, 2020, https://www.vox.com/2020/6/12/21285244/black-lives-matter-global-protests-george-floyd-uk-belgium.

[13]Alex R. Holmes, "World Health Organization Drops Transgender from List of Mental Disorders," *Metro*, May 27, 2019, https://metro.co.uk/2019/05/27/world-health-organisation-drops-transgender-from-list-of-mental-disorders-9698165/.

[14]Sonia Elks, "Tolerance towards LGBT+ People Seen Rising Globally," *Reuters*, November 24, 2019, https://www.reuters.com/article/us-global-lgbt-tolerance/tolerance-towards-lgbt-people-seen-rising-globally-idUSKBN1XZ02M.

BIBLIOGRAPHY

PRIMARY SOURCES

Archival Collections

Records at the Columbia University Libraries Rare Book & Manuscript Library, New York, New York, USA
Amnesty International of the USA, Inc., National Office Records, 1966–2003

Records at GLBT Historical Society, San Francisco, California
Desi Del Valle collection
The Ladder
Newsletters collection
Periodicals collection

Records at the Hall-Carpenter Archives, London School of Economics, London, England
Albany Trust collection
Campaign for Homosexual Equality collection
Gay Liberation Front collection
Ephemera collection
Lisa Power collection

Records at the IHLIA LGBT Heritage, Amsterdam Public Library, Amsterdam, Netherlands
Annual ILGA Conferences – Preconference Papers, Conference Papers, and Conference Reports
Eastern European Information Pool
IGA Informal Meetings
IGA Memoranda
IGA News/*Newsletter*
IGA Summer Meeting
IGA/ILGA Bulletin
ILGA and Pedophilia
ILGA Executive Board Reports
ILGA Reports
ILIS Conferences

Records at the ONE National Gay & Lesbian Archives, Los Angeles, California
The Advocate
Albany Trust

International Committee for Sexual Equality
Mattachine Society Project Collection
ONE, Inc. Records
ONE Calendar/ONE Confidential
ONE Institute, Quarterly Homophile Studies
ONE Magazine

Newspapers and Periodicals

The Advocate
Washington Blade

Other Sources

IGA Pink Book 1985: A Global View of Lesbian and Gay Oppression and
Liberation. Amsterdam: COC-Magazijn, 1985.
The Second ILGA Pink Book: A Global View of Lesbian and Gay Liberation and
Oppression. Utrecht: Interfacultaire Werkgroup Homostudies Utrecht, 1988.
Hendriks, Aart, Rob Tielman, and Evert van der Veen, The Third Pink Book: A
Global View of Lesbian and Gay Liberation and Oppression. Buffalo, NY:
Prometheus Books, 1993.

BOOKS

Adam, Barry D., Jan Willem Duyvendak, and André Krouwel. The Global Emergence
of Gay and Lesbian Politics. Philadelphia: Temple University Press, 1998.
Aldrich, Robert. Colonialism and Homosexuality. New York: Routledge, 2003.
Aldrich, Robert, ed. Gay Life & Culture: A World History. New York: Universe
Publishing, 2006.
Altman, Dennis and Jonathan Symons. Queer Wars: The New Global Polarization
over Gay Rights. Cambridge, UK: Polity Press, 2016.
Ayoub, Phillip. When States Come Out: Europe's Sexual Minorities and the Politics
of Visibility. Cambridge, UK: Cambridge University Press, 2016.
Ayoub, Phillip and David Paternotte, eds. LGBT Activism and the Making of
Europe: A Rainbow Europe? New York: Palgrave Macmillan, 2014.
Bakshi, Sandeep, Suhraiya Jivraj, and Silvia Posoco, eds. Decolonizing Sexualities:
Transnational Perspectives, Critical Interventions. London: Counterpress, 2016.
Bauer, Heike. The Hirschfeld Archives: Violence, Death, and Modern Queer
Culture. Philadelphia: Temple University Press, 2017.
Bauer, Heike and Matt Cook. Queer 1950s: Rethinking Sexuality in the Postwar
Years. London: Palgrave Macmillan, 2012.
Beachy, Robert. Gay Berlin: Birthplace of a Modern Identity. New York: Vintage
Books, 2014.
Benadusi, Lorenzo. The Enemy of the New Man: Homosexuality in Fascist Italy.
Translated by Suzanne Dingee and Jennifer Pudney. Madison: University of
Wisconsin Press, 2012.

Bérubé, Allen. *Coming Out under Fire: The History of Gay Men and Women in World War II*. New York: Penguin Books, 1990.

Borgwardt, Elizabeth. *A New Deal for the World: America's Vision for Human Rights*. Cambridge, MA: Belknap Press, 2007.

Bosia, Michael J., Sandra M. McEvoy, and Momin Rahman, eds. *The Global Handbook of Global LGBT and Sexual Diversity Politics* (Oxford University Press online, 2019), https://www.oxfordhandbooks.com/view/10.1093/oxfordhb/9780190673741.001.0001/oxfordhb-9780190673741.

Boswell, John. *Christianity, Social Tolerance, and Homosexuality: Gay People in Western Europe from the Beginning of the Christian Era to the Fourteenth Century*. Chicago: University of Chicago Press, 1980.

Brady, Sean and Mark Seymour, eds. *From Sodomy Laws to Same-Sex Marriage: International Perspectives since 1789*. London: Bloomsbury Academic, 2019.

Brooks, Adrian, ed. *The Right Side of History: 100 Years of LGBTQI Activism*. New York: Cleis Press, 2015.

Canaday, Margot. *The Straight State: Sexuality and Citizenship in Twentieth-Century America*. Princeton, NJ: Princeton University Press, 2009.

Carter, David. *Stonewall: The Riots That Sparked the Gay Revolution*. New York: St. Martin's, 2004.

Chauncey, George. *Gay New York: Gender, Urban Culture, and the Making of the Gay Male World, 1890–1940*. New York: Basic Books, 1994.

Chiang, Howard, ed. *Global Encyclopedia of Lesbian, Gay, Bisexual, Transgender, and Queer (LGBTQ) History*. 3 vols. Chicago: Gale, 2019.

Choudry, Aziz and Dip Kapoor, eds. *NGOization: Complicity, Contradictions and Prospects*. New York: Zed Books, 2013.

Cook, Matt. *London and the Culture of Homosexuality, 1885–1914*. New York: Cambridge University Press, 2008.

Cook, Matt and Jennifer V. Evans. *Queer Cities, Queer Cultures: Europe since 1945*. London: Bloomsbury, 2014.

Corrales, Javier and Mario Pecheny, eds. *The Politics of Sexuality in Latin America: A Reader on Lesbian, Gay, Bisexual, and Transgender Rights*. Pittsburg: University of Pittsburgh Press, 2010.

Crouthamel, Jason. *An Intimate History of the Front: Masculinity, Sexuality, and German Soldiers in the First World War*. New York: Palgrave Macmillan, 2014.

Currier, Ashley. *Out in Africa: LGBT Organizing in Namibia and South Africa*. Minneapolis: University of Minnesota Press, 2012.

D'Emilio, John. *Sexual Politics, Sexual Communities: The Making of a Homosexual Minority in the United States, 1940–1970*. Chicago: University of Chicago Press, 1983.

Díez, Jordi. *The Politics of Gay Marriage: Argentina, Chile, and Mexico*. New York: Cambridge University Press, 2015.

Dose, Ralf. *Magnus Hirschfeld: The Origins of the Gay Liberation Movement*. New York: Monthly Review Press, 2014.

Duberman, Martin. *Stonewall*. New York: Dutton, 1993.

Duberman, Martin, Martha Vicinus, and George Chauncey, Jr. *Hidden from History: Reclaiming the Gay and Lesbian Past*. New York: Meridan, 1989.

Eder, Franz X, Lesley Hall, and Gert Hekma. *Sexual Cultures in Europe*. Vol. 2. *Themes in Sexuality*. Manchester: University of Manchester Press, 1999.

Edsall, Nicholas. *Toward Stonewall: Homosexuality and Society in the Modern Western World*. Charlottesville: University of Virginia Press, 2003.

El-Rouayheb, Khaled. *Before Homosexuality in the Arab-Islamic World, 1500–1800*. Chicago: University of Chicago Press, 2005.

Encarnación, Omar G. *Out in the Periphery: Latin America's Gay Rights Revolution*. New York: Oxford University Press, 2016.

Epprecht, Marc. *Heterosexual Africa? The History of an Idea from the Age of Exploration to the Age of AIDS*. Athens, OH: Ohio University Press, 2008.

Epprecht, Marc. *Sexuality and Social Justice in Africa: Rethinking Homophobia and Forging Resistance*. London: Zed Books, 2013.

Eskridge, Jr. William N. *Dishonorable Passions: Sodomy Laws in America, 1861–2003*. New York: Viking, 2008.

Foster, Thomas, ed. *Long before Stonewall: Histories of Same-Sex Sexuality in Early America*. New York: New York University, 2007.

France, David. *How to Survive a Plague: The Inside Story of How Citizens and Science Tamed AIDS*. New York: Knopf, 2016.

Froide, Amy M. *Never Married: Singlewomen in Early Modern England*. New York: Oxford University Press, 2005.

Fuechtner, Veronika, Douglas E. Haynes, and Ryan M. Jones, eds. *A Global History of Sexual Science, 1880–1960*. Berkeley: University of California Press, 2018.

Gerassi, John. *The Boys of Boise: Furor, Vice, and Folly in an American City*. New York: Macmillan, 1966.

Gevisser, Mark and Edwin Cameron. *Defiant Desire: Gay and Lesbian Lives in South Africa*. New York: Routledge, 1995.

Goldhaber, Michael D. *A People's History of the European Court of Human Rights*. New Brunswick, NJ: Rutgers University Press, 2009.

Green, James Naylor. *Beyond Carnival: Male Homosexuality in Twentieth-Century Brazil*. Chicago: University of Chicago Press, 1996.

Greenberg, David F. *The Construction of Homosexuality*. Chicago: University of Chicago Press, 1988.

Habib, Samar. *Female Homosexuality in the Middle East*. New York: Routledge, 2007.

Healey, Dan. *Homosexual Desire in Revolutionary Russia: The Regulation of Sexual and Gender Dissent*. Chicago: University of Chicago Press, 2001.

Healey, Dan. *Russian Homophobia from Stalin to Sochi*. London: Bloomsbury Academic, 2017.

Herzog, Dagmar. *Sex after Fascism: Memory and Morality in Twentieth-Century Germany*. Princeton: Princeton University Press, 2005.

Herzog, Dagmar. *Sexuality in Europe: A Twentieth-Century History*. New York: Cambridge University Press, 2011.

Higgins, Patrick. *Heterosexual Dictatorship: Male Homosexuality in Postwar Britain*. London: Fourth Estate, 1996.

Higgs, David, ed. *Queer Sites: Gay Urban Histories since 1600*. London: Routledge, 1999.

Hinsch, Bret. *Passions of the Cut Sleeve: The Male Homosexual Tradition in China*. Berkeley: University of California Press, 1990.

Hobson, Emily K. *Lavender and Red: Liberation and Solidarity in the Gay and Lesbian Left*. Berkeley: University of California Press, 2016.

Hodges, Andrew. *Alan Turing: The Enigma*. Princeton: Princeton University Press, 2012.

Hopgood, Steven. *Keepers of the Flame: Understanding Amnesty International*. Ithaca, NY: Cornell University Press, 2006.

Iriye, Akira, Petra Goedde, and William I. Hitchcock, eds. *The Human Rights Revolution: An International History*. New York: Oxford University Press, 2012.

Irwin, Robert McKee, Edward J. McCaughan, and Michelle Rocio Nasser, eds. *The Famous 41: Sexuality and Social Control in Mexico*. New York: Palgrave Macmillan, 2003.

Jackson, Julian. *Living in Arcadia: Homosexuality, Politics, and Morality in France from the Liberation to AIDS*. Chicago: University of Chicago Press, 2009.

Jeffery-Poulter, Stephen. *Peers, Queers, and Commons: The Struggle for Gay Law Reform from 1950 to the Present*. London, Routledge, 1991.

Jennings, Rebecca. *A Lesbian History of Britain: Love and Sex between Women since 1500*. Westport, CT: Greenwood World Publishing, 2007.

Johnson, David K. *Buying Gay: How Physique Entrepreneurs Sparked a Movement*. New York: Columbia University Press, 2019.

Johnson, David K. *The Lavender Scare: The Cold War Persecution of Gays and Lesbians in the Federal Government*. Chicago: University of Chicago, 2006.

Johnson, Paul. *Homosexuality and the European Court of Human Rights*. Abingdon: Taylor & Francis, 2012.

Kaplan, Morris B. *Sodom on the Thames: Sex, Love, and Scandal in Wilde Times*. Ithaca, NY: Cornell University Press, 2005.

Keck, Margaret E. and Kathryn Sikkink. *Activists beyond Borders: Advocacy Networks in International Politics*. Ithaca, NY: Cornell University Press, 1998.

Kennedy, Hubert. *The Ideal Gay Man: The Story of "Der Kreis."* New York: Haworth, 1999.

Keys, Barbara. *Reclaiming American Virtue: The Human Rights Revolution of the 1970s*. Cambridge, MA: Harvard University Press, 2014.

Kinsman, Gary. *The Regulation of Desire: Homo and Hetero Sexualities*. 2nd ed. rev. Montreal: Black Rose Books, 1996.

Kinsman, Gary and Patrizia Gentile. *The Canadian War on Queers: National Security as Sexual Regulation*. Vancouver: University of British Columbia Press, 2010.

Kollman, Kelly. *The Same-Sex Unions Revolution in Western Democracies: International Norms and Domestic Policy Change*. Manchester: Manchester University Press, 2013.

Kon, Igor S. *The Sexual Revolution in Russia: From the Age of the Czars to Today*. New York: The Free Press, 1995.

Lacey, Brian. *Terrible Queer Creatures: Homosexuality in Irish History*. Dublin: Wordwell Ltd., 2008.

Lauritsen, John and David Thorstad. *The Early Homosexual Rights Movement, 1864–1935*. rev. ed. Novato, CA: Times Change Press, 1995.

Lennox, Corinne and Matthew Waites, eds. *Human Rights, Sexual Orientation, and Gender Identity in the Commonwealth: Struggles for Decriminalization and Change*. London: Human Rights Consortium, Institute of Commonwealth Studies, University of London, 2013.

Lewis, Brian. *Wolfenden's Witnesses: Homosexuality in Postwar Britain*. London: Palgrave Macmillan, 2016.

Loftin, Craig M. *Masked Voices: Gay Men and Lesbians in Cold War America*. Albany: State University of New York Press, 2012.

Long, Michael G. *Gay Is Good: The Life and Letters of Franklin Kameny*. Syracuse, NY: Syracuse University Press, 2014.

Luibhéid, Eithne. *Entry Denied: Controlling Sexuality at the Border*. Minneapolis: University of Minnesota Press, 2002.

Luibhéid, Eithne and Lionel Cantú, Jr., eds. *Queer Migrations: Sexuality, U.S. Citizenship, and Border Crossings*. Minneapolis: University of Minnesota Press, 2005.

Lumsden, Ian. *Machos, Maricones, & Gays: Cuba and Homosexuality*. Philadelphia: Temple University Press, 1996.

Mancini, Elena. *Magnus Hirschfeld and the Quest for Sexual Freedom: A History of the First International Sexual Freedom Movement*. London: Macmillan, 2010.

Manion, Jen. *Female Husbands: A Trans History*. New York: Cambridge University Press, 2020.

Marhoefer, Laurie. *Sex and the Weimar Republic: German Homosexual Emancipation and the Rise of the Nazis*. Toronto: University of Toronto Press, 2015.

Martel, Frédéric. *Global Gay: How Gay Culture Is Changing the World*. Cambridge, MA: MIT Press, 2018.

Martel, Frédéric. *The Pink and the Black: Homosexuals in France since 1968*. Palo Alto: Stanford University Press, 2000.

Massad, Joseph. *Desiring Arabs*. Chicago: University of Chicago Press, 2007.

McAlister, Melani. *The Kingdom of God Has No Borders: A Global History of American Evangelicals*. New York: Oxford University Press, 2018.

McClellan, Josie. *Love in the Time of Communism: Intimacy and Sexuality in the GDR*. New York: Cambridge University Press, 2011.

Meeker, Martin. *Contacts Desired: Gay and Lesbian Communications and Community, 1940–1970s*. Chicago: University of Chicago Press, 2006.

Mendelson, Sara and Patricia Crawford, *Women in Early Modern England, 1550–1720*. New York: Oxford University Press, 1998.

Merrick, Jeffrey and Bryant T. Ragan, eds. *Homosexuality in Modern France*. New York: Oxford University Press, 1996.

Merrick, Jeffrey and Michael Sibalis, eds. *Homosexuality in French History and Culture*. Binghamton, NY: Haworth, 2001.

Meyerowitz, Joanne. *How Sex Changed: A History of Transsexuality in the United States*. Cambridge, UK: Harvard University Press, 2002.

Moyn, Samuel. *The Last Utopia: Human Rights in History*. Cambridge, MA: Belknap Press, 2010.

Murphy, Lawrence R. *Perverts by Official Order: The Campaign against Homosexuals by the United States Navy*. New York: Harrington Park Press, 1988.

Murphy, Timothy, ed. *Reader's Guide to Lesbian and Gay Studies*. New York: Routledge, 2000.

Murray, Stephen O. and Will Roscoe, eds. *Boy-Wives and Female Husbands: Studies of African Homosexualities*. New York: St. Martin's Press, 1998.

Myers, Joanne. *Historical Dictionary of the Lesbian and Gay Movements*. Latham, MD: Scarecrow Press, 2013.

Nicol, Nancy, Adrian Jjuuko, Richard Lusimbo et al., eds. *Envisioning Global LGBT Human Rights: (Neo)colonialism, Neoliberalism, Resistance, and Hope*. London: ICwS, School of Advanced Study, 2018.

O'Dwyer, Conor. *Coming Out of Communism: The Emergence of LGBT Activism in Eastern Europe*. New York: New York University Press, 2018.

Paternotte, David and Manon Tremblay, *The Ashgate Research Companion to Lesbian and Gay Activism*. Burlington, VT: Ashgate, 2015.

Pepin, Jacques. *The Origins of AIDS*. New York: Cambridge University Press, 2011.

Pflugfelder, Gregory M. *Cartographies of Desire: Male-Male Sexuality in Japanese Discourse, 1600–1950*. Berkeley: University of California Press, 1999.

Plant, Richard. *The Pink Triangle: The Nazi War against Homosexuals*. New York: Henry Holt, 1986.

Puar, Jasbir. *Terrorist Assemblages: Homonationalism in Queer Times*. Durham, NC: Duke University Press, 2007.

Puri, Jyoti. *Sexual States: Governance and the Struggle over the Antisodomy Law in India*. Durham, NC: Duke University Press, 2016.

Reumann, Miriam G. *American Sexual Character: Sex, Gender, and National Identity in the Kinsey Reports*. Berkeley: University of California Press, 2005.

Rupp, Leila. *A Desired Past: A Short History of Same-Sex Love in America*. Berkeley: University of California Press, 1999.

Rupp, Leila. *Sapphistries: A Global History of Love between Women*. New York: New York University Press, 2009.

Russo, Vito. *The Celluloid Closet: Homosexuality in the Movies*. rev. ed. New York: Harper & Row, 1987.

Rydström, Jens. *Odd Couples: A History of Gay Marriage in Scandinavia*. Amsterdam: Aksant Academic Publishers, 2011.

Rydström, Jens. *Sinners and Citizens: Bestiality and Homosexuality in Sweden, 1880–1950*. Chicago: University of Chicago Press, 2003.

Rydström, Jens and Kati Mustola, eds. *Criminally Queer: Homosexuality and Criminal Law in Scandinavia, 1842–1999*. Amsterdam: Aksant Academic Publishers, 2007.

Sang, Tze-Ian D. *The Emerging Lesbian: Female Same-Sex Desire in Modern China*. Chicago: University of Chicago Press, 2003.

Schmitt, Arno and Jehoeda Sofer, eds. *Sexuality and Eroticism among Males in Moslem Societies*. New York: Harrington Park Press, 1992.

Shield, Andrew D. J. *Immigrants on Grindr: Race, Sexuality, and Belonging Online*. Cham, Switzerland: Palgrave Macmillan, 2019.

Shilts, Randy. *And the Band Played On: Politics, People, and the AIDS Epidemic*. New York: St. Martin's Press, 1987.

Skidmore, Emily. *True Sex: The Lives of Trans Men at the Turn of the 20th Century*. New York: New York University Press, 2017.

Snyder, Sarah. *Human Rights Activism and the End of the Cold War: A Transnational History of the Helsinki Network*. Cambridge, UK: Cambridge University Press, 2013.

Snyder, Sarah. *From Selma to Moscow: How Human Rights Activists Transformed U.S. Foreign Policy*. New York: Columbia University Press, 2018.

Spencer, Colin. *Homosexuality in History*. New York: Harcourt Brace & Company, 1995.

Sperti, Angioletta. *Constitutional Courts, Gay Rights and Sexual Orientation Equality*. London: Hart Publishing, 2017.

Stein, Marc. *City of Sisterly and Brotherly Loves: Lesbian and Gay Philadelphia, 1945–1972*. Chicago, University of Chicago Press, 2000.

Stein, Mark, ed. *Encyclopedia of Lesbian, Gay, Bisexual, and Transgender History in America*. New York: Charles Scribner's Sons: Thomson Gale, 2003.

Stein, Marc. *Rethinking the Gay and Lesbian Movement*. New York: Routledge, 2012.

Stein, Marc. *Sexual Injustice: Supreme Court Decisions from Griswold to Roe*. Chapel Hill: University of North Carolina Press, 2010.

Stoler, Ann Laura. *Carnal Knowledge and Imperial Power: Race and the Intimate in Colonial Rule*. Berkeley, CA: University of California Press, 2002.

Stryker, Susan. *Queer Pulp: Perverted Passions from the Golden Age of the Paperback*. San Francisco: Chronicle Books, 2001.

Stryker, Susan. *Transgender History: The Roots of Today's Revolution*. 2nd ed. New York: Seal Press, 2017.

Tamagne, Florence. *A History of Homosexuality in Europe. Vol. I & II Berlin, London, Paris, 1919–1939*. New York: Algora Publishing, 2006.

Tarrow, Sidney G. *Power in Movement: Social Movements and Contentious Politics*. Rev. and 3rd ed. New York: Cambridge University Press, 2011.

Teal, Donn. *The Gay Militants*. New York: Stein and Day, 1971.

Thoreson, Ryan *Transnational LGBT Activism: Working for Sexual Rights Worldwide*. Minneapolis: University of Minnesota Press, 2014.

Timm, Annette F. and Joshua A. Sanborn. *Gender, Sex, and the Shaping of Modern Europe*. 2nd ed. New York: Bloomsbury Academic, 2016.

Tin, Louis-Georges. *The Dictionary of Homophobia: A Global History of Gay & Lesbian Experience*. Vancouver, BC: Arsenal Pulp Press, 2008.

Tremblay, Manon, David Paternotte, and Carol Johnson. *The Lesbian and Gay Movement and the State: Comparative Insights into a Transformed Relationship*. Burlington, VT: Ashgate, 2011.

Walkowitz, Judith. *Prostitution and Victorian Society: Women, Class, and the State*. Cambridge, UK: Cambridge University Press, 1980.

Warner, Tom. *Never Going Back: A History of Queer Activism in Canada*. Toronto: University of Toronto Press, 2002.

Weeks, Jeffrey. *Coming Out: Homosexual Politics in Britain from the Nineteenth Century to the Present*. London: Quartet Books, 1977.

Weeks, Jeffrey. *Sex, Politics, and Society: The Regulation of Sexuality since 1800*. London: Longman, 1981.

Weiss, Meredith L. and Michael J. Bosia, eds. *Global Homophobia*. Urbana: University of Illinois Press, 2013.

Wenqing, Kang. *Obsession: Male Same-Sex Relations in China, 1900–1950*. Hong Kong: Hong Kong University Press, 2009.

Wiesner-Hanks, Merry E. *Women and Gender in Early Modern Europe*. 3rd ed. New York: Cambridge University Press, 2008.

Willettt, Graham. *Living Out Loud: A History of Gay and Lesbian Activism in Australia*. Sydney: Allen & Unwin, 2001.

ARTICLES

Alexander, Rustam. "Soviet Legal and Criminological Debates on the Decriminalization of Homosexuality (1965–1975)." *Slavic Review* 77:1 (Spring 2018): 30–52.

Alqaisiya, Walaa. "Decolonial Queering: The Politics of Being Queer in Palestine." *Journal of Palestine Studies* 47:3 (Spring 2018): 29–44.

Altman, Dennis and Jonathan Symons. "International Norm Polarization: Sexuality as a Subject of Human Rights Protection." *International Theory* 7:1 (2015): 61–95.

Arguelles, Lourdes and B. Ruby Rich. "Homosexuality, Homophobia, and Revolution: Notes toward an Understanding of the Cuban Lesbian and Gay Male Experience." In *Hidden from History: Reclaiming the Gay and Lesbian Past*. Martin Duberman, Martha Vicinus, and George Chauncey, Jr., eds., 441–55. New York: Meridan, 1989.

Ayoub, Phillip M. "With Arms Wide Shut: Threat Perception, Norm Reception, and Mobilized Resistance to LGBT Rights." *Journal of Human Rights* 13:3 (2014): 337–62.

Ayoub, Phillip M. "Contested Norms in New-Adopter States: International Determinants of LGBT Rights Legislation." *European Journal of International Relations* 2:2 (2015): 293–322.

Belmonte, Laura A., Mark Philip Bradley, Julio Capó et al. "Colloquy: Queering America and the World." *Diplomatic History* 40:1 (January 2016): 19–80.

Ben, Pablo and Santiago Joaquin Insausti. "Dictatorial Rule and Sexual Politics in Argentina: The Case of the Frente de Liberación Homosexual, 1967–1976." *Hispanic American Historical Review* 97:2 (May 2017): 297–325.

Capó, Julio. "Queering Mariel: Mediating Cold War Foreign Policy and U.S. Citizenship among Cuba's Homosexual Exile Community, 1978–1994." *Journal of American Ethnic History* 29:4 (Summer 2010): 78–106.

Chambers, Stuart. "Pierre Elliott Trudeau and Bill C-150: A Rational Approach to Homosexual Acts, 1968–1969." *Journal of Homosexuality* 57:2 (2010): 249–66.

Churchill, David S. "Transnationalism and Homophile Political Culture in the Postwar Decades." *GLQ: A Journal of Lesbian and Gay Studies* 15:1 (2009): 31–65.

Cohler, Deborah. "Sapphism and Sedition: Producing Female Homosexuality in Great War Britain." *Journal of the History of Sexuality* 16:1 (January 2007): 68–94.

Dixon, Joy. "Havelock Ellis and John Addington Symonds Sexual Inversion (1897)." *Victorian Review* 35:1 (Spring 2009): 72–7.

Doan, Laura. "Queer History/Queer Memory: The Case of Alan Turning." *GLQ: A Journal of Lesbian and Gay Studies* 23:1 (January 2017): 113–36.

Edelberg, Peter. "The Queer Road to Frisind: Copenhagen, 1945–2012." In *Queer Cities, Queer Cultures: Europe since 1945*. Matt Cook and Jennifer V. Evans, eds., 55–74. London: Bloomsbury, 2014.

Evans, Jennifer V. "Decriminalization, Seduction, and 'Unnatural Desire' in East Germany." *Feminist Studies* 36:3 (Fall 2010): 553–77.

Flanders, Sara et al. "On the Subject of Homosexuality: What Freud Said." *International Journal of Psychoanalysis* 97:3 (June 2016): 933–50.

Galeano, Javier Fernández. "Is He a 'Social Danger': The Franco Regime's Judicial Prosecution of Homosexuality in Málaga under the Ley de Vagos y Maleantes." *Journal of the History of Sexuality* 25 (2016): 1–31.

Giles, Geoffrey J. "'The Most Unkindest Cut of All': Castration, Homosexuality, and Nazi Justice." *Journal of Contemporary History* 27 (1992): 41–61.

Girard, Francois. "United Nations: Negotiating Sexual Rights and Sexual Orientation." In *Sex Politics: Reports from the Front Lines*. Richard Parker, Rosalind Petchesky, and Robert Sember, eds., 311–58. Sexuality Policy Watch, 2004, https://www.sxpolitics.org/frontlines/book/pdf/sexpolitics.pdf.

Girard, Philip. "From Subversives to Liberation: Homosexuals and the Immigration Act, 1952–1972." *Canadian Journal of Law & Society* 2 (1987): 1–27.

Jablonski, Olivier. "The Birth of a French Homosexual Press in the 1950s." Journal of Homosexuality 41:3–4(2001): 233–48.

Johnson, David K. "America's Cold War Empire: Exporting the Lavender Scare." In *Global Homophobia*. Meredith L. Weiss and Michael J. Bosia, eds., 55–74. Urbana: University of Illinois Press, 2013.

Johnson, David K. "Physique Pioneers: The Politics of 1960s Gay Consumer Culture." *Journal of Social History* 43 (2010); 867–92.

Kennedy, Hubert C. "The 'Third Sex' Theory of Karl Heinrich Ulrichs." *Journal of Homosexuality* 6:1/2 (Fall/Winter 1980/81): 103–11.

Kimmel, David and Daniel Robinson. "Sex, Crime, Pathology: Homosexuality and Criminal Code Reform in Canada, 1949–1969." *Canadian Journal of Law and Society* 16 (2001): 147–65.

Kinsman, Gary. "'Character Weaknesses' and 'Fruit Machines': Towards an Analysis of the Anti-Homosexual Security Campaign in the Canadian Civil Service." *Labour/Le Travail* 35 (1995): 133–61.

Kollman, Kelly and Matthew Waites. "The Global Politics of Lesbian, Gay, Bisexual, and Trans Rights: An Introduction." *Contemporary Politics* 15:1 (2009):1–37.

Kurimay, Anita and Judit Takács. "Emergence of the Hungarian Homosexual Movement in Late Refrigerator Socialism." *Sexualities* 20:5–6 (2017): 585–602.

LaViolette, Nicole and Sandra Whitworth. "No Safe Haven: Sexuality as a Universal Human Right and Gay and Lesbian Activism in International Politics." *Millennium: Journal of International Studies* 23:3 (1994): 562–88.

Lekus, Ian. "Queer Harvests: Homosexuality, the U.S. New Left, and the Venceremos Brigades to Cuba." *Radical History Review* 89 (Spring 2004): 57–91.

Löfström, Jan. "A Premodern Legacy: The 'Easy' Criminalization of Homosexual Acts between Women in the Finnish Penal Code of 1889." *Journal of Homosexuality*, 35:3–4 (1998): 53–79.

Long, Scott. "The Trials of Culture: Sex and Security in Egypt." *Middle East Report* 230 (2004): 12–20.

Macías-González, Victor M. "The Transnational Homophile Movement and the Development of Domesticity in Mexico City's Homosexual Community, 1930–70." *Gender & History* 26:3 (November 2014): 519–44.

Meyerowitz, Joanne. "AHR Forum: Transnational Sex and U.S. History." *American Historical Review* 114:5 (December 2009): 1273–86.

Minto, David. "Mr. Grey Goes to Washington: The Homophile Internationalism of Britain's Homosexual Law Reform Society." In *British Queer History: New Approaches and Perspectives*. Marie H. Loughlin, ed., 219–43. Manchester: Manchester University Press, 2013.

Minto, David. "Perversion by Penumbras: Wolfenden, Griswold, and the Transatlantic Trajectory of Sexual Privacy." *American Historical Review* 123:4 (October 2018): 1093–121.

Moeller, Robert G. "Private Acts, Public Anxieties, and the Fight to Decriminalize Male Homosexuality in West Germany." *Feminist Studies* 36:3 (Fall 2010): 528–52.

Murphy, James H. "'Disgusted by the Details': Dr. Jekyll and Mr. Hyde and the Dublin Castle Scandals of 1884." In *Back to the Future of Irish Studies*. Maureen O'Connor, ed., 177–90. New York: Peter Lang, 2010.

Ocasio, Rafael. "Gays and the Cuban Revolution: The Case of Reinaldo Arenas." *Latin American Perspectives* 29:2 (March 2002): 78–98.

Olcott, Jocelyn Olcott, "Cold War Conflicts and Cheap Cabaret: Sexual Politics at the 1975 United Nations International Women's Year Conference." *Gender & History* 22:3 (November 2010): 733–54.

Pasquini, Dario. "'This Will Be the Love of the Future': Italian LGBT People and Their Emotions from the Fuori! and Massimo Consoli Archives, 1970–1984." *Journal of the History of Sexuality* 29:1 (January 2020): 51–78.

Peña, Susana. "'Obvious Gays' and the State Gaze: Cuban Gay Visibility and U.S. Immigration Policy during the Mariel Boatlift." *Journal of the History of Sexuality* 16:3 (September 2007): 482–514.

Pratt, Nicola. "The Queen Boat Case in Egypt: Sexuality, National Security, and State Sovereignty." *Review of International Studies* 33:1 (2007): 129–44.

Pyryeskina, Julia. "'A Remarkably Dense Historical and Political Juncture': Anita Bryant, the Body Politic, and the Canadian Gay and Lesbian Community in January 1978." *Canadian Journal of History*, 53:1 (Spring/Summer 2018): 58–85.

Ritchie, Jason. "How Do You Say 'Come Out of the Closet' in Arabic? Queer Activism and the Politics of Visibility in Israel-Palestine." *GLQ: A Journal of Gay and Lesbian Studies* 16:4 (2010): 557–76.

Rupp, Leila. "The Persistence of Transnational Organizing: The Case of the Homophile Movement." *American Historical Review* 116:4 (October 2011): 1014–39.

Schindler, John R. "Redl—Spy of the Century?" *International Journal of Intelligence and CounterIntelligence* 18:3 (2005): 483–507.

Sibalis, Michael. "Gay Liberation Comes to France: The Front Homosexual d'Action Révolutionnaire (FHAR)." *French History and Civilization* (2005): 265–76.

Sibalis, Michael. "Homophobia, Vichy France, and the 'Crime of Homosexuality': The Origins of the Ordinance of 6 August 1942." *GLQ: A Journal of Lesbian and Gay Studies* 8:3 (2002): 301–18.

Stein, Marc. "All the Immigrants Are Straight, All the Homosexuals Are Citizens, but Some of Us Are Queer Aliens: Genealogies of Legal Strategy in Boutilier v. INS." *Journal of American Ethnic History* 29:4 (Summer 2010): 45–77.

Stein, Marc. "Boutilier and the U.S. Supreme Court's Sexual Revolution." *Law and History Review* 23:3 (Fall 2005): 491–536.

Stein, Marc. "Canonizing Homophile Sexual Respectability: Archives, History, and Memory." *Radical History Review* (Fall 2014): 52–73.

Stella, Francesca. "Queer Space, Pride, and Shame in Moscow." *Slavic Review* 72:3 (2013): 458–80.

Stychin, Carl F. "Same-Sex Sexualities and the Globalization of Human Rights Discourse." *McGill Law Journal* 49:4 (2004): 951–68.

Tielman, Rob. "Dutch Gay Emancipation History." *Journal of Homosexuality* 13:2–3 (1986): 9–17.

Wahab, Amar. "'Homosexuality/Homophobia Is Un-African?' Un-Mapping Transnational Discourses in the Context of Uganda's Anti-Homosexuality Bill/ Act." *Journal of Homosexuality* 63:5 (2016): 685–718.

Waites, Matthew. "Critique of 'Sexual Orientation' and 'Gender Identity' in Human Rights Discourse: Global Queer Politics beyond the Yogyakarta Principles." *Contemporary Politics* 15:1 (March 2009): 137–56.

Waters, Chris. "The Homosexual as a Social Being in Britain, 1945–1968." *Journal of British Studies* 51: 3 (July 2010): 685–710.

Willett, Graham. "The Darkest Decade: Homophobia in 1950s Australia." *Australian Historical Studies* 27:109 (1997): 120–32.

Worth, Heather, Jing Jing et al. "'Under the Same Quilt': The Paradoxes of Sex between Men in the Cultural Revolution." *Journal of Homosexuality* 64:1 (2017): 61–74.

Wotherspoon, Gary. "'The Greatest Menace Facing Australia': Homosexuality and the State in NSW during the Cold War." *Labour History* 56 (May 1989): 15–28.

THESES AND DISSERTATIONS

Capó, Julio. "It's Not Queer to Be Gay: Miami and the Emergence of the Gay Rights Movement, 1945–1995." PhD diss., Florida International University, 2011.

de Wals, Joost. "International Diffusion of Movement Mobilization: Dutch Actions against Anita Bryant and the Birth of Dutch Gay Pride." MA Thesis, Katholieke Universiteit Nijmegen, 1996.

Ewing, Christopher. "The Color of Desire: Contradictions of Race, Sex, and Gay Rights in the Federal Republic of Government." PhD diss.: The City University of New York, 2018.

Huneke, Erik. "Morality, Law, and the Socialist Sexual Self in the German Democratic Republic, 1945–1972." PhD diss., University of Michigan, 2013.

Minto, David. "Special Relationships: Transnational Homophile Activism and Anglo-American Sexual Politics." PhD diss., Yale University, 2014.

Newsome, W. Jake. "Homosexuals and the Holocaust: Sexual Citizenship and the Politics of Memory in Germany and the United States, 1945–2008." PhD diss., State University of New York at Buffalo, 2016.

CONFERENCE PAPERS

Judit Takács, "The Double Life of Kertbeny." Conference paper presented at "Past and Present of Radical Sexual Politics," University of Amsterdam, October 3–4, 2003, http://www.policy.hu/takacs/pdf-lib/TheDoubleLifeOfKertbeny.pdf.

INDEX